THE CROWN PLEAS OF THE SUFFOLK EYRE OF 1240

THE CROWN PLEAS OF THE SUFFOLK EYRE OF 1240

Edited by
ERIC GALLAGHER

Revised and with an introduction by
HENRY SUMMERSON

The Boydell Press

Suffolk Records Society
VOLUME LXIV

A Suffolk Records Society publication
First published 2021
The Boydell Press, Woodbridge

ISBN 978-1-78327-600-4

Issued to subscribing members for the year 2021

The Boydell Press is an imprint of Boydell & Brewer Ltd
PO Box 9, Woodbridge, Suffolk IP12 3DF, UK
and of Boydell & Brewer Inc.
668 Mt Hope Avenue, Rochester, NY 14620–2731, USA
website: www.boydellandbrewer.com

A catalogue record for this book is available
from the British Library

This publication is printed on acid-free paper

FSC www.fsc.org MIX Paper from responsible sources FSC® C013056

Printed and bound in Great Britain by TJ Books Limited, Padstow, Cornwall

CONTENTS

PREFACE AND ACKNOWLEDGEMENTS

This volume provides an edition and translation of the crown pleas, largely consisting of criminal proceedings, from the surviving roll made for the King's justices at their eyre held in Suffolk in AD 1240. Its publication completes the process of making available for the first time the earliest such roll to survive in full for Suffolk, complementing the edition of the civil pleas which the Suffolk Records Society published as its volume 52 in 2009. The latter was edited by Dr Eric Gallagher, who laid the essential foundations for the present volume. Circumstances prevented his bringing it to completion, however, and that work has therefore been undertaken by Dr Henry Summerson, who has supplied the introduction and where necessary revised the text and indexes.

Dr Gallagher writes: Much of the research for the edition was done as part of my doctoral thesis on the 1240 civil pleas, and depended on the staff of The National Archives, whom I thank for their advice and help, as I do members of the Suffolk Records Society for guidance with the county's place-names, particularly the late John Blatchly, the late Peter Northeast, David Dymond, David Butcher and Keith Briggs. I am also grateful for the support of the Institute of Historical Research, London, both for its facilities and for the help freely given by scholars attending seminars there. I am obliged, too, to Christopher Whittick and the late Lesley Boatwright for their assistance in transcribing and translating the text.

Dr Summerson adds: The realisation of this text was accomplished in difficult circumstances during the nationwide lockdown which resulted from the Covid-19 pandemic of 2020. It was possible only because essential source material, unpublished and printed, was accessible through the websites of the Anglo-American Legal Tradition project (AALT) and the Institute of Historical Research respectively. My thanks go to them, and also to the British Library and the library of the Society of Antiquaries of London for access to books in the closing stages of work. I, too, am most grateful to Keith Briggs for help with place-names, as I am to Nick Bingham of The Boydell Press for essential help with the production of this book.

Sarston–London
February–October 2020

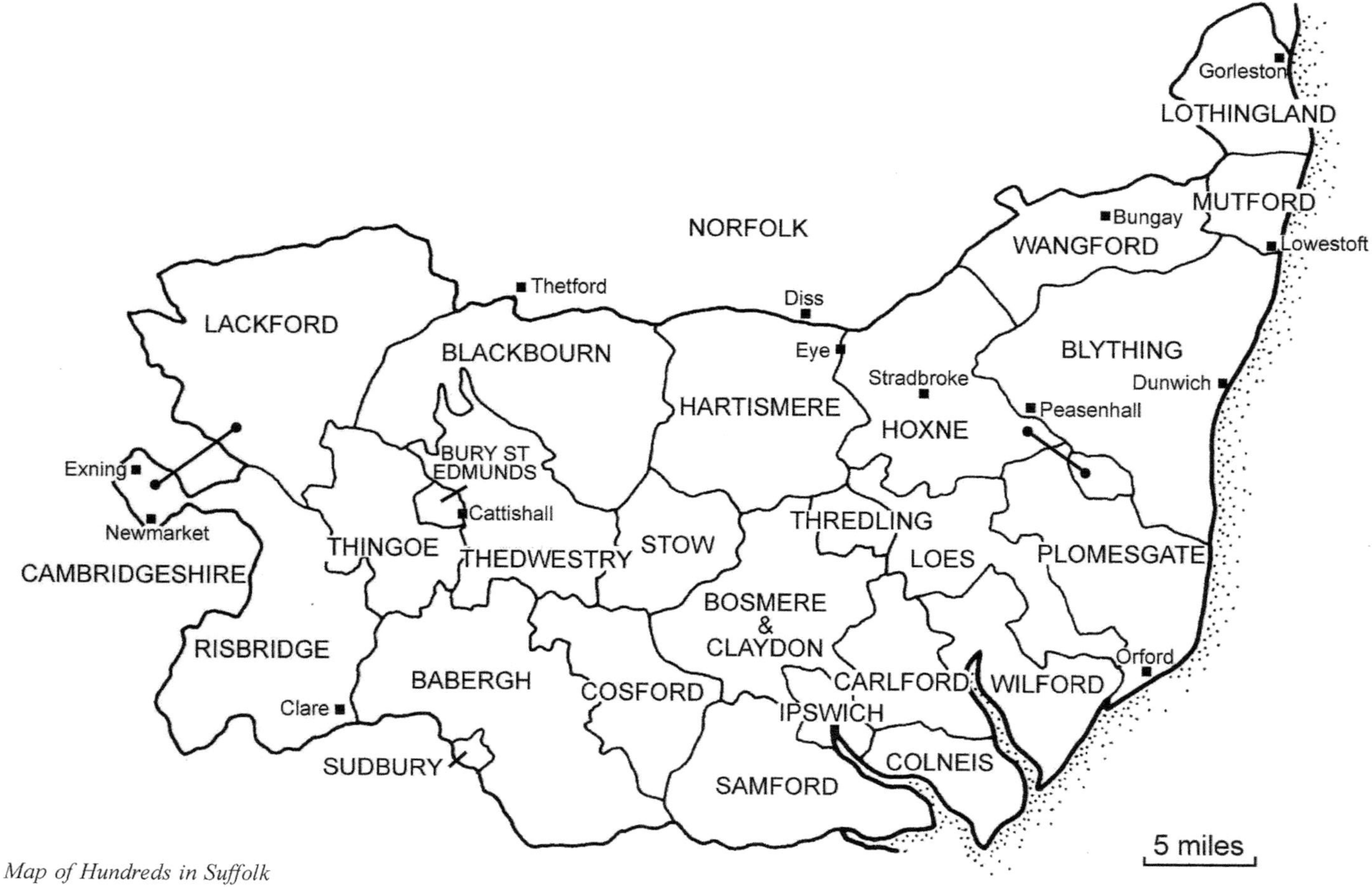

Map of Hundreds in Suffolk

INTRODUCTION[1]

The text which follows constitutes the second and concluding portion of the roll of the Suffolk eyre of 1240, and is made up of the pleas of the crown and the record of their financial yield. The first part of the roll, recording the county's civil pleas, consisted almost entirely of litigation over land. The crown pleas, by contrast, were made up of what today would be described as criminal business, together with matters affecting the government of the county and the interests of the King, and in particular his revenues. A modest number of people involved in civil litigation can be identified as having also taken part in the conduct of criminal proceedings, and a very few suits over land gave rise to, or were associated with, acts of violence which were recorded among pleas of the crown. The two sections are numbered continuously, but overall the differences between them, as well as editorial convenience, are such as to justify their being presented separately.

Suffolk in 1240

The value of an eyre roll does not lie only in the light it can shed on the operations of the medieval legal system, or on the functions of local and central government; it can also illuminate many aspects of the life of a county, and do so at social levels which are otherwise hard to penetrate. For Suffolk in 1240, moreover, it can serve this purpose for decades not especially well provided for by other sources – positively murky, indeed, when looked at between the searchlights provided by Domesday Book at the end of the eleventh century, and the growing numbers of court rolls and estate accounts which from the last decades of the thirteenth century onwards have provided so many insights into the workings of East Anglian society. In its physical shape the county has changed little in the last 800 years, except along its North Sea coast, already fighting a largely losing battle against erosion. Prosperous Dunwich had yet to disappear under the waves, but in 1228 a lawsuit between the men of Yarmouth and the keeper of the royal manor of Lothingland, at Suffolk's north-east tip, found that the latter's market, presumably at Southtown (formerly known as Little Yarmouth), had recently had to be moved to a site where it was less likely to be 'swamped and covered by the sea'.[2] Inland, the landscape then, as now, was one of modest undulations rather than dramatic contrasts of heights and depths. Deeply penetrated by the valleys of a number of rivers, which supplemented networks of roads and tracks, ancient and modern, in enabling the movement of people and goods, and which with their tributaries ensured a plentiful supply of

1 All unpublished documents cited are to be found in The National Archives, London. Numbers in **bold type** are those of pleas of the crown, numbered 1161 to 1601; numbers between 1 and 1160 refer to cases among the civil pleas, published in the first volume of the proceedings of the eyre (SRS volume 52).

2 *Curia Regis Rolls xiii, 1227–1230*, nos. 472–4 (p. 110).

water, Suffolk was fortunate in the fertility of most of its soil, which was such as to make it by 1086 the most heavily populated county in England.[3]

Outside its boroughs most Suffolk people lived by agriculture, or by crafts associated with it. The county was one of mixed farming, though arable predominated over pastoral except on the poor soil of the Brecklands at the north-west corner of the county. By the 1280s, indeed, livestock seem to have been becoming scarce, but fifty years earlier there may have been more; although the goods taken by thieves are only occasionally identified, sheep, cows and horses are all recorded as having been stolen. It would appear that flocks and herds could be found, and therefore taken, anywhere in the county, though the theft of thirteen sheep at Icklingham, where the meagre soil of Lackford hundred was hardly suitable for rearing anything else (**1583**), and the record of what appears to have been a group of sheep-stealers around Thurleston, just outside Ipswich (**1260**), may indicate that these animals, at least, were now especially likely to be found on the sandy ground of the Brecklands and of the south-east of the county. Perhaps shortage of manure, detrimental to the fertility of the soil, was not yet a consequence of a relative lack of cattle and sheep. If it was, a partial compensation was found in the application of marl, used to counteract acidity in the soil – digging it presumably gave a precarious living to Hugh le Marlur, a suspected thief (**1284**), while the pursuit of it left pits into which some unlucky people fell to their deaths (**1171**, **1257**, **1470**, **1566**).

Suffolk was a county with very few magnates – essentially only the abbot of St Edmund's, the prior of Ely and the earls of Gloucester and Norfolk – but large numbers of free landowners, lords of manors or parts of manors, with many of the latter probably hard to distinguish from well-to-do farmers. The possessions of men like Roger de Furnaus (**1550**) and John Thoraud (**1481**), both put in exigent (the term used to define the process of outlawry) at the eyre for theft, and consequently forfeiting chattels valued at 18s. and 16s. respectively, and holding eighteen acres of land in Roger's case and sixteen in John's, can be usefully compared with those of the homicide Warin of Stebbing, who had chattels assessed at £7 8s. 8d., and lands from which the crown raised £4 4s. 4d. (**1196**). The essential difference between them was that whereas Roger and John held their lands by knight's service, Warin was a member of a tithing, and therefore unfree. Socially Warin should have looked up to men like Roger and John, but economically they may well have envied him, not least because as a serf he probably also held unfree lands, subject to the terms of villein tenure but adding to his resources, helping to explain the high value of his chattels. Until he lost everything by killing a man, Warin was probably a man rising in his world, benefiting from conditions in which personal freedom was widespread and becoming more so, and with a flourishing land market in which free and villein holdings alike were easily bought and sold.[4]

In that world the fortunate, the able and the unscrupulous could readily accumulate property, while the unwise and the unlucky could as easily disperse it, helped, moreover, by the widespread practice in Suffolk of partible inheritance, whereby

3 This account of thirteenth-century Suffolk is particularly indebted to M. Bailey, *Medieval Suffolk: an economic and social history, 1200–1500* (Woodbridge, 2007).

4 See M. Bailey, 'Villeinage in England: a regional study, *c.* 1250–*c.* 1349', *EcHR* 62 (2009), pp. 430–57.

lands were not inherited by a single heir but divided among several.[5] Holdings tended to be consolidated rather than scattered across a number of fields, but that did not prevent their being broken up again, and smallholdings proliferated. In an intensely competitive society some men prospered, but many did not, and found their lands barely sufficient to support them and their families. This can be illustrated from the eyre roll, which records a number of the men convicted or put in exigent as having had free lands, which are defined in terms of their extent as well as of their value. Nearly all their possessors were in tithings, and may therefore have had villein holdings as well, but the fact that they are commonly said to have had few or no chattels makes it unlikely that their lands were either valuable or extensive, whatever the terms on which they were held. Forfeitures of two acres and a house, valued at 2s. (**1396**), of three acres, worth 6s. 8d. (**1573**), of five acres, from which the King gained just 3s. 8d. (**1326**) – all point to small holdings and precarious livelihoods. The first two of the men concerned had no chattels, the third goods valued at 6s. 6d. The six acres in Eastbridge forfeited by Nicholas de *Monay,* which provided the exchequer with only 3s., were surely of very poor quality; Nicholas had no chattels and was not in a tithing, though he should have been – perhaps he was newly settled in Eastbridge, taking up the only land available (**1433**).

The small properties and meagre chattels of men like Nicholas de *Monay* are pointers towards the conditions created by the acute land shortage of the late thirteenth century, as the population of Suffolk continued to grow and settlement expanded, and people lived and took in new ground wherever they could. Hence, perhaps, the two encroachments on roads recorded in 1240 as having been made at Little Bricett and Trimley respectively (**1179**, **1311**). The pattern of settlement in the county has been such as to make its characteristic landscape not one of nucleated villages, of the kind typical of midland England, but rather one largely made up of dispersed settlements, of hamlets and isolated farmsteads.[6] Many of the latter were surrounded by moats, a sign of status, actual or aspired to, as was the possession of a park. The growth of population was injurious to Suffolk's woodlands, but trees were too important in the life of the county, providing building material as well as giving shelter to game, not to receive a measure of protection, and a few large and many small acreages survived. Only one charcoal-burner was recorded in 1240 (**1445**) – peat, not wood, was the principal source of fuel (**1243**) – but many carpenters, for in a county without good supplies of building-stone, houses and farm buildings were very largely made of timber, potentially on a substantial scale, like the impressively spacious late thirteenth-century aisled hall which survives at Purton Green.[7] Such a building, perhaps, was the one which Robert Hayl's ex-mistress built next to Robert's home on land he gave her; understandably indignant, his newly-wedded wife had it pulled down, but it may be significant that she had to engage the services of eight men to do it (**1266**). Many others, however, were less well accommodated; when Roger Ful was put in exigent for theft, he was said to have no chattels and just 'a little house', worth one shilling to the exchequer (**1223**).

---

5 Analysed by B. Dodwell, 'Holdings and inheritance in medieval East Anglia', *EcHR* 20 (1967), pp. 53–66.

6 Bailey, *Medieval Suffolk*, pp. 68–72.

7 G. Colman and S. Colman, 'A thirteenth century aisled house: Purton Green Farm, Stansfield, Suffolk', *PSIA* 30:2 (1965), pp. 149–65.

The predominance of timber as a building material inevitably entailed risks, not least the danger from fire. Arson appears to have been a relatively rare crime in thirteenth-century England, but although any eyre might hear of one or two offences, the eight recorded for Suffolk in 1240 was an unusually high number.[8] Standing woodland, when it gave shelter to deer, constituted a temptation to poaching, not always resisted, either by men of a status similar to that of the owner of the park in which they went hunting (**1529**), or by lesser folk who were probably after meat rather than sport (**1239**); the people who took fish from seigneurial ponds, even those belonging to St Edmund's abbey (**1544**), no doubt offended for the same basic reason. Poaching had been a matter for investigation by justices itinerant since the early thirteenth century. It was not itself a felony, but it could give rise to one, as lords and their employees protected their rights, sometimes with excessive force – the 1240 eyre heard how one Gilbert Pot had killed Alard of Wratting 'as he was a poacher in his lord's wood' (**1501**).

Gilbert Pot was said to have no chattels. That should probably not be taken absolutely literally. Gilbert the smith, also in exigent for homicide, was recorded as having chattels worth 18s. 2d., these being his 'gear' (*utensilia*) (**1165**). A smith's working tools, his anvils, hammers and the like, were not of a kind to be easily run away with. Someone like Gilbert Pot, by contrast, may well have had more than the clothes he stood up in – a bag of tools, perhaps, and a horse to help him make his getaway – without this doing much to relieve his poverty. Another eighty-nine people convicted or suspected of felony (twenty-two homicides, sixty-one thieves, three arsonists and three men outlawed by appeals of robbery) were in the same miserable condition, and the true total was probably higher, since in a number of cases nothing was said about a suspect's chattels, most likely because there was nothing to say. Many more such men and women were recorded as having belongings worth only a few pence. A great many people led very precarious lives, and their numbers grew throughout the thirteenth century.

The relationship between poverty and crime is discussed in a later section; all that needs to be said here is that many malefactors were wretchedly poor. Occasional references in the eyre roll show that not everyone living in Suffolk was on the verge of destitution, however. Robert Bude of Bungay was said to have forced his way into the house of Alice Catun and removed rings, brooches, and 'a gallon measure full of money' – seemingly a container of some 265 cubic inches crammed with silver pennies, by any standards a considerable haul (**1252**). Robert the son of William of Peasenhall appears to have been what would later be called a country gentleman; when he appealed – formally accused – Adam the son of Walter of Knodishall of breaking into his house and robbing him of large quantities of barley and malt, clothes for men and women, a basin, a bronze pot, and other, unspecified, goods which he valued at 50s., this gives some idea of what such a man's house might contain (**1445**). It also helps to explain some of the activities of the criminally-inclined, especially those who were both poor and footloose.

Thirty-nine out of 115, or just over a third, of the killings recorded at the 1240 eyre were attributed to unknown criminals, many of them probably in the course of burglaries. Sometimes these evildoers appear to have sheltered, or taken refuge,

---

8 See H. Summerson, 'Burning issues: the law and crime of arson in England, 1200–1350', in S. Jenks, J. Rose and C. Whittick (eds), *Laws, lawyers and texts: studies in medieval legal history in honour of Paul Brand* (Leiden and Boston, 2012), pp. 101–27 (where the number of Suffolk burnings is understated).

in woods. The unknown man found killed in Holbrook park may have been their victim, though it is also possible that he was himself a malefactor, murdered by his accomplices (**1383**). But mostly they seem to have haunted the roads, ambushing other travellers – an unknown woman was said to have been killed at the bridge over the Little Ouse at Brandon, on the boundary between Suffolk and Norfolk, and this may well have been a known danger-spot (**1586**) – or breaking into houses to kill and rob their occupants. They might occasionally penetrate into the boroughs – hence the death of Ralph the son of Alice 'at the church', found killed in the graveyard of Holy Cross church in Bungay (**1247**) – but were more often active in the countryside, where the wide dispersal of houses in much of the county, and the consequent isolation of many of them, made them vulnerable to attack. Dwellings occupied by women seem often to have been chosen for attack; on one occasion no fewer than seven women were killed in a house in Sproughton (**1382**). The danger from bandits probably helps to explain why so many houses were surrounded by moats, which gave defence against marauders as well as proclaiming the status of those whose homes they protected.

The roads which allowed the free movement of evil-minded men and women of no fixed address did the same for traders carrying goods – some of the latter doubtless fell victim to the former. Population growth must have stimulated the development of trade and encouraged the growth of urban communities.[9] Outside the borough of St Edmund's, a special case thanks to its association with one of England's greatest monasteries, the most important towns in Suffolk were seaports – Ipswich, Orford and Dunwich. All were represented by their own juries at the 1240 eyre, along with six other, lesser, communities, those of Eye, Beccles, Bungay, South Elmham, Clare and Sudbury. Bungay had been granted a market and fair in 1228, but though such a grant was commonly regarded as conferring at least the beginnings of burghal status, many other growing communities received the same privileges in thirteenth-century Suffolk, and Bungay's ability to answer by itself before the King's justices was probably due principally to its association with one of the county's greatest lordships, that of the Bigod earls of Norfolk. The same was probably at least partly true of three other, much older, boroughs – Eye, granted in 1230 with its associated lordship to Earl Richard, the King's brother, Clare, held by the earls of Gloucester, and South Elmham, a manor, and sometimes the residence, of the bishops of Norwich. Beccles, on the River Waveney, and Sudbury, in the Stour valley, both recorded as boroughs in Domesday Book, may have owed their standing more particularly to the commerce which their geographical positions facilitated.

The seaports, headed by Ipswich, prospered through trade with the Continent, with the Low Countries, northern France and the Rhineland. Flemings were sometimes found further inland. William Maperelenebolle, a Fleming with a probably garbled name, who with his master, also a Fleming, killed a woman somewhere in Plomesgate hundred, may have come ashore at Orford, at that hundred's southern tip (**1277**). Two Flemings who took part in the slaying of Geoffrey the chaplain at Livermere in Blackbourn hundred, in the north of the county and a long way from the sea, could have landed anywhere on the Suffolk coast, but Dunwich seems the

9 What follows is indebted to B. Brodt, 'East Anglia', in D.M. Palliser (ed.), *The Cambridge urban history of Britain i, 600–1540* (Cambridge, 2000), pp. 639–56, as well as to Bailey, *Medieval Suffolk*, chapter 6.

likeliest place (**1539**). The ports prospered through coastal shipping and fishing as well as foreign trade. It was probably from Dunwich that William Spekeman of Thetford set off westward with a cartload of herrings, as far as possible keeping to the Waveney valley, though he came to grief in Hoxne, some twenty miles from the coast, when he was drowned in a ditch after his cart overturned. Unusually, it was drawn by two horses, which suggests a large vehicle and a heavy load, as does the high value of 29s. which was set on cart, horses and fish together (**1368**).

On the evidence of other occasions when they were involved in fatal accidents, goods were more often moved in carts which were drawn by single horses (**1365**, **1438**, **1440**, **1580**), and were seldom of any great value; when Robert Bunne was killed by falling from his cart, it and its horse were assessed at just 2s. 6d. (**1387**). Packhorses were doubtless also employed, in the hands of men like Martin le Sumeter (**1529**). These relatively modest methods of transport were appropriate for a county whose commercial life consisted largely of small-scale trading carried on in many small towns. The number of towns granted the right to hold markets and fairs grew considerably during the thirteenth century – forty-nine were empowered to hold weekly markets, and fifty-one to hold annual fairs, in the half-century between 1225 and 1275.[10] The difference between the activities of a market and of a fair was well set out in a lawsuit heard in 1228 between the men of Yarmouth and the keeper of the royal manor of Lothingland, when it was explained that those who attended the market at Yarmouth traded in 'corn, malt, meat and victuals, nets and ropes and other little things', whereas its fair was the occasion for buying 'horses, oxen and sheep and other larger things …'.[11]

Sheep may have been bought and sold at fairs, but it seems likely it was at weekly markets that their wool was traded in shearing time, bought by men and women who wove it into cloth, before it was finished by the process of fulling. For many of those concerned, these were probably secondary occupations, a useful way of helping to make ends meet, but on the evidence of the eyre roll there were some for whom such employment represented their essential livelihood – not always a very profitable one. Benedict the weaver, in exigent for killing a woman in Elmham, was relatively prosperous, with chattels worth 13s. 4d. (**1342**), at least by comparison with Stephen the weaver, hanged for theft, whose belongings were valued at only 3s. (**1535**), just as Simon the fuller, in exigent for theft (**1398**), with chattels worth 20s. was better off than John the fuller, who ran away after stealing a foal, and had no chattels at all (**1256**). The cloth which men like these, and their less violent, or more honest, contemporaries, produced seems to have been largely, though not entirely, disposed of in the county's major towns, principally the ones represented at the eyre by juries. These named at least twenty-nine drapers as having infringed the assize of cloth, by selling cloth which did not conform to the two-yard breadth prescribed for it in 1196. Eye recorded five offenders (**1187**), Clare six (**1509**), and Orford eight (**1317**), and there were certainly others at Ipswich, Sudbury and Dunwich, where the drapers escaped individual amercements when their communities chose to negotiate fines which would cover their as yet undiscovered delinquencies (**1406**, **1512**, **1590**).

Drapers did not themselves make the cloth they sold. Some of them were described as merchants, and overall it seems likely that they were effectively entrepreneurs, buying up the produce of their localities and selling it on, in many cases

10 Bailey, *Medieval Suffolk*, pp. 116–17.

11 *Curia Regis Rolls xiii, 1227–1230*, no. 472 (p. 110).

probably to tailors, of a kind occasionally referred to in the eyre roll. Clothing seems to have been more often bought in shops and stalls than made at home.[12] Some tailors, at least, seem to have prospered from this trade. Reynold the tailor also sold wine at Clare (**1510**). Andrew the tailor was in a position to litigate over land at Framlingham (**1337**). William the tailor of Kelsale, a man of rather lower standing, was at least the chief pledge of his tithing (**1373**). Men such as these made garments for those who attended the 1240 eyre, not to mention the annual fairs where more substantial trading took place. It is noteworthy, however, that infringements of the assize of wine were far fewer than those of the assize of cloth, with only ten offenders being named. Wine was a luxury, principally demanded by men of wealth and power. Four out of the ten men amerced for selling wine at a price contrary to the assize did so at Clare (**1510**), where no doubt they met the needs of the establishment maintained in the castle by the earl of Gloucester.[13] The commercial life of Suffolk was busy, but precisely because it dealt primarily in relatively inexpensive necessities it may not always have been particularly profitable, so that even seemingly prosperous communities might feel the need to protect themselves against competition. In 1240 the men of Dunwich complained at the eyre that a newly-established market at Southwold, five miles up the coast (it was granted to the abbot of St Edmund's in 1223),[14] was harmful to their merchants (**1599**). Like the wealth of the county in general, Suffolk's internal trade may have been spread dangerously thin.

The eyre and its record

The eyre, a searching review conducted by royal justices, was the first to be held in the county since the conclusion of its predecessor, in January 1235, and, though it could look further back in time if the need arose, was therefore essentially concerned with matters arising during the previous five years.[15] The disappearance of most of the records of the royal chancery for the years 1238/9 and 1239/40 has deprived posterity of information concerning the preparations for this eyre, so that it is impossible to say how much notice was given to the sheriff, John de Ulecote, and through him to the people of Suffolk, that a judicial visitation was imminent. But since John was also sheriff of Norfolk, which the justices visited immediately before they began their sessions for Suffolk, it seems likely that the two counties were given due warning at the same time, and that Suffolk was therefore the better prepared of the two.

The attendance required at an eyre was considerable. As well as past and present sheriffs and coroners with their records, the presence was demanded of all free landholders, great and small, representatives of boroughs and vills, men and women with litigation in progress or with lawsuits in preparation, prisoners and suspects who had earlier been released on bail, finders of corpses – everybody, in fact, who

12 C. Dyer, *Making a living in the middle ages: the people of Britain, 850–1520* (London, 2002), pp. 172–3.

13 See J.C. Ward, 'The honour of Clare in Suffolk in the early middle ages', *PSIA* 30:1 (1964), pp. 94–111.

14 T.D. Hardy (ed.), *Rotuli litterarum clausarum ii, 1224–1227* (Record Commission, 1834), p. 545. The grant was confirmed in 1227. *Calendar of Charter Rolls 1226–1257*, p. 30.

15 For the dates, places and personnel of Suffolk eyres I have relied upon D. Crook, *Records of the general eyre*, Public Record Office Handbook 20 (London, 1982).

had been in some way caught up in a system of law enforcement which depended for its effectiveness on the involvement in its workings of countless people from every level of society. Not everyone who was summoned turned up. Lists of defaults name many individuals as having failed to attend, often important people who chose to pay a modest amercement (in present-day parlance, a fine) rather than make the journey, but sometimes the representatives of vills (**1370, 1429**). But despite such absenteeism, several thousand people must have been present when the eyre opened on around 29 April 1240, and when the hearing of the crown pleas began on 6 May following.

Five justices had been appointed to conduct proceedings. Their nominal head was Ranulf Brito, abbot of Ramsey in Huntingdonshire. Although in 1236 he had acted as a justice at eyres for Bedfordshire and Buckinghamshire, he did not attend all the Suffolk sessions, and was probably chosen more for his local eminence than for his legal skills. That cannot be said of his colleagues, all of whom enjoyed distinguished careers as royal justices. Their leader in 1240, William of York, had been serving regularly on eyres since the mid-1220s; a cleric who eventually became bishop of Salisbury, he probably heard the civil pleas, with Roger of Thirkleby, a younger man who subsequently gained a high reputation as a judge, as his likely colleague. Henry of Bath, who had made his early career in administration rather than jurisprudence (he acted as sheriff in several counties), probably heard the pleas of the crown, along with Gilbert of Preston; as laymen the two men would not have been inhibited from passing sentences of death, a consideration which, by contrast, would have obliged Abbot Ranulf to sit alongside York and Thirkleby when he was present in court.

The eyre over which these men presided was held in three separate places. It started in Ipswich, the county town. Many eyres held their sessions in royal castles, but there was none such in Ipswich, and proceedings most likely took place in buildings belonging to Holy Trinity Priory, the larger of the town's two Augustinian houses, where they lasted for just over a fortnight. The justices then moved to Cattishall, where around 21 May they began to hold the pleas for that considerable part of the county, later defined as West Suffolk, which constituted the liberty of St Edmund's abbey. That liberty's privileges were such that the borough at its centre, and its immediate surroundings, or *banleuca*, were completely exempt from the jurisdiction of the King's justices – at the 1228 Suffolk eyre the knights of the county had declared that civil and crown pleas alike 'should be terminated by the abbot within the borough', and that the necessary writs should be handed over to him.[16] The justices therefore held their own sessions at Cattishall, a hamlet about three miles east of St Edmund's which seems to have been the site of the liberty's gaol. They had rather less business to transact there than at Ipswich, for they concluded their main session only ten days later, on 31 May (there were some additional proceedings on 4 June), and by 10 June they were at Dunwich, hearing that borough's pleas there in accordance with privileges granted by King John in his charter of 6 July 1215.[17] For this a single day seems to have sufficed, and the justices soon moved on – by 17 June they were at Chelmsford, for the beginning of an eyre for Essex.

16 JUST 1/819 m. 28.

17 T.D. Hardy (ed.), *Rotuli chartarum, 1199–1216* (Record Commission, 1837), p. 211.

The record of their crown pleas sessions in Suffolk is preserved in a single manuscript preserved in The National Archives at Kew, London, as JUST 1/818, in which the hearing of the pleas occupies both sides of membranes 45 to 55. These are immediately followed by three more membranes, 56 to 58, containing all the issues of the crown pleas except those for Dunwich, which are entered at the end of the roll on membrane 62 – these four membranes make up the 'amercements section' of the crown pleas. A number of hands wrote the civil pleas, but a single clerk appears to have been responsible for the entire text of the crown pleas, except for those for Dunwich. The parchment on which he wrote is flawed several times by holes and tears, and also by later rubbing, which has rendered illegible the margins of the lower portions of several membranes. But the sense of the text is rarely lost, while many names of both persons and places which cannot now be read in it have been recovered from entries in the amercements section. The roll is not the one kept for William of York, effectively the eyre's principal justice, which would be distinguished by its having marginal notes of debts and dues struck through as these were entered in the record of financial issues which was drawn up when proceedings ended, and must therefore have been compiled by one of the clerks employed by colleagues of York's.

It cannot be said that the clerk responsible for nearly all the crown pleas did a very good job. His hand, though unremarkable, is usually clear enough; his 'c's and 't's, and his 'n's and 'u's, can be hard to distinguish, but where there is obscurity it is usually due more to carelessness than to bad penmanship. The proceedings recorded in the roll will have been largely conducted in Anglo-Norman French, as the language of government and of the landowning classes, though English must sometimes also have been spoken, and taken down in note-form in court, before being turned into a formal record composed in Latin.[18] The clerk more than once did this part of his work so badly as to make it difficult – in one case impossible (**1553**) – to tell exactly what had happened (**1433**, **1539**, **1583**). His record of a single appeal omitted part of the proceedings, and in a list of sureties ran two names into one (**1445**). Richard son of William of Bergholt was described as having killed Fulk son of Arnold, who was then said to have appealed Richard of his own death (**1395**), and the death of a chaplain was recorded as having taken place among sheep (*bidentibus*) instead of among men drinking (*bibentibus*) (**1224**). A fugitive's chattels might be recorded in shillings in the main text, and in the same number of pence in the margin (**1417**). This last case can at least be resolved by checking in the amercements list, but comparisons of these two parts of the roll more often show that the clerk had persistent problems with the rendering of names, which frequently appear in different forms. Thus Brun de *Latguine* and John le Chinnere in the main text appear respectively as Bruning of Grimston and John Ikin in the amercements section, and the man variously named John de Geraunvile and John de Gerardvile in the entry in which he was appealed of wounding and robbery was finally recorded as owing 10s. for his trespass under the name of John de Crammaville (**1200**, **1605**). Ivo was turned into Guy and Walter into William, while Godiva changed sex to become Godwin. Although such variations seldom create insoluble problems, the historian who uses this record needs to be constantly aware of the technical shortcomings of the clerk who compiled it.

18 For the language of the courts see P.A. Brand, *Observing and recording the medieval bar and bench at work*, Selden Society lecture (1999).

A crown pleas session revolved around presentments by juries.[19] For Suffolk in 1240 there were thirty-three of these, of which twenty-four represented the ancient administrative units known as hundreds into which the county was divided, while the remaining nine spoke on behalf of urban communities of varying size and importance. In Suffolk eyre rolls the latter are referred to throughout as 'vills', but in the headings to their pleas, as well as in this introduction, they have been designated 'boroughs' to emphasise their distinctive status. Most juries had twelve members, but there was no uniformity. Babergh and Blackbourn were considered to be double hundreds and had twenty-four jurors apiece, while Plomesgate and Samford each had eighteen jurors as a result of their both consisting of one and a half hundreds. At the other end of the scale, Mutford, Lothingland, Exning and Cosford all ranked as half-hundreds and therefore had only six jurors each. And in between came two fragmented hundreds. The bishop of Norwich's lordship of South Elmham was called a borough, but it answered as a quarter of the hundred of Wangford, with a jury of six men according to the text but of only three according to the amercements section; the latter figure is more likely to be correct, since the rest of the hundred was represented by nine jurors, so that the entire hundred would have had a conventional twelve-strong jury. And Claydon and Thredling, units in the centre of the county on either side of the hundred of Bosmere, answered as a single hundred of which Claydon constituted two-thirds and Thredling the rest – the roll of the 1286/7 Suffolk eyre spelt out that this entailed Claydon contributing eight men to the common jury and Thredling the remaining four.

The protocols of an eyre required the bailiff of each hundred or borough to nominate two men, who should be knights, to select a further ten (or more, or fewer, as was required) to make up its jury. These, too, should be knights, if such were available, otherwise they were to be 'free and law-abiding men'. No kalendar listing the 1240 eyre's juries has survived. The twelve men who represented Dunwich are for some reason entered among the civil pleas (**1146**). Of the remaining 383 jurors, one can be identified from his having failed to turn up, an offence which cost him 6s. 8d. (**1465**, **1630**), while the names of some of the others can be recovered from the amercements section, as a result of their having been penalised for shortcomings in the performance of their duties. A number of these men can be found among the civil pleas, which show that some knights were indeed chosen as jurors. Bosmere, Hartismere, Samford and Babergh had two apiece, Blything and Blackbourn one each; since their names appear at the heads of these lists, they had probably all been electors of their various juries. Neither of the presumed electors for Lothingland, on the other hand, is recorded as having been a knight, but one of them, Robert of Blundeston, is recorded as litigating over land at the eyre (**231**), as are a number of the known jurors for other hundreds, so that it seems likely that most jurors, and perhaps all of them, were men of property, to an extent sufficient to give them weight within their communities. In the phrasing of a later age, they represented the squirearchy of the county. The jurors who spoke for the boroughs will likewise have been among their foremost inhabitants.

All these men swore before the justices that they would speak the truth in response to questions put to them in a set of formal articles, the *Capitula Itineris* or

[19] The best and fullest accounts of the conduct of an eyre's crown pleas sessions remain those of C.A.F. Meekings, in his introductions to *Crown pleas of the Wiltshire eyre, 1249*, Wiltshire Archaeological and Natural History Society, Records Branch xvi (1960), and *The 1235 Surrey eyre*, 3 vols, Surrey Record Society xxxi–xxxii, xxxvii (1979–2002).

'Articles of the Eyre'. When first drawn up in 1194 there had been about twenty of these, and although several of them were subsequently dropped as obsolete, others were added, and although precision is difficult, it can be said that in 1240 there were about forty articles to which the juries were required to answer. They have been analysed in detail elsewhere,[20] so that it is only necessary to say here that where serious crime – in medieval parlance felonies, potentially entailing judgment of death for those convicted of them – was concerned, the most important were the first, involving cases left unfinished at the previous eyre, and the second, relating to offences committed since that last eyre, in the five years since 1235. Presentments under the first article were always rare, and only two were made at this eyre (**1273**, **1431**), but the second was of all the articles the most productive of judicial business. Some of the others were also relevant to crime and law enforcement, for example escapes of suspects from prisons and offences against the coinage. But most were concerned with the protection of royal rights and revenues, and the conduct of the officials required variously to maintain and collect them, and with other matters of concern to the King's government, like attendance at local courts and – since this affected the nation's trade – the observance of the assizes of wine and cloth. On all these issues the juries prepared answers which were then delivered in the form of *veredicta*. The word means 'true speakings', but despite the name they were presented in writing as well as orally, so that the justices could check the information which the juries provided by word of mouth against the texts which those same juries had also submitted to them.

The eyre roll shows that they did so with determination, both by detecting errors and omissions in what jurors told them and by using the other means at their disposal in pursuit of the facts. The number of lapses on the part of juries was not in fact very great – eighteen in all, two of them in a single case. It was the judgment of a notable scholar of eyre rolls that 'The more we study the omissions and substantial misstatements of fact, the more we are likely to conclude that they were made deliberately and not from forgetfulness',[21] and on the whole a close examination of the Suffolk pleas bears out his finding. One of the earliest entries, for instance, shows the Bosmere jury making a cursory presentment of an appeal of homicide, which the justices were then able to amplify by reference to the coroners' rolls, which revealed that the killing had stemmed from a quarrel involving a local landowner who would doubtless have been glad to have his involvement passed over in silence. The jurors were therefore put in mercy for having 'falsely concealed this', and also for having wrongly declared that Englishry had not been presented and that a murder fine was therefore due – perhaps they hoped that conceding the King's right to money from the case would avert that examination of the coroners' records which might, and indeed did, bring their attempted deceit to light (**1162**). Three further cases entailed false presentments of Englishry (**1191**, **1226**, **1527**), and it is easy to see how transgressions like these, and others such as failing to name a man who had infringed the assize of cloth (**1464**), or undervaluing an abjuror's chattels (**1258**), or omitting to name a neighbour to a death (**1367**) or the first finders of corpses (**1414**, **1470**), could have been welcomed by individuals or communities who were spared an amercement, or loss of goods, or just a troublesome appearance at the eyre.

20 By Meekings, in the introductions cited in note 19 above. The articles to which the jurors answered at the 1240 eyre are set out below on p. lxvii.

21 Meekings, *Crown pleas of the Wiltshire eyre, 1249*, p. 35.

Inevitably there were occasions on which it is hard to see how a jury could have hoped to benefit either themselves or anybody else through silence or misrepresentation, and which may in fact be best explained as resulting from ignorance or carelessness. The Loes jurors, for instance, who had said all that was required of them about lands formerly held by a Norman at Brandeston (**1340**), but were then amerced in the very next entry for presenting nothing about an estate similarly held at Cretingham (**1341**), may simply have forgotten about it, though it is also possible that they were less than fully prepared to respond to what in 1240 was a novelty among the *Capitula Itineris*. How the justices discovered the omission of Cretingham is not explained. For serjeanties and churches they could have consulted the records of the previous eyre, which they will have had at their disposal, while for the many other matters in which they found fault with vills and individuals, as well as juries, they could have referred to the rolls of the coroners and sheriffs. These records, along with juries' *veredicta*, must have provided the justices which much of the information they needed for the conduct of the eyre, but there are entries in which the appearance of additional detail suggests that they had applied themselves to discovering more about a case. In that of an unknown man found dead in Steeple Creeting graveyard, for instance, the Stow jurors probably reported no more than the event and added that they did not know who the dead man was, though they may also have conceded that a murder fine was due. They failed to mention that he had been buried without a coroner's view, and were therefore put in mercy, as was the vill itself. But the justices continued to probe, and though the dead man's name did not come to light, they were still able to establish that he came either from Steeple Creeting itself or from one of the cluster of nearby vills named Creeting, that he had suffered from epilepsy, that he had been found dead in the church, and finally that the priest had had his body taken out and buried (**1241**).

It should not be thought, however, that the conduct of this or any other crown pleas session entailed ceaseless skirmishing between justices and jurors, with the former striving endlessly to ferret out what the latter were determined to conceal. Not only was the number of recorded errors and omissions small at this eyre, but some of the presentments made by jurors constitute striking evidence for their being both willing and able to provide the kind of facts which the justices called for, and in so doing illustrate the way in which a system of law enforcement based on continuous presentments to courts and officials both generated information and worked against its concealment. The justices could never have known about the unknown lad who abjured the realm for theft from Dalham church, for instance, if the Risebridge jury had not presented it, since the coroner did not oversee the event; he might have sent his clerk instead, but even if he did, the abjuration was not recorded in his roll (**1497**). No less significant in this context is the killing of John the son of the smith of Boxford. Two men had been outlawed for this felony before the eyre began, but the Babergh jurors found there was more to say about it, telling how one of the killers, an Essex man, had spent a single night in Boxford, 'at the house of John le Chinnere, who is similarly suspected of having connived in John's death, on account of disputes at one time between them'. He was therefore put in exigent, in the process showing how communal alertness both to the movements of strangers and to relations between villagers could afterwards enable a jury to bring a man's involvement in felony home to him (**1468**).

The presentment of their *veredicta* was not the only contribution made by juries to the conduct of an eyre. Another preliminary task was the making of indictments, by preparing what were known as *privata* or *secreta* – lists of suspected felons which they handed in to the justices, who in turn transmitted them to the sheriff, so that he and his subordinates could try to arrest the men and women named, and produce them at the eyre. The word most commonly used of people indicted, *rettatus* (translated as 'charged'), could be applied both to suspects who stood trial and to those who escaped arrest; the eyre roll probably names as many of the latter as of the former, showing that indictment did not always achieve its purpose. Nor, when suspects came into court, were they always, or even often, convicted. The trial jury seems usually to have consisted of the hundred jury, reinforced in a number of cases by the representatives of four vills, presumably those nearest to the scene of the alleged crime. Both with and without such additions, jurors acquitted suspects far more often than they convicted them. It may seem strange that they should clear those whom they had themselves apparently accused, and occasionally (though not at this eyre) they were penalised for contradicting themselves, but more often the justices appear to have accepted that it was the task of juries to pass on the allegations and suspicions of others so that these could be tested in court, where, however, they might then be found to be baseless.

Many voices might be heard in the court over which it is assumed that Bath and Preston presided. The steady recital of juries' *veredicta* might be interrupted at any time as something he heard caused a justice to give an order (**1344**) or ask a question (**1181**). A *veredictum* would be constantly checked against the rolls of the sheriff, and especially of the coroner, and also against the presentments of other juries. The jury for Orford presented that Baldwin of Glemham and Reynold, the son of Gilbert the miller, had been seen at the town mill one evening but never afterwards, and then, presumably under pressure from the bench, that Baldwin had been drowned in a fit of insanity, while Reynold ran away for fear of being charged with his death. Either the justices remained suspicious or others were determined to bring the truth to light, for the jury for the inland hundred of Loes, supported by four nearby vills, established that Reynold had indeed killed Baldwin, and that the deed had been covered up not only at the eyre by the Orford jury, but earlier by the borough of Orford itself, when it failed to present Baldwin's death in the county court. Reynold was therefore put in exigent, while proceedings ended with the borough of Eye, in the north-east corner of Hartismere hundred, near Suffolk's boundary with Norfolk, being put in mercy for harbouring him outside frankpledge – in their pursuit of the facts the justices had tracked the case across a large part of the county (**1320**).

Those who came into court in any capacity were liable to be questioned, or at least called upon to testify. The reeve and four men representing Laxfield vill declared that two women attached as neighbours to the killing of Walter Nobelet had died, only to be shown up when the women came to the eyre (**1362**). It may have been as a neighbour to an accidental death that Robert de Suzleboys (*alias* Underwode) presented that Thomas son of Walter, another neighbour, had died, when he had merely failed to attend (**1436**). Some participants, indeed, spoke up for themselves without waiting to be asked – the man whom the Lothingland jury said had been the first to find the bodies of men killed in Hobland mill promptly protested 'that he was not the first to find him because many found him before he saw him', an obviously indignant claim which the jurors found themselves unable to deny (**1414**).

Similar objections might be made by suspects claiming that they had been maliciously indicted. This was a possibility which all the participants in an eyre had to keep in mind. The Thredling jurors who acquitted Roger Onhund and Roger the smith of Debenham of harbouring felons added to their verdict a declaration that the charges against the two men had originated in the malice of John Blackeye and Roger of Winston, who consequently had to make fine for their offence (**1268–9**), and the Lackford jury did the same in disclosing that Peter the son of Henry of Livermere had been indicted for theft at the instigation of his own father, with whom he was at odds over land (**1589**). The justices, too, were expected to be alert for signs of rancour which if undetected could send an accused person to the gallows, and to be ready to investigate accordingly. The case of Robert le Franceys, charged by the Babergh jurors with killing Alan the servant of Walter Wild, but acquitted by them and four vills, may provide an example of their having done so, for after his acquittal Robert was found to have been indicted 'out of hatred' by two named men (unfortunately it is impossible to say whether they were themselves members of the jury), one of whom had to make a one-mark fine (**1474**). And in one dramatic case the initiative was taken by the accused, when two men and a woman, charged with various kinds of theft by the jurors for Beccles, refused to put themselves on the jury of that borough, which they claimed had a grudge against them, but instead demanded trial by the twelve of Wangford hundred. There may well have been a good deal of shouting while accusations were made and rebutted, but the accused had their way, and the record of their eventual acquittal concludes with a summary of the issues which underlay their indictment – one man was detested because he had taken at farm (for a fixed rent), and so had sole use of, a piece of land in which the men of the borough had been accustomed to enjoy common rights, and the wife of the other man had been in the habit of quarrelling with her neighbours, while the husband of the accused woman, a former bailiff of Beccles, had similarly engaged in disputes with its inhabitants (**1221**). The case illustrates one of the ways in which animosities common in medieval English communities, both rural and urban, could find expression, as well as showing how they could be detected and punished – their malignancy cost the Beccles jurors as least £1 13s. 4d. (**1607**).

Many suspects escaped arrest following their indictment, and though a few were cleared *in absentia*, most were put in exigent, to be outlawed (men) or waived (women) if they failed to surrender to the King's peace and stand trial. A very few did so before the eyre had ended. Aylwin Punche, indicted and in exigent for harbouring thieves, subsequently came before the justices and was acquitted by the Thingoe jurors responsible for his indictment (**1518**), while Eustace the miller, charged in Babergh hundred with killing his wife, was able to clear himself in the most conclusive way possible by presenting himself in court in the company of his supposedly dead spouse (**1483**). More are likely to have sought acquittal at subsequent gaol deliveries, or at special sessions like one held at Thetford on 9 September 1235.[22] Arranged specifically to try suspects indicted at recent eyres for Norfolk and Suffolk, people from the former county predominate in its record, but thirty men and women from Suffolk were said to have either surrendered themselves or been arrested after the county's latest eyre ended on 14 January, nearly eight months earlier. All were suspected of theft except for two men charged with homicide; these last had remained in prison, but the other twenty-eight were released after finding sureties for their attendance; of these, two men and a woman did not show up and were put in exigent again, while no verdict was recorded on two women who also failed to appear. Of the rest, seven were convicted and hanged, and a further six

22 JUST 1/1173 mm. 6d–7d.

were convicted of petty thefts, conventionally involving goods valued at 12d. or less, and were instructed to find guarantors for their future good behaviour. The remaining twelve, including the suspected killers, were acquitted altogether.

There is no way of telling how many fugitives had declined to take their chance in court, but remained at large in 1235 after being put in exigent. But it can at least be said that on the evidence of the figures from Thetford there were good grounds for suspicion against at least half the men and women who made off but later came into court. Of those who persisted in staying out of the reach of royal justice the proportion who would probably have been convicted is likely to have been higher. It thus seems reasonable to suggest that in spite of some obvious failings, the presenting juries at the 1240 Suffolk eyre were in general careful and conscientious in making indictments, and the same can probably be said of their performance in giving verdicts and making presentments. Of their verdicts, indeed, nothing can be usefully said, since like the ordeals they replaced they constituted the judgments of God, and were similarly inscrutable.[23] Suspects could attempt to take precautions against possible bias before a verdict was taken, by challenging a jury or by paying for an especially searching inquest (**1434**), but not afterwards. But the presentments which juries made in their *veredicta* were clearly subjected to close scrutiny.

It is hazardous, and indeed impossible, for want of the necessary evidence, to assess either the completeness or the reliability of the 1240 Suffolk crown pleas as a whole.[24] On the evidence of other such records, many more accidental deaths were probably presented than were entered on the roll, and some killings by unknown malefactors may also have been omitted. Lower courts will have heard of many acts of violence, and heard suits against numerous suspected thieves, of which no mention was made at the eyre – the proceedings at Thetford in 1235, for instance. Evidence has been cited for determined efforts to misrepresent or conceal criminal acts, and to bring capital charges against men and women which could have brought them to the gallows. It is impossible to be certain that other attempts did not succeed. It has been estimated, largely on the basis of evidence from later in the thirteenth century, that up to fifteen per cent of the homicides committed in a county may have been omitted from the average crown pleas roll, either because their inclusion served no purpose or because they were concealed from the justices. Applying that estimate to Suffolk between 1235 and 1240 would not invalidate any statistical conclusions that could be drawn from the roll, though it might make it necessary to modify them. But perhaps more important than any possible shortfall in completeness is the evidence which the 1240 crown pleas provide for the determination of the justices to uncover the facts, to obtain the information, which it was the purpose of their eyre to collect. And with that determination went the willingness of juries – except when particular interests were involved, of course – to assist them in their task, impelled, in the last resort, by an understanding that the King's peace was also their own.

23 T.F.T. Plucknett, *Edward I and criminal law* (Cambridge, 1960), pp. 72–6.

24 The reliability of crown pleas rolls is assessed by H. Summerson, '"A photograph of English life"? The trustworthiness of the thirteenth-century crown pleas rolls', in D. Ibbetson, N. Jones and N. Ramsay (eds), *English legal history and its sources: essays in honour of Sir John Baker* (Cambridge, 2019), pp. 100–20.

Keeping the peace and enforcing the law

The peace which the Suffolk eyre served to uphold was that of God, and under God that of the King, the fount of justice in England. The King appointed justices itinerant, and also, with very few exceptions, the sheriffs, the men who directed the government of the counties of England in his name and under whom there existed a variety of officials, of whom in the present context the coroners were the most important. Serjeants, bailiffs and beadles made up the lowest level of the administrative hierarchy. Since the previous eyre, three men, Thomas de Hemmegrave, Thomas of Ingoldisthorpe and Robert de Briwes, had held the joint shrievalty of Norfolk and Suffolk, with each of them serving for between eighteen months and two years; its present incumbent, John de Ulecote, had only recently taken up office when the eyre began, having been appointed at Michaelmas 1239.[25] All government in England was ultimately the King's, but in administering it in Suffolk the sheriff had powerful competitors, in the prior of Ely and the abbot of St Edmund's.[26] All over the country rights of government, of varying consequence and value, had fallen into private hands, either by long usage or by royal grant. Few had accumulated franchises, as such privileges are conventionally known, on the scale of these two prelates. Both enjoyed that of return of writs, which gave them the right to receive from the sheriff any writ instructing him to take action of some kind within their immense estates – eight and a half hundreds in the case of St Edmund's, five and a half in the case of Ely – and themselves execute the order contained in it, only notifying him afterwards that it had been carried out, while the abbot could even exclude royal justices from the borough at the centre of his liberty – the name given to the whole aggregate of lands within which he exercised his franchises.

This is not to say that the holder of a liberty exercised unrestricted power within it. A disregarded writ could be the occasion of a follow-up, a writ of *non omittas* to the sheriff commanding him to enter the liberty from which he had at first been excluded, and there execute the King's orders. And procedures of government and proceedings in courts within liberties were in all important matters required to keep in step with those in force outside their boundaries. This was made plain in the case of St Edmund's by the rules for the hearing of crown pleas laid down by a charter of Henry III's granted in 1231, dealing with uncertainties created by the abolition of trial by ordeal in 1219.[27] Appeals could be terminated in the abbey court, either by combat or by an inquest, but men and women charged with felony by presentment or indictment were only to be tried before justices itinerant. These regulations appear to have been observed. A presentment at the outset of the liberty's pleas not only recorded that the presentments of Englishry were to be made exactly as they were elsewhere in the county, but also followed the 1231 charter in setting out procedure for the hearing of appeals (**1466**). And so it was that two men appealed of homicide were recorded in 1240 as having been acquitted 'in the court of St Edmund', but a third suspect was put in exigent at the eyre – this was not left to the liberty (**1579**). Similarly William Thwosogod, a suspected thief, was imprisoned at St Edmund's for production at the eyre – the justices called for judgment on the borough when he failed to appear (**1570**). Equally significant, though it dealt with a less serious

25 Details from *1240 Suffolk Civil Pleas*, p. lxxiii.

26 See H. Cam, 'The king's government as administered by the greater abbots of East Anglia', in *Liberties and communities in medieval England* (London, 1963), pp. 183–204.

27 *Calendar of Charter Rolls 1226–1257*, pp. 131–2.

kind of transgression, was an order for the arrest of five suspected poachers, which was directed simultaneously to the sheriff and to the steward of St Edmund's, and which further demonstrates how all liberties, however great their lords and high their privileges, still formed part of a national system of government, with powers which might be extensive but were not unlimited (**1529**).

On 1 June 1233, at a time of growing political tension, the government issued peace-keeping ordinances which were sent to all sheriffs and were to be observed everywhere, within liberties as well as outside them.[28] They were primarily directed towards the humblest components of the national system of law enforcement, the rural communities known as vills and their adult inhabitants. Proclamation was to be made throughout each county that until Michaelmas vills were to have at least four watchmen, with a particular responsibility for controlling the movements of strangers, who were to be arrested if possible, and pursued with hue and cry if they ran away. Those who stood their ground were not to be lodged for more than one night. When in 1240 the Babergh jurors presented that Gilbert Heved from Essex was suspected of killing a man at Boxford, and averred that he was 'never harboured in Boxford except for one night', it was probably this peace-keeping measure, or one very like it, that they had in mind (**1468**).

Alongside the exclusion and constraint of outsiders, and the call to action against the potentially or actually lawless represented by the hue and cry, there went the controls exerted upon those who lived in vills by the system known as frankpledge. In a county like Suffolk this entailed the enrolment of every male who reached the age of twelve in a tithing, conventionally a group of ten men who were sworn both to keep the peace themselves and to keep law-abiding the other members of their tithings (in Dunwich known as leets). Women were not in frankpledge, presumably because they were regarded as being under the control of their husbands, nor were children; William Bule, who ran away because he was suspected of stealing malt, and was licensed to return because the value of his theft was small, was said to be 'not in a tithing because he was under age' (**1315**). Others exempted from being in frankpledge included strangers from other counties (**1468**, **1569**) or even countries (**1277**, **1539**), clerics (**1237**, **1248**, **1366**, **1408**, **1511**, **1522**) and men in the households of men or women of substance who were expected, and indeed required, to enforce good behaviour among their agents or servants, and were amerced if they failed to do so. Such households, also known as 'mainpasts' meaning literally those who ate the bread of their lords, could be those of men as great as the earl of Norfolk (**1324**), or of heads of religious houses like the abbot of Leiston (**1445**) and the prioress of Wix (**1486**). Some were minor landowners, like Thomas de Haya (**1539**) and William de Colville (**1264**), while others appear to have been no more than fathers of families, unable, as it turned out, to control their own sons (**1346**, **1366**, **1511**).

One further exemption from frankpledge is problematic. In 1240 (**1195**), and again at the 1286/7 eyre,[29] men committing felony were said not to have been in a tithing because they were free. Suffolk, however, was a county in which personal freedom is generally agreed to have been unusually widespread, and to have become more so as the thirteenth century progressed. It is very hard to see how frankpledge could have functioned, or indeed served any useful purpose, if only a diminishing

28 *Close Rolls of Henry III, 1231–1234*, pp. 309–10.

29 E.g. JUST 1/833 mm. 15, 28d, 44d, 45.

minority of the county's male population was included in it. Yet although it failed on numerous occasions to prevent men in tithings from committing acts of felony, their recorded numbers, at both eyres, provide clear evidence that considerable numbers of adult males were indeed in frankpledge, and therefore ostensibly unfree. Since many felons in tithings had no chattels, it is possible that their low standing, socially and economically, has made them largely invisible to historians. It is also possible that free men who bought villein lands, as they did in increasing numbers, also took on with their acquisitions obligations associated with unfreedom, and that these included recruitment into tithings. The enigma seems insoluble, and it can only be said that to outward appearances, frankpledge was still a major factor in 1240 in the maintenance of law and order in Suffolk.

The engagement of vills, and those who lived in them, in the task of peace-keeping was supervised and controlled through a network of inquests and courts.[30] The significance of the latter did not lie only in their jurisdictions, which were limited, but also in their role in receiving and disseminating information. It was for this reason, as well as because it had a modest financial consequence, that an eyre might hear presentments concerning the performance of suit, that is, the attendance at courts due by certain people by reason of the lands they held; its withdrawal could hinder the receipt and distribution of particulars concerning the keeping of the peace (**1356**, **1405**). The hundred court, meeting every three weeks, could hang thieves caught in the act, and though in general its competence was mostly limited to actions over brawls and debts of less than 40s., it could also become involved in more important matters. Probably in 1238 or 1239, Adam of Boulogne, in dispute with the locally influential William de Cyresy, who had taken his cattle in distraint, 'claimed the King's peace' against William in Bosmere hundred court, with the result that he was obliged to give assurances there before the King's bailiffs that he would do no harm to Adam, and to find sureties for observing his undertaking. The precaution failed, for on the very next day William sent men to make a further distraint upon Adam, thereby precipitating a fight in which William the son of Nicholas de *Westwode* was killed, but the case shows how a hundred court could serve as a public forum for a peace-keeping measure (**1162**).

The circumstances surrounding William's death were largely revealed at the eyre by the coroners. Then and later, Suffolk had two royal coroners; the abbot of St Edmund's, too, had a coroner for the hundreds under his jurisdiction (**1497**), while at the end of the eyre the men of Lothingland hundred negotiated the right to have two coroners of their own, paying twenty marks for the privilege (**1430**). Holding inquests into deaths caused by violence or misadventure, or simply occurring in suspicious circumstances, was one of a coroner's most important functions. Summoned to the scene by someone from the place where a death took place, he was required to convoke all the adult male inhabitants of at least four neighbouring vills, and then conduct an inquest to establish the cause of death and, if necessary, assign responsibility for it. Should anyone be charged, or need to be attached – obliged to find guarantors for his or her appearance at the next eyre, when the death ought to be presented – the coroner was expected to give the necessary instructions. The only royal coroner to be named at the 1240 eyre was Robert Malet, as a knight

30 See H. Summerson, 'The structure of law enforcement in thirteenth century England', *American Journal of Legal History* 23 (1979), pp. 313–27; idem, 'Maitland and the criminal law in the age of Bracton', in J. Hudson (ed.), *The history of English law: centenary essays on 'Pollock and Maitland'* (Oxford, 1996), pp. 115–43.

and minor landowner a typical member of the county squirearchy from which such officials were usually recruited, who was identified by being amerced for failing to arrange the attachment of four neighbours to an accidental death (**1309**).[31]

When a death was felonious, the large attendance at an inquest was a means of publicising it as well as of identifying those responsible for it. If a killer was named but remained at large, the coroner's inquest was a means of ensuring that a whole neighbourhood knew about the deed and its perpetrator, putting its inhabitants on their guard and increasing the chances of an arrest being made. The exclusion of the coroner from the half-hundred of Exning was thus potentially a serious matter (**1460**). Much the same purpose was served by the similarly large attendance required at another of the coroner's major functions, namely an abjuration of the realm. The suspected thief or killer who took advantage of this extension of the right of sanctuary by fleeing to a church and refusing to surrender to the King's peace, opting instead to swear to leave the country and never return, made his promise before all the inhabitants of the neighbouring vills who had gathered to prevent his escape from the church in which he had taken refuge.[32] All could hear his oath and mark his departure, and so be ready to pursue and capture him if he left his assigned path to the coast, or returned to the vicinity he had sworn to leave.

This was not all, however, for suspicious deaths and attendant inquests, abjurations, indeed anything that led to the raising of the hue, were subject to a further series of regular inquests, in the form of the sheriff's tourn. Every six months, at Easter and Michaelmas, the sheriff (or the abbot's steward in the liberty of St Edmund) circulated the county hundred by hundred, holding an especially well-attended meeting of their courts. Part of his purpose was to ensure that all were in frankpledge who ought to be. A necessary precaution, implementing it was no easy task. Along with those rightfully exempted from membership of tithings, the 1240 roll contains references to a number of men who should have been enrolled but were not, thanks to oversight or omission on the part of vills. Some, indeed, had avoided becoming members of tithings for a long time. Gilbert the smith, in exigent for homicide, was found to have been living in Gisleham for nearly five years outside frankpledge (**1165**). His profession should have made him a well-known member of the community, and the same is true of John the miller of Rede, another killer, who was allowed to live at Brockley, a short distance away, likewise without joining a tithing (**1516**). In the case of William of Eleigh, who had land and houses as well as chattels worth 42s., uncertainty as to his status may have allowed him to remain outside frankpledge (**1198**), while others may simply have escaped enrolment because they were birds of passage, never long in one place. Such, perhaps, were John le Waleys and his presumed son Walter, who had been residing respectively in Glemsford and its near neighbour Cavendish before they both abjured the realm from Somerton church. John had chattels worth just 5s. while Walter had none; both may well have been Welsh, as their name suggests, outsiders moving through Suffolk in pursuit of a livelihood (**1480**, **1489**).

The tourn was not only a means of checking whether all who should be were members of tithings, it also provided a way of obtaining and circulating information about criminality and disorder, and it achieved this by exploiting that system of

---

31 For Robert Malet see P. Brown (ed.), *Sibton Abbey cartularies and charters* i, SRS, Suffolk Charters 7 (1985), pp. 71–2.

32 R.F. Hunnisett, *The medieval coroner* (Cambridge, 1961), p. 41.

frankpledge which it was also designed to supervise. Suffolk records are uninformative about the holding of the tourn, but it is unlikely that its procedure differed from that of Norfolk, where in 1257 a jury for East Flegg hundred, at the eastern end of that county's border with Suffolk, told how until recently 'the sheriffs of this county were accustomed to make inquests at their tourns by free men of this hundred, who were wont to be informed by vills on articles put to them …'.[33] It was the usual practice for the heads of tithings, who could be expected to be respectable men in their vills – in 1240 one of them was also recorded as having been a beadle, a minor official (**1517**) – to answer to those articles, under which presentments were then made to the sheriff, and those articles in their turn closely resembled those to which hundred juries answered at the eyre. Indeed, those of the tourn, on the evidence of a set circulating in Devon, were in some respects even more wide-ranging, for in addition to the 'old and new pleas of the crown', the tithingmen were expected to report every occasion on which the hue had been raised, however trivial the disorder behind it might turn out to be.[34]

Through these same channels the sheriff also received indictments against suspected felons, just as the justices did at eyres, so that efforts could be made to capture them – later records of gaol deliveries, and indeed of eyres, contain many cases of suspects having been arrested on such grounds. But no less important was the publicity which proceedings at the tourn gave to recent felonies and offences against the peace, alerting those who attended it to crimes and suspects. The county court, too, at its monthly meetings, could serve the same purpose. Here the vills were required to make presentments directly, and could expect to be penalised if they failed to do so. In 1240, for instance, Aldeburgh vill was amerced for failing to present an accidental death by drowning (**1279**), and Syleham vill was similarly punished because it did not present that a woman had run away after leaving her stillborn child in a marlpit (**1369**).

This was not the only way in which the county court served to give notice to those attending it of events potentially relevant to their peace, for it was there that appeals of felony were usually begun and often ended. More is said about appeals in a later section; it is only necessary to say here that they were formulaic actions brought by individuals against at least one other person, alleging a felony which might be homicide or rape, but could be something less serious, perhaps wounding or assault; that their validity depended on the hue having been raised upon and pursuit made after the alleged felon; and that after a first prosecution the action had to be repeated at the next four sessions of the county. The person accused thus who came to the county could expect to be imprisoned if the charge was homicide; for other offences he or she would be required to find pledges for appearing at the next eyre. Appellees who did not present themselves there would be outlawed (if men – women were waived, but the status was the same) at what would be, in all, the fifth court at which the appeal had been made.

In a number of cases presented in 1240, it was recorded that an appeal had been made and that the accused person, having fled, had now been outlawed, liable to arrest and execution if captured. In other cases, appeals still undetermined when they came to the eyre were concluded there, while in a few instances a prosecutor

---

33 JUST 1/568 m. 36d.

34 H. Summerson (ed.), *Crown pleas of the Devon eyre of 1238*, Devon and Cornwall Record Society new series 28 (1985), p. 129.

was told to continue his or her action against an appellee who had failed to turn up until the latter was either attached or outlawed (**1211**, **1246**, **1328**). In at least one case, indeed, the threat of outlawry seems to have been sufficient to bring to the eyre an appellee who had at first stayed away from it (**1202**). Not every outlaw was forced out into the wilds, to live like the wolf whose head he was said to bear – Roger the son of Hugh of Rendham, whose outlawry was referred to at the eyre (**1274**), managed to survive for seventeen years before receiving a royal pardon, though it seems likely that he achieved this by moving to another county. Nonetheless, the extended process inherent in the appeal provided one more way of facilitating arrests and making sentences of outlawry effective, involving as it did repeated presentments and allegations in public courts. Following the raising of the hue, which should afterwards have been presented at the tourn, each appeal was then formally commenced in the county court, where it might be repeated several times. If it came to the eyre, it was given a further airing, before an even larger attendance, though by then it should already have been common knowledge. Word of other acts of violence – burglaries, for instance, or highway robberies – which were not the subject of appeals, should have been similarly circulated through the same system of presentment and inquiry in local courts. The names of suspects were disseminated by the same means. It was on these grounds, when taken together with their personal awareness of events in their own localities, that jurors could be expected to fill up their *veredicta* and make indictments when an eyre began.

Seen in this context, the eyre was the last in a sequence of local courts, to which it added a wider, even national, dimension. It had the highest jurisdiction, and one that was also well-nigh exclusive. Chapter 24 of Magna Carta had laid down that crown pleas – a term embracing all felonies as well as many other matters – were not to be heard by sheriffs or other officials, so that from 1215 onwards they could only be dealt with by royal justices. The abbot of St Edmund's enjoyed a parallel jurisdiction at the heart of his liberty, but nowhere else. The killing of two women 'within the liberty and vill of St Edmund's' was entered on the eyre roll after at least a cursory inquiry into their deaths (**1519**), and though an inquest held at St Edmund's acquitted Godfrey the son of Peter of the death of John de *Ambir'*, he was still entrusted to sureties to be produced at the eyre (**1571**). As noted above, the justices kept a close eye on the abbot's liberty, and did not allow it to exceed its proper bounds, and they treated the liberty of the prior of Ely with similar firmness. The court for the prior's liberty may have enjoyed a jurisdiction equivalent to that of the county court, but it does not appear for that reason to have been allowed to stand apart from it, since the justices called for discussion at the eyre when they discovered that an appeal of wounding made there had not been presented to the county (**1330**). They did the same when the Thredling jury presented that the prior's bailiff had heard an appeal of wounding, in direct contravention of Magna Carta, and the bailiff asserted that it was 'entirely lawful' for him to hear and decide the case; since the claim was not repeated at the 1286/7 eyre, it would seem that they refused to allow it (**1267**).

It was the business of the King's justices in 1240 to ensure, among other things, that the eyre retained its place at the centre of a network of royal and private courts, whose workings they were empowered to review. Many functions of government had come under the control of liberties, but they had not for that reason ceased to form part of a system of government which ultimately owed its authority to the King, so that their operations were of concern only to the lords who held them. On the contrary, the rest of the county needed to be kept informed about what happened within them, regardless of their extent, so that information relevant to peace-keeping in the shire as a whole could continue to be circulated. By 1240 many lords had acquired the franchise of view of frankpledge, giving them jurisdiction over minor offences presented to the sheriff at his tourn – infringements of the assizes of bread and ale, for instance. Procedure varied from vill to vill, but in all cases it was essential that presentments of lawbreaking should be made and communicated to the authorities. Failures to make the necessary arrangements, or to observe arrangements already made, could be corrected at the eyre; hence the presentment by the Samford jury that two powerful lords, Earl Warenne and Margery de Rivers, had been holding views of frankpledge in Holbrook and Harkstead respectively, 'without the King's bailiff' (**1402**). His attendance will have been required, not only, in the case of Harkstead, to collect a modest amount of money, but also to receive and pass on information concerning breaches of the King's peace in those two vills. It will have been at least partly for the same reason that a number of men and women of Wangford and Samford hundreds were named as having withdrawn their suits to – attendance at – hundred and county courts (**1356**, **1405**); their presence was required to give weight to proceedings there, but also to provide a way of communicating those proceedings to others. Indeed, it was by such means that the whole county was kept informed.

The processes of inquest and presentment were not endangered only by lords. The role of officials, and their ability to work with the men of the vills, was also important. Suspects, once named, had to be arrested, and once arrested, had to be either imprisoned or, in most circumstances, required to find sureties for their future appearance in court. The prominence of sureties is a striking feature of any crown pleas roll, and not only for their role in guaranteeing the appearance at the eyre of litigants and others whose presence was required for procedural reasons. Penal imprisonment played little part in the early thirteenth-century system of criminal justice; prisons were basically where suspects were held before they stood trial, and then only if they were charged with particularly serious offences – essentially homicide and theft for those caught in possession of stolen goods.[35] What usually happened when arrests were made can be illustrated from the case of Wyot of Kettlebaston, arrested on suspicion of theft, who was imprisoned in his own home, no doubt by the villagers of Kettlebaston, until he was released by the serjeant of Cosford hundred, who handed him over to his tithing and a couple of others – twelve men in all – who were made responsible for producing Wyot at the eyre (**1523**). They failed to do so, and were put in mercy, but the number of suspects who did attend shows that this procedure was not always ineffective.

Prisons in the sense of lock-ups were scarce. Suffolk's main prison was at Ipswich (**1162**), there was a gaol at St Edmund's (**1570**), from where prisoners could be transferred for trial at Cattishall, and suspects could also be held in Orford Castle (**1319**). All three could be the scene for gaol delivery proceedings. The eyre was the most important, but it was not the only kind of judicial visitation to be commissioned by the central government. Officials may have wanted to keep suspects out of their prisons, but they still needed to be cleared from time to time of those unavoidably held in them, and this was managed through commissions of gaol delivery, usually of four men, appointed to hold sessions at which suspects could

35 For prisons generally see R.B. Pugh, *Imprisonment in medieval England* (Cambridge, 1968).

be brought for trial. Assessing how often such proceedings took place in Suffolk in the years around 1240 has been made impossible by the disappearance of the chancery records for 1238/9 and 1239/40, and there is no way of telling how soon a gaol delivery took place after the 1240 eyre, or whether there was a special session for suspects arrested after it as there had been following the 1235 eyre. Only two hangings from the period between 1235 and 1240 were referred to in the latter year (**1380**, **1583**). That does not necessarily mean that few gaol deliveries took place, however, since most of those convicted would have had no chattels, leaving no reason for their being mentioned at the eyre, and the evidence from 1241 onwards suggests that, though hardly frequent, deliveries of Suffolk gaols were held with at least a degree of regularity. In March 1241 four local men were commissioned to deliver Ipswich gaol, while Roger of Thirkleby was appointed to deliver it again in May 1242, and then again in July that year. An interval of well over a year followed, until another commission to local men was issued in November 1243, this time for Orford gaol, while Thirkleby was yet again appointed to clear Ipswich gaol in the following month. Not long afterwards he received a further commission, to deliver the gaols of both St Edmund's and Ipswich at Cattishall on 19 May 1244, but no more such commissions appear to have been issued before justices itinerant visited Suffolk once more in 1245.[36]

The gaols delivered by royal commissioners would have been solid, perhaps even purpose-built, structures. But the term 'prison' was capable of a broad interpretation, especially in the context of escapes, which usually entailed a 100s. amercement on whoever was to blame. Stocks could be used to detain suspected felons as well as recalcitrant villeins. Hugh le Marlur's break-out from the stocks at Kelton led to a dispute between the bailiffs of the prior of Ely and William de Auberville, the joint lords of Plomesgate hundred, as to whose the stocks were and so who was responsible for Hugh's escape from them. Eventually it was decided that they had equal rights, and so the amercement was divided equally between them (**1284**, **1612**). But any convenient building might be pressed into service to hold a suspicious person, whether it was the earl of Norfolk's residence at Peasenhall (**1451**) or the house, probably that of the lord of Icklingham manor, in which Katherine of Icklingham was held as a suspected sheep-stealer – though bound in chains she managed to break out of them and then through the wall of the house (**1583**).

In securing as well as identifying and bringing charges against suspected malefactors, it was necessary that the inhabitants of vills should be both willing and able to cooperate with the sheriff and his subordinates. The minor officials of Suffolk are not well documented in the 1240 eyre roll, which may indicate that in general they were efficient and well-conducted, since their activities were most often recorded when they were found to have been incompetent or dishonest. In Suffolk they can occasionally be observed making attachments and arrests, or failing to do so. When a woman on pilgrimage fell dead in the road, it was the serjeant of Cosford hundred whom the coroner ordered to attach her husband, though he failed to act (**1521**). The bailiff of Wangford did no better, failing to attach a Bungay man appealed of rape (**1246**). In other cases it was the officials of boroughs and liberties who can be seen fulfilling similar police functions, whether it was the bailiffs of Ipswich, arresting and imprisoning two suspected killers (**1408**), or the bailiff of the bishop of Ely arresting a man caught in his employer's granary (**1480**). When Ralph the son of

[36] Details from C 66/49 m. 10d; C 66/50 m. 1d; C 66/51 mm. 2d, 7d, 12d.

Roger of Clare gave Richard the chaplain's son a fatal blow on the head with a cowl-staff, the men of Clare acted as they should by arresting Ralph and handing him over to the constable of Clare Castle, who, however, released him (**1511**). Cumulatively these failings do not amount to much, but they underline the way in which vills and officials were expected to work together.

As the eyre roll repeatedly demonstrates, the system which itinerant justices reviewed depended very heavily on the involvement of vills. In many cases they did all that was expected of them, if the silence of the eyre roll be taken as evidence. But there were also a number of occasions on which they were amerced for failings of various kinds – for not making presentments, for burying bodies without a coroner's view, for harbouring men outside frankpledge, and especially for failing to raise the hue upon suspects or failing to pursue them, most often both; some twenty-five vills were penalised for this. Such shortcomings may show that vills sometimes met their responsibilities grudgingly, if at all. They also show that the justices often failed to take circumstances, geography, or even basic human nature, into account. Eyke vill was amerced for failing to pursue a killer who fled to its church and abjured the realm, though if he had not been pursued he would presumably not have taken flight (**1324**). Holbrook vill was amerced because it neither raised the hue nor pursued after an unknown man was found killed in Holbrook park – one may wonder how long it took for his death to come to light (**1383**). In a county in which dispersed settlement was common, so that vills were frequently made up of widely separated houses, it must often have been hard for their inhabitants to come to the aid of one another when they were attacked by outsiders or when a fight broke out, or, indeed, to know that such aid was needed. And for those who heard shouts and screams from neighbouring houses, it was asking much that they should risk their lives, possibly in hours of darkness, by confronting armed and dangerous men, for instance by trying to capture the 'unknown thieves' who killed a woman in Earl Stonham (**1170**), or the malefactors who slew seven women in a single house in Sproughton (**1382**), or the killers of a man and two women in Barnham (**1551**), or those who waylaid the two men whose bodies were found in the road at Wetherden (**1227**). But the justices made no allowances in any of these cases, and put all those vills in mercy. Maintaining law and order in thirteenth-century Suffolk was a demanding business, often too demanding, it would seem, for the men and women whose shortcomings were so relentlessly recorded at the 1240 eyre. The various felonies which they were unable to prevent are considered in the following section.

Crimes and criminals

Accidental deaths, homicide and suicide

Death makes many appearances among the 1240 crown pleas, testimony to the insecurity of life even in a prosperous part of a country which had been at peace for the previous five years, having recovered from the civil war at the beginning of Henry III's reign, and from the briefer outbreaks of violence which troubled the early 1230s. Among the eighty deaths recorded at the eyre as caused by misadventure, drownings occur frequently, in rivers, marshes, ditches, fishponds, and the pits created by diggings for marl and peat. Many of those who perished thus were probably children, distinguished by being identified only as the son or daughter of a father or mother; in the case of an eighteen-month-old boy who drowned in a ditch in Wenham, the eyre roll spells out his age, and with it his vulnerability (**1379**). For adults, life was hardly more secure. They too might die by drowning, but also as they went about their daily business. Men and women lost their lives when they fell from horses or were run over by carts. Mills were dangerous places to work in – four men, two of them millers and a third the son of a miller, were killed by watermills (**1310**, **1386**, **1436**, **1565**), and a woman was struck dead by a windmill (**1584**). Perhaps William Luvered of Saxmundham thought himself safe in the barn of the prioress of Campsey Ash, until a beam fell on him and crushed him (**1325**). Edric of Debenham, a carpenter, fell over a beam and died as a result (**1265**), and Walter the mason was working on a building belonging to the Knights Templar in Dunwich when he fell from the top of it and was killed (**1596**). A maidservant named Basilia was crushed to death when a stack of corn fell on her (**1548**). Disease in the form of the 'falling sickness' – the name given to epilepsy, and also to other unexplained seizures – claimed a number of lives (**1171**, **1189**, **1241**, **1460**, **1598**).

Along with these hazards, and others like them (probably including many that were presented but not recorded at the eyre), the people of Suffolk were also exposed to the perils which arose from their dealings with their fellow human beings, many of them their relations and neighbours, but others who were strangers to them and their communities. As well as eighty accidental deaths, the eyre roll records 115 deaths which can be plausibly described as felonious, that is, resulting from malice or at any rate from acts of violence. That figure has to be qualified by an acknowledgement that imprecisions in the roll prevent complete statistical certainty; in the case of the death of Basilia the daughter of Gilbert Aylwin, for instance, the record leaves it unclear whether Stephen the son of William Threin deliberately killed her by chasing her into a ditch and then falling on her, or if he killed her accidentally in trying to rescue her (**1553**). But since the jury found that his action, whatever its motives, was the cause of her death, so that he was put in exigent, she has been included among the victims of homicide. Also included are two killings which took place in Norfolk (**1424**, **1530**) and one committed in Essex (**1525**) – the killers all appear to have been Suffolk men – and thirteen cases in which accusations of homicide led to those against whom they were made being acquitted, without anyone else being named as responsible; the record is usually sufficiently detailed to make it clear that a death had taken place, and is sometimes explicit that the circumstances had been violent, but not always. When John the son of Geoffrey appealed Elyas de Prato of causing the death of his sister Sabina, the wife of Elyas, by beating her when she was pregnant, and Elyas was acquitted by the Blything hundred jury, it seems safe to assume that Sabina was indeed dead, and also that she died in childbirth (**1441**). But when the Thedwestry jurors cleared Richard the son of Ranulf of the death of Roger le Furmager, and named no other suspect, all that it is possible to say is that Roger, too, was probably dead (**1576**). He has therefore been counted in the total of felonious deaths for the hundred and the eyre, but it is impossible to be certain that he should be so included.

Entries in the 1240 roll are rarely dated, and so it is impossible to say how many killings were committed in Suffolk during each of the five years covered by the eyre. What can be said is that if every alleged killing is included, then the average number was twenty-three per annum, and that both total and average were much higher than those recorded in similar sources for other counties in the years on either side of 1240. The 1238 Devon eyre, covering a period of ten years, heard of 149 killings, an average of almost exactly fifteen per annum; the 1241 Surrey eyre, covering six years, had only forty-seven killings, at an annual rate of between seven and eight; and the 1241 Berkshire eyre heard of sixty-four killings, also from six years, at an average rate of just over ten (damage to the record means that details of a few more may have been lost).[37] After the total figures, the most striking differences lie in the numbers of killings attributed to unknown malefactors – thirty-nine for Suffolk, just over a third of the total, but only thirteen for Devon, eleven for Surrey and sixteen for Berkshire. Berkshire was more prosperous than Surrey, and so more attractive to the criminally-inclined, but Suffolk was wealthier still, with the same dangerous consequences.

Taken as a whole, there is no obvious pattern for the distribution of homicide in Suffolk. The highest numbers were recorded in Blackbourn hundred, in the north of the county, with fourteen killings, seven of them by unknown criminals, and Samford, with thirteen, nine of them by unidentified marauders (seven of them in a single attack – **1382**), at its southern end. Bosmere and Claydon hundreds, in the centre of the shire, if taken together as they were later, had ten killings, but Colneis, next to Samford, recorded none. The boroughs were relatively safe, with only thirteen among all nine of them; neither Beccles nor Sudbury recorded any; Ipswich, unsurprisingly, had the most, with four. The danger of a violent death may overall have been greatest in the hundreds along the county's northern border with Norfolk, and was clearly least in those at the western end of the shire, with only two killings in Lackford and three apiece in Thingoe and Risbridge – a reflection, no doubt, of the relatively sparse population, and meagre resources, of the Brecklands. But overall it would appear that the people of Suffolk could be exposed to the violence of others anywhere in the county.

The eyre roll seldom provides much detail about the circumstances of homicide, and neither justices nor jurors tried to distinguish between what today would be defined respectively as murder and manslaughter, between premeditated killings carried out in cold blood, and deaths which, though still culpable, were the unintended results of sudden confrontations and brawls. A mechanism for doing so developed later in the thirteenth century,[38] but in 1240, in so far as it is possible to tell, the two kinds of killing were treated with the same severity. Both slayers and slain were predominantly men, with only five women being named among the former, but thirty-eight among the latter. Women were often targeted by unknown malefactors; they were probably seen as less likely to be able to defend themselves, and may also have been more likely to be at home, and vulnerable to attack there, when their husbands were at work; hence, perhaps, the death of Matilda the wife of Roger le Daneys, killed by unidentified evildoers who broke into Roger's house. Belstead vill was amerced for failing to raise the hue and pursue, but perhaps most of its inhabitants had been out in the fields with Roger (**1388**).

Of the killers who *were* identified, eleven had been outlawed before the eyre began, and twelve were recorded as having abjured the realm, while forty-three suspects were put in exigent, and thirty-one were acquitted, either in court or *in absentia* – licensed to return if they had run away. A man named Burghard, convicted of killing his unnamed brother, was sentenced to be hanged (**1209**), the fate already suffered for killing a woman by Matthew the son of Godfrey, hanged at a delivery of Cattishall gaol (**1380**). Sabina of Creeting, convicted of infanticide, was sentenced to be burnt (**1233**). The treatment of the clergy is discussed in a separate section,

---

37 Statistics from H.R.T. Summerson, 'The maintenance of law and order in England, 1227–1263', unpublished Cambridge PhD dissertation (1976).

38 See T.A. Green, *Verdict according to conscience: perspectives on the English criminal trial jury, 1200–1800* (Chicago, 1985), pp. 35–59.

and it is only necessary to say here that of the seven clerics who came into court on homicide charges, one was remanded because it was uncertain whether he had been ordained, and two were acquitted outright. Four were handed over to the bishop's representative, one having come into court after being put in exigent. A second was unequivocally convicted, while a third had been described as preventing a killer's arrest. Procedure in such cases had not yet become completely settled, and in the fourth case, that of Walter the parson of Blaxhall, suspected of killing a man found dead in his cattle-shed, the Plomesgate jurors are not said to have given a verdict; but since it was recorded that no one else was suspected, Walter may plausibly be described as having been convicted by implication (**1271**).

Fourteen killings were prosecuted by appeals of felony, of which seven were made by widows ('the death of her husband slain within her arms' was one of just two felonies for which, according to the letter of the law, a woman had the right to make an appeal), three by mothers, two by fathers and the rest respectively by a husband, a brother and a sister. The rest were presented by juries, who named, and sometimes indicted, the people suspected of them. The details which jurors provided of those they named as convicted or suspected killers show that, with few exceptions, they were poor. Twenty-three had no chattels, numerous others had chattels valued at only a few shillings or even pence. Many were also unfree, since forty-one were said to have been members either of tithings or of the households of men and women of local consequence, while a further seven should have been members of tithings but were not. Five were described as strangers, to set alongside all the malefactors who could not be identified.

Not every violent death was the work of peasants assailing or murdering one another. Of special interest in this context is a killing presented by the Blackbourn jury, which is unusual in that it plainly arose from a dispute between two landowners whose litigation is recorded among the civil pleas of the 1240 eyre. Henry of Livermere sued against Thomas de Haya over property in Little Livermere, in proceedings which clearly gave rise to considerable ill-feeling (**765–6**). Not only land but also fishing rights in Livermere itself – now Broad Water – appear to have been at issue, and when three of Thomas's men went out onto the lake in a boat, Henry's chaplain Geoffrey resolved to stop them. He accosted them as they came ashore, only for one of them to stab him to the heart. The killer fled to Great Livermere church and abjured the realm, while two Flemings, also members of Thomas's household, were put in exigent for abetting the felony; the misdeeds of his men cost Thomas a fine of ten marks (**1539**).

Social significance no doubt helps to explain the unusual detail with which this case was recorded. In most other cases it is hardly possible even to speculate as to the causes of violent death. The very fact that four of the men killed were millers may reflect the distrust and resentment which their occupation tended to generate (**1302**, **1410**, **1414**, **1437**).[39] Sudden anger or long-festering hatred presumably explain outbreaks of violence within families, when a husband killed his wife (**1409**) or a man his brother (**1209**), or even between them, as when Miles Sugge, with his wife, son and two other women killed four members of the Cockel family in their home in Weybread (**1366**). When Gilbert the smith killed Thomas the son of Matilda in Easton, one Alice of Westleton was said to have colluded in Thomas's death, and then to have fled to Easton church, where she abjured the realm after acknowledging

39 As noted by J.B. Given, *Society and homicide in thirteenth-century England* (Stanford, 1977), p. 87.

that Thomas had been killed 'on her account' (*propter eam*), a phrase suggesting that it was over her that the two men had come to blows (**1165**). The deaths of Richard the son of Gilbert Algar (**1324**) and Alard of Wratting (**1501**) appear to have been the work of gamekeepers overzealously protecting their lords' game. Presumably jurors who named suspects sometimes did so because they knew about quarrels between them and their alleged victims, but they are practically never recorded as saying so; when the Babergh jurors found that John le Chinnere had connived in the death of John the son of the smith of Boxford 'on account of disputes at one time between them', they offered no explanation of what those disputes had been about (**1468**).

The roll's silence about motives is particularly unfortunate with regard to what is probably the most dismaying, even shocking, entry on it. Sabina of Creeting was charged by the Stow jurors with killing her newborn son. She pleaded that he had been stillborn, and also that she had been out of her mind at the time, but the jury would have none of it, returning that she had been in full possession of her faculties, and so she was sentenced to be burnt (**1233**). It is impossible to say why she was treated so harshly. Since no husband is referred to, presumably Sabina was an unmarried mother, unlikely as such to be regarded with much favour at a time of population growth. When another woman came into court accused of killing her son in a fit of madness, it may have helped Alice the wife of John Maynard that she could claim the respectability of marriage; as it was, the Carlford jurors testified that she had indeed been insane, and the justices remanded her to prison 'until it is decided what should be done' (**1285**). It may also be relevant that burning was the conventional punishment for women convicted of petty treason, inflicted on wives who killed their husbands. Possibly the fact that Sabina had killed her son at the very moment of his birth, before he had even been baptised (he bore no name) and when he was at his most vulnerable, was regarded as a like act of betrayal, meriting an exceptionally rigorous punishment. But like so much in the record of the 1240 eyre, the circumstances behind both the crime and its punishment are ultimately irrecoverable.

The same is largely true of another kind of felony, namely suicide. This was a felony committed against oneself, and therefore constituting a breach of the King's peace and entailing forfeiture of chattels. It was also a mortal sin, condemned as such by the church, and for that reason, if for no other, appears to have been rare. Six suicides were presented at the eyre, all of them by hanging, a form of self-destruction well-nigh impossible to conceal. It is possible that some of the many drownings presented as misadventures at the eyre were in fact suicides, but that can only be supposition. Of the six people recorded as having put an end to their own lives, two were men and four women. Of the latter, two were widows, with chattels worth 2s. and 6s. respectively – poverty and loneliness seem sufficient explanation for their having killed themselves (**1435**, **1582**). One other woman (**1299**), and one of the men, were also said to have no chattels when they died; John de *Tulleberghe*, indeed, hanged himself in his own barn, but presumably at a time when there was nothing in it (**1280**). But why William the tailor should have killed himself in his mother's barn, leaving chattels worth 16s. 6d. (**1254**), or Ivetta the daughter of Robert of Bures, with chattels worth 20s., should have done the same in another man's brewhouse (**1347**), it is impossible to tell. It was not the business of the court to investigate the unhappiness which underlay such actions.

Rape

There is no way of knowing how often rape was committed in Suffolk between 1235 and 1240. Homicide could be prosecuted both privately and publicly, by an appeal or through the process of indictment, and an eyre roll was expected to record every felonious killing committed in a county since its previous visitation. But there was no such requirement where rape was concerned, for in Henry III's reign, at least, his justices heard only such actions as women who had been sexually assaulted chose to bring. The procedure involved was such as to ensure that few did so – only eight prosecutions were recorded in 1240, and for one of them jurisdiction was claimed for the court of the abbot of St Edmund's, preventing further proceedings at the eyre (**1502**). Rape was one of only two offences against the King's peace for which women were by strict law permitted to sue against men in royal courts.[40] But it was rape of a particular kind, for the appellor had to claim that she had been a virgin until being forcibly deflowered. She had also to raise the hue immediately after being attacked, and then show visible evidence of the injury done to her, in the form of bloodstains and torn clothes, to men of the neighbourhood, to show how she had been dishonoured to a series of officials, including the coroners and sheriff, and finally to initiate an appeal in the county court, prosecuting it thereafter until her assailant was either outlawed or attached by sureties to attend the next eyre. For the man convicted of rape the penalty laid down by law was blinding and castration. No examples of its being inflicted have been reliably recorded, but the possibility remained. The woman who appealed a man of rape was thus asking a jury made up of men to give a verdict which might expose one of their own sex to a dreadful mutilation; if she failed to achieve this, after having publicly and repeatedly let it be known that she was no longer a virgin, she would be open to a charge of fornication, with potentially dire consequences for her reputation.

Of the seven remaining appeals, one had been partly concluded before the previous eyre, when Philip the Scot was recorded as having been outlawed at the suit of Leviva la Wyte. But she had also appealed William Choure of abetting Philip, and was instructed in 1235 to continue her appeal against him, which she did until he was attached to appear at the following eyre. He did not come, however, probably because he knew that Leviva was in no state to prosecute him – when his case came up for trial she was in childbirth, and her appeal probably lapsed (**1431**). Three further appeals had more certainly lapsed by the time the 1240 eyre began. In two of them the appellor's suit was said to have been insufficient, probably meaning that they had prosecuted at only one or two county courts before giving up (**1197**, **1578**). In the third, Matilda the daughter of Leofric of Oakley had at least secured the attachment of William the son of John of Eleigh, but he did not attend, and neither did she. William found two sureties for his appearance, but she was only able to take oath that she would come to the eyre, a sure sign of poverty (**1190**).

No better off was another Matilda, the daughter of Richard del Hill, who claimed that Gilbert the son of Humphrey had deflowered her in Orford fields, and also robbed her of 18d. – a capital offence, if proved. But she was non-suited for having been slow to initiate her appeal, and though Gilbert still had to stand trial, a jury acquitted him of rape. He was indeed found to have taken Matilda's money, but the offence was rated as only a 'trespass', so that he was remanded to gaol instead of

40 For what follows see S.E. Thorne (ed. and trans.), *Bracton on the laws and customs of England*, 4 vols (Cambridge, MA, 1968–77), ii, pp. 414–19.

being hanged. Matilda, in mercy for her false claim, was too poor to be amerced (**1329**). Rose Roffa, who appealed Robert del Heth of raping her in Benacre fields on Palm Sunday 1237, was similarly non-suited, and was then humiliated by the jury's finding that she and Robert had been lovers, and that therefore no rape had taken place (**1432**). He went quit, she was remanded, but she is not recorded as having been amerced, suggesting that like the two Matildas she was too poor to pay anything. The closest to a successful appeal of rape was the one which Agnes the daughter of Ralph Becke brought against Robert Bond of Bungay, in which she persevered up to the eyre, when she came and sued against him. He did not appear, and the justices, clearly thinking that he should have been attached to face his accuser, told Agnes to continue her appeal until he was either attached or outlawed (**1246**), thereby raising the possibility that she obtained some kind of justice for the assault on her.

The justice sought by women making appeals of rape could take more than one form. A woman like Agnes may have sought retribution, publicly delivered in a form that would also protect her good name. Others may have prosecuted in the hope of securing some kind of settlement – a payment of money or a promise of marriage. Perhaps this was Rose Roffa's hope, that by shaming Robert del Heth in open court, or threatening to do so, she could induce him to marry her. Appellors secured such settlements at other eyres, but not in Suffolk in 1240, where the outcomes of their suits only underlined the difficulties they faced, arising primarily from the stress on violated chastity inherent in the form of the appeal. For any woman with a reputation to lose, this stress was probably in itself a serious disincentive to prosecution, one which can only have been intensified by an awareness of the likely consequences for her standing should she fail to secure a conviction, as she very well might. As a result, it was women who were either poor or of dubious repute who brought the great majority of appeals, a consideration which had the inevitable result of making juries even more reluctant to convict the men they accused. The scarcity of appeals and of convictions had the same basic cause.

Thieves and thefts

As with rapes, so with thefts, though for different reasons, it is impossible to tell how many were committed in Suffolk during the five years covered by the 1240 eyre, for the latter's record registered only suspected and convicted thieves, and usually refers to their misdeeds only in generalised terms. William Champeneys, hanged for being 'a thief of many thefts', was typical in that respect (**1507**). Burglaries may well have been numerous, but they are seldom identified as such. The attack on the house of John Griche of Stoke-by-Nayland, which may have been a major criminal enterprise since it involved at least four men, is a rare exception (**1481–2**). It seems very probable that many of the killings attributed to unknown malefactors were accompanied by the robbery of their victims' houses, but only occasionally does the eyre roll say so, even by implication – the killing of Matilda the widow of William de *Northage* and her son Geoffrey in their home at Stradbroke, said to be the work of two unknown thieves, is an example (**1360**). It is highly likely, moreover, that any amount of pilfering was dealt with by lower courts, while many more serious offenders will have been tried at periodic gaol deliveries, leaving nothing further for the eyre to deal with. The 1240 roll refers to a forger who had been hanged at London (**1425**) and a member of a group of sheep-stealers who was not put in exigent with his fellows because he, too, had been already hanged, it is not said where (**1583**); it may be significant that in both these cases there were chattels still to be accounted for. That the roll is manifestly incomplete, as a record either of thieves or of thefts, does not, however, make it valueless.

Eighty-two men and women were put in exigent for theft at the 1240 eyre, and though only five abjurations were recorded, thirteen thieves were hanged, in addition to the two referred to as previously executed. Fifty-three suspects were acquitted, either in court or *in absentia*. Of the 102 convicted or suspected felons, twelve were women, and one was a cleric. These figures do not include another cleric, described as having thrown a woman out of her house and taken her valuables, since it is impossible to say precisely what his offence was – no certain action was taken against him, for what may have been an episode in a lawsuit rather than a robbery (**1252**). Nor do they take into account the people accused in the fifteen appeals of felony which added theft or robbery to their alleged offences, since such charges were usually intended to serve as aggravating factors to other issues. The appeal which Robert the son of William of Peasenhall brought against Adam the son of Walter of Knodishall, for evicting him from his house in Knodishall and taking a quantity of his goods, accused Adam of acting 'wickedly and in felony', and went so far as to include preparations for a duel. But it was essentially the by-product of a property dispute, in the end there was no fighting, and the justices, presumably accepting that no robbery had taken place, did not ask the Blything jury to give a verdict on it (**1445**).

Well before 1240 it appears to have become accepted that theft became a capital offence only when the value of the goods stolen exceeded 12d. – a sum which in the late thirteenth century was said to be enough to keep a man or woman alive for a week.[41] It must have been for that reason that three suspects who had run away, charged variously with stealing 'a very little corn' (**1216**), two bushels of malt (**1315**) and some fish (**1557**), were licensed to return, their thefts being too small to justify their outlawry. In a further entry the value of a foal stolen by John the fuller is recorded as 17d. – perhaps the jurors provided this detail to justify their having indicted John, or the justices may have asked for it before they were prepared to have him put in exigent (**1256**). John was one out of sixty-one suspected or convicted thieves recorded at the eyre as having no chattels. The connection between poverty and theft was well understood in thirteenth-century England. When protesting against papal taxation in 1246, the English clergy asserted that the pope's demands would severely diminish their ability to give alms to the poor, of whom there was an infinite number, with the result that some would die of hunger, while others would out of necessity turn to 'thefts, rapines and robberies'.[42]

The clergy were making a case, not presenting a sociological argument. A great many people probably kept their heads above water by means which included picking and stealing. Richard le Ko, acquitted at the eyre of stealing sheaves, a bundle of flax and a single sheep, but required to find sureties for his future good behaviour (**1255**), and Henry and William Pelehaste, cleared of theft but convicted of poaching in the abbot of St Edmund's fishponds, may have been occasional thieves of this kind (**1544**). Small-scale delinquents like these were probably often

41 See R. Groot, 'Petit larceny, jury lenity and parliament', in J.W. Cairns and G. McLeod (eds), *'The dearest birthright of the people of England': the jury in the history of the common law* (Oxford, 2002), pp. 47–61.

42 F.M. Powicke and C.R. Cheney (eds), *Councils & Synods with other documents relating to the English church ii, A.D. 1205–1313*, 2 vols (Oxford, 1964), i, p. 400.

dealt with by local courts, and could be put up with as long as they were only occasional offenders, but would become liable to arrest, if possible, or to expulsion and outlawry if they managed to flee, when their thieving became intolerable. William Keyloc, hanged at the eyre after being convicted of 'stealing clothes and of burglary, and of many other larcenies', may have been such a thief; perhaps his theft of clothes, not obviously the most heinous of offences, was the one which finally moved his community to get rid of him (**1308**).

Of course, some poor people will have stolen under the impulse of a combination of want and opportunity. This may well have been the case with the unnamed lad who abjured the realm for stealing a linen sheet (**1497**), and perhaps also with Richard the son of Andrew of Easton, in exigent for breaking into the house of his brother and stealing some nine marks – £6, or 1,440 silver pennies (**1336**). For a man with no chattels that hoard of money may have constituted a temptation he could not resist. Others who were not completely destitute may have slipped into felonious habits as the influence of moral or religious constraints was undermined by the constantly precarious circumstances of their lives. Men with next to nothing to fall back on, like Peter the son of Ailwin, with chattels worth 2s. and a messuage which yielded 12d. to the crown (**1238**), or Humphrey the son of Joscelin, whose chattels, too, were worth only 2s. (**1517**), must have felt endlessly under pressure to save themselves by crime from utter destitution. Other poor folk may have been corrupted by their associates, perhaps even by members of their own family. William the son of Leofric, and his sister Edith, convicted and hanged for theft and burglary, appear to have formed a small family group along with their father, Leofric Dyrunt, who was put in exigent for harbouring thieves, the latter presumably being his own children. All were said to have no chattels, and it is easy to see how they might have taken to thieving together (**1210**). In the case of a group of four sheep-stealers, put in exigent in Claydon hundred, and the fact that two were brothers and that all were seemingly inhabitants of Thurleston, family ties may have been reinforced by neighbourly ones, carrying the four men into criminality together, the more readily, perhaps, because none had any chattels (**1260**).

By 1240 Leofric and his children, and the thieves of Thurleston, had clearly come to be seen as the sort of people against whom the apparatus of law enforcement was principally directed, that is, they were suspected of being habitual evildoers, stealers of livestock and burglars of houses, men and women who consorted with and filled the ranks of the 'unknown malefactors' to whom so many homicides were attributed, and of whose activities, it seems clear, the law-abiding – with very good reason – went in dread. It was such men who killed Mabel the wife of Hubert Kembel in her own home in Cotton (**1201**), and who slew Geoffrey of Holbeach in Ixworth (**1546**). That vill's position on the Black Bourn river and in the local road system was such as to bring wayfarers continually through it, not all of them honest journeymen and traders. The felons who killed Geoffrey wounded two other men in the same incursion, but apart from that, nothing could be said about them. On the evidence of the Suffolk eyre roll it must often have been hard to identify the criminally-inclined. Of the men named as thieves, sixty were members of tithings, and another six should have been, while only two were defined as strangers. Roger de Furnaus (**1195, 1550**) and John Thoraud (**1481**), two *déclassé* malefactors, were not in tithings because they held land by military service. How Reynold the shepherd and Ralph the son of Richard of Chedburgh had formerly been perceived it is impossible to say. At the eyre the Risbridge jury presented that Reynold had abjured the realm for the theft of twelve sheep, probably those of his employer. He had chattels worth 10s. and was a member of a tithing, showing that he had a place, if at a very humble level, in the local machinery of law enforcement (**1499**). Ralph, in exigent for stealing two bullocks and two cows, was also in a tithing, but as a man with no chattels may have been in danger of losing his place in society, and of being forced out into the company of drifters and fugitives to which outlawry will in fact have condemned him (**1503**).

Perhaps Ralph was familiar with that world already. Where law enforcement was concerned, men and women were judged by the company they kept as well as by their actions. To associate with felons, or to harbour them, was in itself a felony. Joss Stute was arrested, convicted and hanged for associating with thieves (**1428**), and two others were put in exigent for harbouring them (**1292**, **1491**). Robert Ordrich, when giving lodging to an unknown man and woman in his house in Barnham, may have investigated their origins and reputation, so causing the man to run away, leaving his horse behind, and the woman to flee to Barnham church, where she abjured the realm (**1552**), but perhaps others were less careful. Aylwin Punche of Lackford, also in exigent for harbouring thieves, subsequently came to the eyre and was acquitted (**1518**), as were another nine men and women charged with the same offence – possibly they were able to show the court that they had no means of knowing what sort of people they had accommodated.

Of course, some evildoers were identified. The poverty of so many of them having probably already made them the objects of suspicion, they might be recognised at the scenes of their crimes, perhaps, or betrayed by some incautious word or action, or simply by their possession of stolen goods. William Keyloc, hanged for stealing clothes, may have been arrested when trying to sell a stolen garment, or even while wearing one. William was not said to have had a partner in crime, but that was not true of all malefactors. Two brothers and a sister, along with another man, were hanged following their conviction by the Blackbourn jury of 'larceny, burglary and burning houses' (**1535**). They seem, indeed, to have been hardened criminals, since the same jury later imputed to them the killing of two men in Stanton, and a break-in there, during which a man and his wife were tied up – they were probably lucky to escape with their lives (**1542**). Medieval criminal bands were not on the whole very large, usually just three or four strong. Typical in this respect was the group of three men who stole thirteen sheep in Icklingham, and took them to the house of Katherine of Icklingham, a confederate who was doubtless able to provide them with shelter and also with a place where the sheep could be slaughtered – the skins of some of them were discovered under her bed. They must have been followed, however, for Katherine herself was arrested, though she later managed to escape, and one of the thieves was captured and hanged. The other two, who were put in exigent, were members of the same tithing, suggesting that frankpledge could sometimes be a means of strengthening links between felons rather than working to undermine them (**1583**).

Katherine and her associates were probably habitual thieves, active in a part of Suffolk in which sheep-farming was widely practised and opportunities for stealing sheep were accordingly widespread, and they may well have been under suspicion for some time before they could be caught in the act. The 1240 eyre provides a good example of another of the ways by which the authorities could take action against evildoers, namely the approver. The approver was a suspect, almost invariably a man, who on being arrested chose, or was persuaded, to confess his crimes to a coroner and undertake to secure the conviction of an agreed number of his associates, whom he was to accuse of having acted alongside him in his acknowledged felonies, proving their guilt either by defeating them in duels or by securing their conviction through juries' verdicts.[43] While such proceedings as followed were in progress, he was to be maintained at the King's expense, and if he kept his part of the bargain, he was permitted to abjure the realm; but if he failed to do so he was hanged. Such a man was William Thurbern of Monk Soham, who made appeals against eight (and almost certainly eleven) men, starting with Richard the son of Roger of Kettleburgh, whom he charged with being his accomplice in breaking into Kettleburgh church and stealing the goods – probably vestments and plate – they found in it; from this robbery, so William claimed, Richard's share had been worth 3s.

Richard denied the charge. He could have opted for jury trial, but instead he chose to fight, and so a day was appointed for their combat, when the two men, presumably in the archaic dress traditionally worn by approvers and those they accused – white leather tunics and cross-gartered legs, with pudding-bowl haircuts, and carrying double-headed war-hammers and large rectangular shields – came back into court and fought for their lives. Richard prevailed, and so William, having failed to make good his accusations, was hanged on the basis of his confession. This was not, however, the end of the matter for Richard. The very fact that he had not put himself on a jury's verdict was held against him, marking him out as a suspicious character, and he was told that he must find sureties both that he would stand trial if anyone wished to sue against him, and also that in future he would either lead a law-abiding life or abjure the realm. This he was unable to do, but instead returned to court, and in a desperate attempt to clear himself voluntarily put himself on a jury's verdict. The move did him no good, for the jurors found that he had committed many thefts, and so he followed William Thurbern to the gallows. Richard was not destitute; he had chattels valued at 36s. 2d., and also five acres of land, but that would not have been enough for even the barest subsistence, and so he appears to have turned to crime – notoriously so, judging by his inability to find the sureties who would have saved his life (**1293**).

The appeals of an unsuccessful approver did not die with him, and those he had accused still needed to clear themselves. The entry on the eyre roll which follows the record of the hangings of William Thurbern and of the man who defeated him names another seven men who had also been appealed by William, and who now came up for trial. All were acquitted, in two batches – four in the first and three in the second. The likelihood is that they had been appealed by William of having been involved with him in two separate crimes, which were not recorded on the roll because after his execution the details had become irrelevant. It was enough that the seven accused had appeared in court, denied felony and put themselves on a jury (**1294**). Later in the eyre another three men came before the justices, described as having been indicted by 'William the approver', without much doubt William Thurbern, and probably for yet another crime. They, too, were acquitted, this time by a Hoxne jury, as was appropriate when their accuser was a man from Monk Soham (**1374**). William's low success rate is not surprising, for most approvers' appeals failed, and nothing is known about those he accused, though it seems unlikely that they were all men of the utmost respectability. Therein, perhaps, lies

43 For approvers see M.T. Clanchy, 'Highway robbery and trial by battle in the Hampshire eyre of 1249', in R.F. Hunnisett and J.B. Post (eds), *Medieval legal records edited in memory of C.A.F. Meekings* (HMSO, 1978), pp. 25–61.

much of the significance of William's appeals, that he should have been the crown's agent in bringing charges of felony against up to eleven men, concerning whom the conventional processes of presentment and indictment had said nothing. He and the people he consorted with constituted what a later age would call 'the dangerous classes', and inhabited a world largely hidden from the King's government and its agents. The approver, as a thief set to catch a thief, provided them with one of the few ways by which they could hope to penetrate it.

Arson

Fire, in an age when most houses were built of wood and had roofs made of thatch or shingles, was as much a threat to communities as thieves, the more so, indeed, because it could be the result of accident as well as felony. The legal text commonly known as *Bracton*, which was largely composed in the 1220s and 1230s, carefully distinguished between malicious arson and the kind of burning which resulted from accident or negligence, and expected the former to be prosecuted by appeals of felony.[44] Only one accidental fire is recorded in the 1240 roll; it claimed two lives, probably those of children, and may have called for investigation because they were not the offspring of the owner of the house in which they perished; but nothing suspicious was discovered and the deaths were entered as misadventure (**1230**). But also recorded at the eyre were eight cases of deliberate arson, a much higher number than usual – it was a crime greatly feared for its destructive capacity, but does not appear to have been very often committed.

Of those eight cases, only two were the subject of appeals. One of them, unusually, was prosecuted by two people together, with a man and a woman accusing Adam the son of Geoffrey Osmund of burning their houses, probably in Easton, and continuing their suit until he was outlawed (**1326**). His action and his victims' response to it suggest a neighbourhood quarrel, and the same is true of the other appeal, made by Alice de *Hendeseye* against three men and four women, again for burning her house. One of the women had already been waived (the equivalent of outlawry for women) by the time of the eyre, but the other six appellees came into court, and when Alice continued to sue they gave 40s. for an inquest into the case, which acquitted them. Their proffer was doubtless intended to ensure an impartial investigation, but may also have been designed to suggest that Alice's continuance of her action was unwarranted and malicious, and needed close scrutiny for that reason (**1434**).

The remaining six cases of arson were recorded as either presentments or indictments. William the son of Nicholas was simply said to have burnt the house of Alice le Ko and run away, so he was put in exigent (**1282**), while the Cosford jury, as recorded, presented that the house of Agnes of Cosford had been burnt, and then, perhaps in response to a question from the bench, said that Robert of Lindsay was suspected of the deed (**1522**). Neither man appears to have been formally indicted, and the background to their crimes remains obscure, though the fact that their victims were both women is suggestive. In the case of Henry the smith of West Stow, it is obviously possible that professional rivalry caused him to set fire to the house of Robert the smith of West Stow (**1537**), but the brief entries recording the indictments of Beatrice the daughter of Robert Blok and Walter Prat, in each case as 'suspected of burning houses', offer no motives, only the implication that they

44 Thorne, *Bracton on the laws and customs of England* ii, p. 414.

were regarded as anti-social threats to their communities (**1458, 1490**). The same can perhaps be said of Hugh le Seyte of Thorpe, suspected of burning an unidentified house in Thorpe (possibly Thorpe Ixworth), and particularly 'as he brought strangers with him who burnt that house' (**1545**). Hugh was not put in exigent, however, and though he fled it is possible that unrecorded grounds were found for dissociating him from the outsiders who had carried out the burning. As with larceny, it was the activities of strangers, people to whom no names could be given and with no fixed address, which posed the greatest threat to the relatively ordered world of the Suffolk vills.

Appeals and plaints

Homicide, rape, theft and arson were all indisputably felonies and therefore pleas of the crown. Rape, however, only came within the cognisance of the eyre if individually prosecuted, and the same was true of many other acts of larceny and violence, which were not presented by juries or subjects for indictment, but which could be brought to the attention of the King's justices through the process known as the appeal of felony. It seems certain that the offences prosecuted in this way were a small proportion of the number committed, and that many fist-fights and petty thefts were dealt with in lower courts, while others never came into court at all, but were settled informally between the parties. The appeals heard at the 1240 Suffolk eyre represented only the tip of an iceberg of local disorder, of widely varying seriousness.

The procedure involved in the appeal was essentially the same used in the prosecution of undoubted felonies. It involved a highly formalised accusation, in which the appellor asserted that the person or persons he named had robbed or wounded him – often both – at a particular place and a particular time, identifying in detail the injuries inflicted and the weapons used to inflict them. Consistency in every detail was required between an appeal as initiated in the county court and as continued at the eyre. Any omission or mistake would lead to the appeal being declared invalid and its maker being put in mercy. Grounds for doing this were clearly sought by the justices and were almost always found. The appellor conventionally offered to prove his accusations by his body, that is, by combat, and the appellee was expected to offer to defend himself in like manner. In theory only those who could show that they were too young to fight, or too old (over sixty years of age), or were incapable of fighting due to some physical disability, were exempted from combat. In practice duels were extremely rare; probably very few appeals were made with the intention of fighting one, while the justices certainly did their best to discourage and prevent them. Until the late 1220s the invalidation of an appeal brought proceedings to an end and thereby acquitted the accused.[45] But during the 1230s it became normal practice for the proof which an appellor had been unable to provide to be supplied instead by a jury, so ensuring that disputes were in some sense concluded; when the appeal of wounding which John the smith of Sharpstone brought against Adam Bullok was quashed at the 1240 eyre, the case was put before a jury specifically 'for the maintenance of the King's peace …'. Proceedings ended with Adam and three other appellees putting themselves in the King's mercy and making a four-mark fine – possibly a satisfactory outcome for John (**1253**).

45 E.g. JUST 1/54 m. 12; JUST 1/229 m. 14d; JUST 1/358 mm. 20d, 22.

When Geoffrey Pepper appealed Hugh the son of Camilla of Henham of wounding him, his appeal was ruled out of order 'because he does not offer to prove against him by his body, nor specifies felony ...' (**1456**). The objection looks disingenuous, for it seems certain that if Geoffrey had offered to fight, the justices would have found a way of preventing his doing so. The 1240 eyre does, however, offer what may be called a near-exception to this development, which has the added value of illustrating the whole process of an appeal. Robert the son of William of Peasenhall appealed Adam the son of Walter of Knodishall of breaking into his house on 22 May 1239 and removing a number of his possessions, all duly listed, and offered to prove his case by his body. Adam came into court, made a detailed defence (somewhat garbled in the eyre roll), and offered to defend himself by his body. A number of other men, whom Robert had appealed of abetting Adam, also appeared in court, but proceedings against them could not proceed until the case against Adam had been settled. So far both parties had followed the protocols correctly. The justices may have looked for grounds for objection, since they checked, by reference to the coroners and the wider community ('the country'), that earlier proceedings – during which one man had been outlawed – had been properly conducted, but they were assured that the hue had been duly raised and pursuit made, and so they directed that a duel should take place, and named a day for it. The two principals may have so hated each other that they were eager to fight. If so, their tempers evidently cooled, for although they appeared at the prescribed time, with their weapons, it was not in order to do battle, but instead they put themselves in the King's mercy and made individual fines – the fact that they did not make a joint fine (as often happened) suggests that though they had decided not to fight, they were far from reconciled (**1445**).

Probably only a few appellors looked forward to a trial by battle, indeed, in 1240 no fewer than thirty-three of them either failed to come to the eyre or attended only to abandon their suits. Of those who persevered, another six had their appeals invalidated on technical grounds; among them were two women, whose appeals were quashed on the grounds that they could lawfully sue only for the deaths of their husbands and the rape of their virginity (**1173**, **1385**). The justification for the limitation appears to have been that since women could not offer to prove their claims by combat, there was a danger that they might be put up to making appeals against men at no risk to themselves. The restriction must have appeared increasingly irrelevant in view of the hostility of the King's justices to judicial combat, and of the fact that an appeal, once begun, would be decided by jury trial. In such cases much probably depended on the response of the accused; some may have wished by objecting to embarrass their accusers, financially or otherwise, while others may have been content to let proceedings take their course. It is certain that many appeals were made at eyres by women, without objections being raised – the appeal of arson brought by Alice de *Hendeseye* is an example (**1434**).

In all, forty-five appeals alleging offences other than the ones already discussed separately were made at the 1240 eyre – this total excludes one relating to an offence committed in Norfolk (**1274**), but includes another found among the civil pleas, possibly because it became essentially a plea about the status of the appellor, who was allegedly a villein (**1104**). Of these appeals, thirty-four alleged wounding or physical assault and six robbery, while five involved accusations of wounding and robbery together. They were brought by forty-one men and four women against a total of 174 people, all but eleven of them men. The imbalance between appellors and appellees was due to a number of prosecutions being made against several people; in most cases, indeed, one man or woman sued against one, two or three others, but in the appeal of Robert the son of William of Peasenhall cited above there were sixteen appellees all together, and in the next entry on the roll there were eleven (**1446**), while Godfrey the smith of Beccles brought an appeal of robbery against twenty-four men and a woman (**1222**).

This multiplication of numbers was often caused by the practice of appealing one or two men of committing the alleged offence, and accusing others of abetting it – the charges were separated in this way in twenty-five appeals. Allegations of abetment were not tried until after the charges against the principal appellee had been disposed of; when William the son of Burghard appealed Gilbert the son of William de *Caketon* of wounding, and Everard de *Caketon* and his wife Olive of abetting him, and Gilbert failed to appear, the justices could only tell William to continue his action in the county court until Gilbert either stood trial or was outlawed, and respited proceedings against Everard and Olive until the case against Gilbert was decided (**1202**). If he was convicted, then the appeal against them could go forward. When a principal was acquitted, his alleged abettors could normally expect to go quit as well; the appeal which Humphrey of Earsham brought against Thomas Sharp was unusual in this respect, in that it ended with two alleged abettors being convicted of the wounding imputed to Thomas, who was himself acquitted of it (**1361**).

There is no way of knowing if Humphrey was satisfied with the outcome of his appeal. Probably he sued because he wanted to see his adversaries convicted and punished, and there must have been others who did the same, but some appeals, and perhaps many, will have been made in the hope of forcing a settlement giving reparations for an injury. To outward appearances the appeal was poorly designed for the purpose. The convicted appellee would be required to pay the King for the breach of his peace, but not to give damages to his accuser. If an appeal was prosecuted to the point of outlawry, the possessions of the accused person were forfeit to the crown and the appellor got nothing; some appeals may have been broken off for this reason. But in some cases they achieved their purpose, for the parties were said to have reached an agreement in twelve of the thirty-three discontinued appeals, and it would be rash to assume this was all, even though this was a process which the justices sought to control. Once an appeal had begun they wanted to prevent the King's name being taken in vain, and to ensure that alleged breaches of his peace were appropriately punished. If the parties to an appeal wished to settle their differences, it must be with their consent, which would usually be granted only in return for an appropriate payment.

Forty appellees were formally acquitted at the eyre, whereas ninety-six were convicted of all or part of the offences alleged against them, and fifty-three of these negotiated fines after being put in mercy. Only three appellees were outlawed. The justices may have reflected with satisfaction on the money such proceedings made for the crown. It may also have pleased them to think that there was no distinction of persons where the appeal was concerned, anybody could make one. Geoffrey of Henham, in mercy because he withdrew in court from his appeal of wounding, was described as 'very poor' and therefore spared amercement (**1454**); he may also have been a man of doubtful reputation, since he had only just been cleared of homicide (**1452**). But he was not prevented from prosecuting for either reason. Nothing is recorded of whatever dispute underlay his appeal, however, and this is true of many such actions, though it is possible that the appeal of wounding which Baldwin the reeve of Thorington brought against two men of that vill reflected strained relations between a manorial official and some of the men whose labours he directed;

Baldwin failed to prosecute at the eyre, but the appellees were convicted (**1439**). And Godwin Bullock's appeal of wounding and robbery against three other Bullocks bears all the hallmarks of a family quarrel – the fact that a jury rejected his allegations does not mean that there was no dispute behind them (**1378**). Like any other form of litigation the appeal was capable of being abused, and Godwin's may be an example of an accusation without substance launched by a man with a grievance. Another such, perhaps, was the appeal of wounding which William of Toftes made against three men but did not come to the eyre to prosecute. The emphatic way in which the Blackbourn jurors dismissed it, attesting 'that Robert did not give him a wound, that Master William did not abet him, and that Henry is not guilty of giving the order', suggests that they regarded William's injury as pure invention (**1540**).

Most of the appeals made at the 1240 eyre seem to have been brought by men of modest means and standing, but a few involved men of somewhat greater consequence. Roger de Ripa and William of Badley appear to have been minor landowners in Sproughton, involved in disputes which spilled over into both the civil and crown pleas. William's appeal against Roger, alleging that he had taken a large quantity of his corn, was dismissed after Roger asserted, with a jury's support, that the corn was his own, a legacy from his mother whose executor he was (**1381**). But his action against Roger for three and a half acres of land in Sproughton was successful, and brought him 6s. 8d. in damages as well as the recovery of his property (**427**). A dispute over land also seems to have been behind the appeal of housebreaking which John de Hauville brought against Robert the son of Gilbert de la More, accusing him of vandalising a stable built on land in Creeting St Mary (**1168**). John had purchased the land from Robert's father, and an action of mort d'ancestor which Robert brought against John for lands and rents in that same vill suggests that he resented the loss of the property and was trying to recover it, though without any success (**163**). His knocking down a dyke on John's land in Creeting was doubtless another episode in this dispute (**166**).

Of the knights and squires directly involved in the 1240 proceedings by way of an appeal, the most important was Guy de Verdon. The head of an East Anglian branch of an important baronial family powerful in the English midlands and in Ireland, he was primarily a Norfolk landowner but also had properties in Suffolk.[46] Too grand a figure to descend to assault and battery himself, he sent others to inflict violence on his behalf. Hence the appeal of wounding which Robert of Boxted brought against Roger Spurecat for wounding him, against six other men for abetting Roger, and against Guy for ordering the attack on him. The Hartismere jurors convicted the appellees of wounding Robert and giving him a severe beating on Guy's orders, and they also found that when Robert fled to a neighbouring house, one of his assailants had followed him there and attacked the householder's wife as well. His role in this violent affair cost Guy a £20 fine 'for himself and his men' (**1192**, **1193**). Abuses of local power were probably common enough, and a few others came to light at the eyre. But it took a brave man to denounce a man of Verdon's eminence as Robert of Boxted did, and such offences had usually to be exposed in other ways.

46 See M.S. Hagger, *The fortunes of a Norman family: the de Verduns in England, Ireland and Wales, 1066–1316* (Dublin, 2001), pp. 244–5; Brown, *Sibton Abbey cartularies and charters* i, pp. 108–9; F. Blomefield, *An essay towards the topographical history of the county of Norfolk* i (2nd edn, London, 1805), pp. 49–73.

One such way was the plaint, an informal petition for redress made to the King, as the fount of justice, or to one of the King's chosen representatives.[47] Its use was subject to limitations, and as a rule would-be litigants were expected to acquire writs or bring appeals of felony if they wished to sue for injuries. But neither form of action was appropriate for all eventualities, and many eyres heard at least one plaint; the 1240 Suffolk eyre heard two. Both were brought by women, who stood at a particular disadvantage where the appeal was concerned, and indeed, the circumstances in both cases were such that it would have been hard for the plaintiffs to use an appeal in their pursuit of justice. This was particularly the case with the first plaint, in which Beatrice the daughter of Gilbert Algor complained that eight named men had knocked her house down and taken clothes and bedding. The justices had no recorded qualms about hearing her suit, and so the defendants put themselves on a jury's verdict. It came in the form of a story of acute domestic complication. Beatrice had been the mistress of one Robert Hayl, with whom she had a son and who gave her a plot of land next to his house, on which she built a house of her own. But at some point Robert married, and his wife took grave exception to having her husband's ex-mistress living literally next door, so much so that she arranged for the accused men to come one night and demolish Beatrice's house – an act which cost them four marks (**1266**).

The fact that the litigant making a plaint was not obliged to use the rigid formulae required for a legitimate appeal helps to explain the unusual amount of detail contained in Beatrice's action. And the same is true, if to a somewhat lesser extent, of the second plaint, this time brought by two women, who complained that they had been seized by six men and taken by them into Westhall wood, where they hung them up, presumably on trees, and mistreated them in some undefined way. This time the defendants had the better of it, however, for a jury found that the plaintiffs had broken into the park of John the son of Ranulf, no doubt a landowner in Blything hundred, and that the park-keeper had taken a pledge from them – security either that they would appear in court to answer for their trespass or that they would not transgress again in future. No harm had been done to them, and so they ended up having to make fine by 6s. 8d. for their unfounded accusation (**1455**). A plaint against a park-keeper illustrates one of the ways in which men and women could try to obtain justice at an eyre against a lord or his employees. But more often the task was left to the presenting juries.

The church and clergy

Society in thirteenth-century England was permeated by the practices and values of the Christian religion, accepted, however nominally, by all its inhabitants except for members of Jewish communities. Their omnipresence affected the administration of justice at every level, from the King downwards – at his coronation each new ruler, 'having taken an oath in the name of Jesus Christ', swore, in the words of *Bracton*, 'that he will cause all judgments to be given with equity and mercy, so that he may himself be shown the mercy of a clement and merciful God, in order that by his justice all men may enjoy unbroken peace'.[48] It was to uphold that peace – which

47 Analysed by H.G. Richardson and G.O. Sayles (eds), *Select cases of procedure without writ under Henry III*, Selden Society 60 (1941).

48 Thorne, *Bracton on the laws and customs of England* ii, p. 204.

in appeals of felony might be explicitly described as that of God as well as of the King – that justices like those who held an eyre in Suffolk in 1240 were sent round the English counties. When juries were enrolled at the beginning of an eyre, their members swore on relics that they would speak the truth, and they took a similar oath when trying indictments. The approver accusing an associate of breaking into a church with him, and the accused man denying the charge, will both have invoked God before they fought (**1293**). Much else that was recorded at the eyre bore a religious imprint. The practice of abjuration was an extension of the right of sanctuary traditionally allowed to consecrated buildings. Deodands, the causes of accidental deaths, were so named because they were given to God, that is to charity, in acts of propitiation. The appellor specifying when an assault or robbery had taken place named the year in secular terms – that of the King's reign – but identified the time within it in ecclesiastical terms. John the smith of Sharpstone, accusing Adam Bullok of wounding him, alleged that Adam had attacked him 'on the Saturday next after the Nativity of the Blessed Mary about the hour of Vespers ...' (**1253**).

Viewed as an institution, the buildings and personnel of the church were well in evidence in mid-thirteenth-century Suffolk. Over 500 medieval churches have survived from the middle ages, most of them serving parishes which long predated Henry III's reign. Many of these were very small, but each had its church and parson, and usually ancillary clergy as well. In 1240 the county also contained twenty-eight abbeys and priories, four nunneries, and perhaps four preceptories staffed by knights of the Hospital of St John and of the Temple.[49] The newly-arrived mendicants had as yet only one friary, at Ipswich (**1258**), but six towns maintained hospitals, which were at least as much religious as medical institutions. The lists of defaults at the eyre show that a number of monasteries in other shires, or even, in the case of some Norman houses, in another country (**1183**, **1403**), also had lands in Suffolk. The religious varied greatly in wealth and importance. The abbot of St Edmund's was the greatest lord in the county, with the prior of Ely probably his nearest rival. Many of the other houses were small, even tiny, but all were in a position to wield influence in their localities, as landlords and employers, and as dispensers of spiritual benefits in an age which valued them. As far as the 1240 eyre is concerned, the power wielded by the abbot of St Edmund's and the prior of Ely is reflected in many entries on the roll, but the other houses are seldom mentioned – there was a killing in the prior of Butley's mill (**1302**), and an accidental death in the prioress of Campsey Ash's barn (**1325**), while a servant of the abbot of Leiston was outlawed for robbery (**1445**).

The ecclesiastics who make the most frequent appearances in the 1240 roll were members of the secular clergy, men who had taken holy orders and enjoyed the privileges which came from having done so. In the immediate aftermath of Henry II's quarrel with Thomas Becket, and the latter's murder in 1170, it was conceded by Henry that members of the clergy charged in royal courts with offences against the King's peace should not stand trial there, but should be handed over to Court Christian – the church's court – to be tried there. In the words of *Bracton*, written around 1230, a clerk arrested for homicide or any other crime, who came into court and was claimed by, or on behalf of, the bishop, was to be 'delivered to them at

49 Details from D. Knowles and R.N. Hadcock, *Medieval religious houses: England and Wales* (2nd edn, London, 1971).

once, without calling any inquest ...'.[50] By 1240, however, procedure in such cases had changed considerably, with the King's justices exercising a much wider jurisdiction over offences allegedly committed by members of the clergy; at the Suffolk eyre the latter were, indeed, still handed over to a representative of their diocesan, the bishop of Norwich, so that they could appear in Court Christian, but only after juries had given verdicts on them. In fact the authority of the justices could go beyond this. They could question whether the man claiming this 'benefit of clergy' had any right to it. When Geoffrey the son of Sarah of Eye, arrested for the death of Adam of Worlingworth, came into court and said he was a clerk, he was sent back to gaol because 'it is not known if it is true that he has been ordained ...' (**1186**). And they might also take appropriately firm action if Court Christian failed to deal effectively with a suspect. Roger Bretun of Iken, a clerk arrested on suspicion of killing Richard Wickerman, had been handed over to the bishop at the previous eyre: 'But because it was established that no justice was done on him by Court Christian and he has fled, it is adjudged that he is to be exacted and outlawed' (**1273**).

Not everybody appears to have noticed how the King's courts were extending their authority in cases involving members of the clergy. When Robert Temprenoyse brought an appeal of wounding against William the son of Geoffrey Gikel at the Suffolk eyre, he let it be known that he was a clerk, and that he only wished to prosecute William, who was also a clerk, in Court Christian. Ten years earlier the justices might have agreed to this, but in 1240 they were not prepared to do so. Instead they put Robert and his sureties in mercy and took a jury's verdict which convicted William. Only then did Robert obtain his wish, for William was handed over to the bishop's representative, Master Geoffrey of Walpole, leaving the way open for his accuser to sue against him in Court Christian, should he still wish to do so (**1448**). Justice in the church courts was done by compurgation, whereby the suspect had to find a prescribed number of men of standing who were willing to swear, not to his guilt or innocence on a particular charge, but to his good reputation in general. An adverse finding by such 'oath-helpers' might indeed be something to be feared by a notorious reprobate, not least because it would probably lead to close confinement in the bishop's prison, but overall there seems to be little doubt that most of those who stood trial in this way were cleared.[51] The requirement that clerical suspects should first face trial in a lay court was presumably introduced in the hope of limiting the number of such acquittals.

Twenty-two men described as clerics came before the justices at the 1240 Suffolk eyre, having been indicted or appealed of offences against the King's peace. As noted above, no verdict was given on Geoffrey the son of Sarah of Eye because of doubts about his status. Of the others, fifteen were convicted, three of them of homicide and one of helping a killer to escape his pursuers, the others of wounding or assault, while six were acquitted, two of them of homicide. One cleric had been outlawed for homicide, and two more were put in exigent for it, as were one man for arson and another man for larceny. William Puleyn, appealed of abetting assault in two related actions, failed to appear in court and was convicted *in absentia* in both cases (**1249, 1250**). Robert Bude of Bungay, charged with breaking into a house by night, ejecting its occupants, and carrying off the money and jewellery of its owner,

[50] Thorne, *Bracton on the laws and customs of England* ii, p. 348.

[51] L.C. Gabel, *Benefit of clergy in England in the later middle ages* (New York, 1969), though needing revision on a number of points, remains the fullest study.

was said to be a clerk. But it is unclear precisely what his offence was thought to be, for it was not described as a felony, and though the sheriff was ordered to sequestrate his lands, no further action appears to have followed (**1252**). Order was given for the arrest of a chaplain named Simon, said to have poached a deer in Ralph de Arderne's park, but again it is not known what action resulted (**1239**).

On the evidence of these figures, the contribution made by the clergy of Suffolk to the record of crime presented to the 1240 eyre was a variable one. Only one cleric was put in exigent for theft and one for arson, and none were appealed of rape, but men in orders were involved in twelve out of 115 killings, or nearly ten per cent, and in eight of the assaults and affrays which gave rise to appeals. However, it is necessary to make distinctions between offenders before reaching conclusions about their actions. Out of the clerics convicted, only Walter the parson of Blaxhall, found to have killed a man found dead in his cowshed (**1271**), and Robert the parson of Livermere, presented as having rescued a fugitive killer from his pursuers by getting him into a church where he abjured the realm, were the incumbents of parishes (**1539**). Another cleric, convicted of wounding, may have been a man of consequence, since he bore the title of *magister*, indicating that he had attended the schools (**1393**). The parson of Stoven was acquitted of wounding (**1454**), as was another *magister* (**1540**). All the other members of the clergy recorded as either convicted or acquitted at the eyre were defined simply as clerks – *clerici* – meaning that they had taken orders but not necessarily any more than that. A cure of souls was most likely to be entrusted to a man in one of the three major orders, those of subdeacon, deacon and priest. Many ordained men did not rise so far, and remained only in minor orders, but were still entitled to benefit of clergy.

It seems highly likely that, with a few exceptions, the parish clergy in mid-thirteenth-century Suffolk led respectable and orderly lives, and that the great majority of the clerics recorded as troubling the peace of Suffolk in the years between 1235 and 1240 were men in minor orders. Judging by their names, they were nearly all men from that county, recorded under names like Roger Pinchun of Bungay (**1248**) and Theobald the clerk of Rendlesham (**1321**). The unknown Irish clerk who was arrested by the earl of Norfolk's bailiff and later escaped from imprisonment in the earl's residence was a rarity (**1451**). A parson like the vicar of Exning, for whom Bishop Blundeville in 1229 prescribed an income of £11 8s. in cash and kind, along with the provision of a house, could expect to live in comfort.[52] But for *clerici* who had yet to receive preferment, life must often have been bleak, as, indeed, the eyre roll suggests by what it records of their possessions; Osbert Sugge, a member of a penniless family of killers (**1366**), Robert of Lindsey, in exigent for burning a woman's house in Hadleigh (**1522**), and Robert Crowe, in exigent in Stow hundred for larceny (**1237**), were probably typical in having no chattels, and also in being members of this clerical underclass, with hopes of preferment but no certainty of their being fulfilled, and in constant danger of being drawn into criminality as the easiest way of keeping body and soul together – further tempted, perhaps, by the consideration that their orders would protect them from the gallows. It was with good reason that Thomas of Chobham, writing in the second decade of the thirteenth century, warned that men competing for benefices in a church in which candi-

52 C. Harper-Bill (ed.), *English episcopal acta 21: Norwich 1215–1243* (Oxford, 2000), no. 31 (pp. 26–7).

dates for livings substantially outnumbered the supply risked ending up as thieves, robbers and sorcerers.[53]

The quality and behaviour of the church's ministers was a matter of continual concern to English bishops. The set of statutes which William Raleigh, bishop of Norwich, issued between 1240 and 1243 is one of many which both illuminates episcopal expectations of the clergy and also points to some of the ways in which members of the clerical order could influence the behaviour of the laity.[54] Many statutes were addressed to parish priests, setting out the need for them to lead honourable and praiseworthy lives, in a manner which distinguished them from the laity among whom they lived, the better to enable them to set an example and to proclaim the message of salvation to their flocks. That message was by no means irrelevant to the maintenance of law and order. Each pastor of souls, for instance, was required not only to know the Ten Commandments, with their injunctions against murder and theft, and the Seven Deadly Sins, which included wrath, lust and avarice, but also to preach upon them, exhorting their flocks to observe the one and flee the other. And every three months, in every parish church, sentence of excommunication was to be pronounced against all disturbers of the peace of the realm, all bearers of false witness, and all who maliciously defamed their neighbours. Equally pertinent were some of the statutes which were not concerned only with parish priests, but were addressed to men 'beneficed or in holy orders', that is, to the whole body of the clergy of Norwich diocese. All were commanded, for instance, not to haunt taverns – a statute which might have been ignored by Robert the chaplain of Buxhall, perhaps an assistant to the parson, who fell dead one day amid a company of men drinking (**1224**) – and all *clerici* were forbidden to carry weapons, while being also required to be dressed and tonsured as befitted their calling.

The eyre roll has nothing to say about what clerics wore, but provides plentiful evidence of their capacity for violence. They could break the laws of God and man in other ways as well. A chaplain who poached a deer is referred to above; perhaps Adam the priest of Lindsey was also poaching when he drowned in a fishpond in Polstead (**1469**). Sexual incontinence, though ceaselessly denounced by the church, was a sin which not all Suffolk clerics were able to shun; they eschewed rape, indeed, but the eyre roll contains a number of references to their children, though here too it is necessary to make distinctions before pronouncing judgments. Men in minor orders could lawfully marry. Simon the son of Walter the chaplain of Kembroke, for instance, who found the body of his father when he drowned in Nacton marsh (**1309**), may have been of legitimate birth, unlike John the son of the parson of Somerleyton, who was presented by the Lothingland jury as having imprisoned John de Stert for a day and a night, ostensibly because he suspected him of being a thief, but in fact because he resented John de Stert's affair with his sister. John and his sister were most likely the parson's illegitimate children; the fact that Stert was imprisoned in their mother's house at Fritton, a neighbouring vill, rather than at Somerleyton itself, may indicate that their father had been making a bid for respectability by trying to distance himself from his offspring and the transgression which produced them (**1423**).

53 H.M. Thomas, *The secular clergy in England, 1066–1216* (Oxford, 2014), p. 70.

54 Powicke and Cheney, *Councils & Synods* i, pp. 342–64 (these pages include additional statutes of uncertain date).

Such failings mattered because they were capable of bringing the church into disrepute and weakening its ability to guide its flocks into leading peaceful and law-abiding lives. That ecclesiastical teaching could be effective is surely demonstrated by the low number of suicides, only six being presented at the eyre. It is possible that a few more were concealed or disguised as accidental deaths, but it seems certain that acts of self-destruction were rare. How in other respects the laity regarded the church, as opposed to how they interacted with its ministers, it is usually impossible to say. But even vagrants who had no parish to call their own will have understood that the humblest church was a sanctuary to which a fugitive could escape from his or her pursuers, though they must also have seen it as a potential target for robbery, worth breaking into for the valuables it might contain (**1293**) – Raleigh's statutes included one ordering rectors and vicars to see that appropriate provision was made for the safe-keeping of sacred vessels and vestments. An unknown man found dead in Steeple Creeting churchyard was found to have died in the church – perhaps he had taken shelter in it, or turned aside for rest or prayer, when oppressed by the sickness which killed him (**1241**). But the equally sudden death of a woman named Elviva, who collapsed in the road in Kersey when on a pilgrimage with her husband which would probably have taken them to Italy, along with references to minor land-owners who went to the Holy Land on pilgrimage or crusade (**1178**, **1355**), are the only clear glimpses provided by the eyre roll of the kind of piety which the church called for from the faithful, in Elviva's case recorded only for its tragic ending (**1521**). The roll is of its nature a record of failings, in the present context of clerics who failed to meet the demands of their calling, and of crimes which the generally accepted teachings of the church failed to prevent. There is no way of knowing how many men and women were dissuaded by those teachings from acts of violence and theft, but it would probably be unwise to assume that none were.

Royal responsibilities, interests and rights

At the time of the 1240 Suffolk eyre, Henry III was thirty-two years old and in the twenty-fourth year of his reign. After many earlier difficulties, he was now to outward appearances a well-established monarch, generally on good terms with the baronage and the church hierarchy, and the father of a son and heir. The record of the eyre provides a way of examining his kingship from different perspectives, those of the localities rather than the centre, and of his humbler subjects rather than the men and women whom he could expect to meet at court or in the council chamber, people, indeed, whom he might never set eyes on, but who might be affected by his upholding, or pursuit, of his rights and by his understanding of his duties. As far as those duties were concerned, it is seldom possible to make a clear distinction between Henry's own attitude towards them and that of his representatives, above all his justices, whose task it was to interpret and implement them, but that may be because they were in basic agreement in matters of both outlook and policy.

The King's authority and his peace extended throughout the realm, and could be invoked by, and extended to, anyone except for those who rejected them. According to Humphrey of Earsham, he had been on his way to church and 'in the peace of the lord King' when Thomas Sharp attacked him (**1361**). When Eustace the miller came into court with the wife he had been charged with killing, the sheriff was instructed to receive him into the King's peace from which he had initially fled, and of which outlawry would have deprived him (**1483**). Important roads were royal ones, like the King's highway on which two men were found killed in Wetherden (**1227**) – it was probably the thoroughfare from Ipswich to St Edmund's. All coin circulating in England was the King's, and he was everywhere responsible for its integrity. The abbot of St Edmund's franchises included the right to strike coins, but his mint used a die issued at the royal exchequer, and in weight and value the pennies it struck were identical with those made in London.[55] So when Walter le Blund was convicted and hanged in London for forging money, it would have made no difference to his offence whether the false coin was fabricated in the capital or in Suffolk (**1425**). The trade which money facilitated was also supervised by the central government, showing itself concerned to protect the King's subjects against being cheated as well as against being murdered or robbed, by following Magna Carta in enforcing the use of a standardised measure for the sale of cloth, while also setting maximum prices for the sale of wine.[56] Numerous offenders against these regulations – 'assizes' – were named at the Suffolk eyre, along with two Beccles men who were amerced of half a mark for using false measuring-rods when selling cloth (**1218**, **1607**). A less precise charge against the men of Ipswich, Bricett and Needham, that they had been buying by a greater measure than they sold by, did not lead to any penalty being imposed and perhaps proved impossible to maintain (**1180**). But it further illustrates the scope of the eyre, and the range of possible wrongdoings that it might be called upon to remedy, that the accusation should have been made and recorded.

As the fount of justice, the King had the power to pardon, either directly or through his justices, who like their master might have to exercise their discretion in deciding how to act. In the case of John the son of Goda of Theberton, put in exigent for killing a man in a Leiston church, they called for discussion when it was realised that John was only seven years old, and may have referred the matter to the King, but there is no record of John's receiving a pardon (**1443**), whereas they remanded Alice the wife of John Maynard, who had killed her son when insane, 'until it is decided what should be done' – a choice of words which makes it clear that they had resolved to be merciful (**1285**). It was similarly through justices itinerant that the King could investigate and respond to acts of injustice by officials and local magnates, of a kind which lesser folk would otherwise have found it hard to either resist or remedy. With one exception, the offences presented at the 1240 eyre were not particularly serious: one of the brethren of the Hospital of St John of Jerusalem at Battisford had put three men in the stocks for keeping an ox badly (**1184**); the employee of a local grandee had imprisoned a man and made him pay half a mark for his release (**1357**); another man, whose position is unstated in the roll, raised a whole mark by similar means, binding his victim hand and foot until he bought his freedom (**1559**). Three unauthorised tumbrels – devices commonly used to discipline offenders against the assizes of bread and ale – were challenged, and in one case ordered to be pulled down (**1259**, **1339**, **1353**). Such presentments, and the responses to them, are noteworthy principally because they underline the willingness of justices acting in the King's name to hear about malpractices which in the context of government activity as a whole were relatively trivial, though not neces-

55 M. Allen, 'Ecclesiastical mints in thirteenth-century England', in *Thirteenth Century England* viii, ed. M. Prestwich, R. Britnell and R. Frame (Woodbridge, 2001), pp. 113–22.

56 Meekings, *The 1235 Surrey eyre* i, pp. 100–1.

sarily trivial to those who suffered from them. But they also took cognisance of, and responded firmly to, another abuse of power which was anything but insignificant.

The Lothingland jurors told a dreadful story of how some time between January 1235 and December 1237 William le Sauvage, a bailiff of that half-hundred, arrested two men and a woman and imprisoned them at Gorleston. He probably put them into stocks, in a manner preventing the circulation of blood, for by the time he saw fit to produce them in Lothingland's court, one man had died, the other man had lost a foot, and the woman had lost both feet, 'from putrefaction'. To make matters even worse, the court had refused to give a judgment on the surviving cripples, on the grounds that they had not been arrested for any offence which fell within its jurisdiction – presumably William had arrested them purely on suspicion, and not because they were possessed of stolen goods – and so they were allowed to depart as best they could. The justices did not go so far as to have William arraigned for homicide, but his offence cost him the heavy fine of £20, and that was seemingly conditional on his standing trial if occasion arose in future (**1416**). Whether he had to do so is unknown.

As well as dealing with abuses of power, the justices were also concerned with the maintenance of the King's administrative rights. The presentments they received concerning these often had fiscal implications – it is a measure of the closeness of the eyre's scrutiny that they should have included a withdrawal of the traditional due known as sheriff's aid which deprived the King of 3d. per annum (**1215**) – but they could also be significant for their potential effects upon the workings of government. The exclusion of the coroners from the half-hundred of Exning, so that they could neither make summonses and distraints nor hold an inquest into a death at Newmarket (**1460**), was bound to be detrimental to the exercise of royal authority in that part of the county, as was the refusal of the bailiffs of Orford – even though they were said to be 'the King's' – to allow the sheriff's men to take distraints demanded by the exchequer in Orford's suburb of Gedgrave (**1338**). But although the King needed to protect both his rule and his revenues – as part of his coronation oath he swore to preserve his rights and recover such as had been lost[57] – his power in thirteenth-century England did not depend only on money. It was exercised through the people he chose to employ, but also through the men – and they almost always were men – to whom the accident of birth had given authority in their localities, and with whom he was obliged to work if his own authority was to be maintained. His position was strengthened in his dealings with them by his having at his disposal a variety of material assets which could be distributed as rewards or signs of favour, instruments of patronage which when skilfully deployed could enhance his position in the shires and make his rule more effective. Details of a number of these were presented at the 1240 eyre. The five serjeanties were the least important of them. Consisting of lands held in return for specific services, four of them were military in character, while the fifth involved a bizarre display of Yuletide exhibitionism which proved so little to Henry III's liking that around 1256 he abolished it, commuting the service for a money payment (**1178**).[58]

Serjeanty tenures were almost entirely the creation of the twelfth century. They may have been still regarded as serving a useful purpose in 1198, when an article concerning them was added to the *Capitula Itineris*, but forty years later serjeanties

57 D.A. Carpenter, *The minority of Henry III* (London, 1990), p. 189.

58 JUST 1/833 m. 11.

like those of John Cordebof and Richard de Auyllers, requiring their presence for forty days on campaigns in Wales, were largely obsolete (**1213**, **1397**). That did not mean, however, that there was no point in the government's requiring information about them, about their holders and values, and about alienations from them. Apart from the possibility, however remote, that their holders might after all be called upon to provide the services due from them, there were other ways in which they could be useful to the King. If a campaign was planned, serjeants, like the holders of knight's fees, could be called upon to pay scutage, commuting military service for money, and if a serjeant died leaving an under-age heir, the King could dispose of the latter's wardship and marriage.[59] Those were occasional assets, but the King could also give a serjeanty away, along with the land which supported it. In 1240 Ralph de Burgo was said to hold by serjeanty what had once been a valuable property at Burgh Castle (in Domesday Book it was recorded as an estate of four carucates, or nearly 500 acres).[60] For this he could be called upon to supply the King's army with a crossbowman for forty days at his own expense. At the eyre the serjeanty was said to have been formerly worth £15 per annum, but its value had dropped to £5, while by 1240 Ralph had sold so much of it that his holding was worth only 5s. (**1420**). Litigation between Ralph and the purchaser, one Gilbert of Weasenham, followed, and in 1244 the King intervened, precisely because a serjeanty was at issue.[61] The upshot was that Gilbert transferred his rights to Henry III, who in turn gave the serjeanty, with all its land, to Broomholm Priory in Norfolk, which was to hold it 'as the said Ralph held it'.[62] In 1286/7 it was presented as owing the same services as in 1240, but the value of the land had risen to £30 per annum.[63]

Churches were more valuable and, in the circumstances of the time, more useful to the King, than serjeanties, since he could use them to reward his servants, or to allow others to reward theirs. They also became available more often, the church having set its face against hereditary succession in ecclesiastical positions. Details of fourteen churches said to be in the King's gift were presented at the eyre, showing that they varied considerably in value, and also that those with small revenues were seldom held by important people – it is not surprising that nothing can be said about Robert who held two Ipswich churches in 1240, when together they were worth only four marks per annum (**1412**). But Master Nicholas of St Albans, who held Kettleburgh church in 1240 (**1331**), was presumably a clerk in the exchequer, where in 1248 he was appointed King's remembrancer,[64] while Martin de la Wardrobe, who in 1240 occupied the church at Cove, worth twelve marks (£8) per annum (**1351**), was without much doubt an employee of the royal household; it was because they could be used to reward such men for their services that a king wished to retain his control over these benefices. When Chelmondiston church (**1389**) fell vacant in 1244, Henry III presented one of his chaplains to it.[65] Churches could also constitute rewards for services at much higher levels of government, as with that of Hintlesham, a valuable living worth £20 per annum, which formed part of

59 E.G. Kimball, *Serjeanty tenure in medieval England* (New Haven, 1936), pp. 138–9, 170–5.

60 Little Domesday Book, fol. 165.

61 *Curia Regis Rolls xvii, 1242–1243*, no. 139 (pp. 36–7), *Curia Regis Rolls xviii, 1243–1245*, no. 893 (p. 85).

62 *Calendar of Charter Rolls 1226–1257*, p. 283.

63 JUST 1/833 m. 27.

64 E 159/24 m. 5d.

65 *Cal. Pat. Rolls 1232–1247*, p. 432.

the ecclesiastical portfolio assembled by Master Michael Belet, a royal official and justice (**1389**), while Easton church appears (the phrasing is unclear) to have been at some point in the hands of no less a figure than William of Savoy, the uncle of Queen Eleanor of Provence (**1332**).

It can be seen that from the King's point of view, his rights in his churches were well worth protecting. The extent to which an eyre could help him in doing this is suggested by what was discovered in 1240 concerning Tattingstone church, namely that it was held by the dean of Rockland, not at the King's presentation but at that of the archdeacon of Norfolk (**1389**). The Samford jurors said nothing about this, and the church may have been in danger of slipping out of the hands of the King, for in 1243 he was recorded as suing against the archdeacon of Suffolk for trying to hinder his presenting to the now-vacant church.[66] It may well have been the record of the 1240 eyre which alerted the crown's agents to their master's rights in Tattingstone church, and led to a lawsuit aimed at safeguarding them.

Widows and heiresses could also be included among the assets of the English crown, though a much less profitable one than they had been under Henry III's predecessors. Chapter 8 of Magna Carta (chapter 7 in the 1225 reissue) had laid down that the widows of tenants-in-chief were not to be forced into remarriage, though it also enacted that when they did wish to remarry, they needed to have the King's consent. That consent was unlikely to be given for nothing, but the price paid was nothing like the sums for which King John, in particular, had sold the marriages of widows to the highest bidders, always assuming that he did not simply give them to whoever he wished to favour. Six widows who were nominally in Henry III's gift were named at the 1240 Suffolk eyre. In three cases the women concerned were landowners of modest importance, at any rate in Suffolk – Katherine of Eleigh (**1479**), Alice de Helyun (**1504**) and Margery, widow of Henry de Kemesec (**1462**), all had properties in more than one county. None of them seem to have remarried, while Lauretta de Pontibus, the widow of a former seneschal of Gascony, who held £10 worth of lands in Withermarsh which were themselves a royal escheat (**1476**), was probably unlikely to do so. Each of the two most important ladies concerned had previously paid to avoid being remarried against her will, in the case of Hillary Trussebut, who was an old woman by 1240, as long ago as 1203, after the death of her husband Robert de Boullers (**1504**). Margery de Rivers, a great heiress (in 1242 she was described in litigation as 'countess of Wight'),[67] had married first the heir to the earldom of Devon, and then King John's principal captain Falkes de Bréauté. She later claimed that this was against her will, and in 1229 she paid 200 marks for quittance from certain military obligations and 'so that she shall not be compelled to marry for so long as she wishes to live without a husband'.[68] In the light of Magna Carta this last provision should have been unnecessary, and in the event she remained single until her death in 1252.

Margery's land in Little Fakenham (**1555**) constituted an insignificant fraction of her estates. The same may also have been true of Hillary Trussebut's manor of Badmondisfield, but it was a valuable property, worth £15 per annum, and its fortunes after Hillary's death in the spring of 1241 help to show why it was worth

66 *Curia Regis Rolls xviii, 1243–1245*, no. 983 (p. 205).

67 *Curia Regis Rolls xvi, 1237–1242*, no. 1915 (p. 392); C 60/38 m. 12.

68 *Patent Rolls of the reign of Henry III, 1225–1232*, p. 269; C 60/28 m. 4; S.L. Waugh, *The lordship of England: royal wardships and marriages in English society and politics, 1217–1327* (Princeton, 1988), p. 86 n. 90.

the King's while to keep wealthy widows and their properties under observation. Badmondisfield had been part of her dower, and as such it was claimed in the court *coram rege* by William de Cantilupe and Vitalis Engayne, men whose rights descended from Hillary's husband's grandfather's first marriage, back in the reign of Henry I. So complicated were the details that the court commissioned a special inquest to sort them out, and it is not certain that they were truly unravelled. What is clear is that the two claimants won their case, supported by a proffer of money – in December 1241 they agreed to pay 100 marks for the manor, which was presumably in the King's hand as a possible escheat, Hillary having died childless. Cantilupe was pardoned his share of the joint fine, but Henry III was still richer by fifty marks when the litigation ended,[69] a conclusion which again demonstrates the potential value of the eyre as an instrument for pursuing and establishing the interests of the crown.

The same was especially true of the last of the assets to be considered in this section, consisting of escheats and Normans' lands. At the Suffolk eyre presentments concerning the latter were sometimes made under the heading of the former (**1234**, **1304**, **1477**), but they were inherently distinct. Escheats, the lands of tenants-in-chief which fell into the King's hands when their holders forfeited them or died without legitimate heirs, had been the subject of an article among the *Capitula Itineris* since 1194, and the King's right to them was uncontested. But inquiries concerning the English estates forfeited by Norman knights and lords, because in the years around 1204 they had chosen to adhere to the French king rather than to the English one, were new to the eyres which started in 1239, and constituted a potentially controversial extension of investigations begun three years earlier. This was above all because grants of such lands were usually made only 'during pleasure', and could therefore be revoked, with the estates involved being granted elsewhere.[70] In 1240 the manor of Haughley, at £40 per annum the most valuable of the former Norman estates presented at the eyre, was said to be in the hands of Henry III's brother Richard, earl of Cornwall (**1234**). Once the possession of Thomas, count of Perche (killed in 1217 fighting for the French at the battle of Lincoln), King John had granted it (with its attendant honour) to Hubert de Burgh in 1215, but only during pleasure, and though in 1227 Hubert had exploited his justiciarship to have his tenure made hereditary, that was revoked when he fell from power in 1232.[71] When King Henry gave the manor of Haughley to his brother in 1234, it was at first to be again held only during pleasure.[72] The grant was swiftly made hereditary,[73] and in any case it seems unlikely that Henry would have dispossessed his own brother, but that could have happened with other former lands of the Normans, as long as the King knew what they were and who held them.

The 1240 eyre heard eleven presentments of Normans' lands in twelve places, and also one of an ordinary escheat, the estate of Hugh de Cantilupe in Finborough, forfeited by the felony for which Hugh was hanged in 1225, and in 1227

69 *Curia Regis Rolls, xvi*, no. 1611 (pp. 313–16).

70 D. Power, 'The treaty of Paris (1259) and the aristocracy of England and Normandy', in *Thirteenth Century England* xiii, ed. J. Burton, F. Lachaud, P. Schofield and K. Stöber (Woodbridge, 2011), pp. 141–58; T.K. Moore, 'The loss of Normandy and the invention of *Terre Normannorum*', *EHR* 125 (2010), pp. 1071–109; D. Carpenter, *Henry III: the rise to power and personal rule, 1207–1258* (New Haven, 2020), p. 95.

71 *Book of Fees* i, p. 282; Carpenter, *Minority of Henry III*, pp. 141, 244, 389, 395.

72 N. Denholm-Young, *Richard of Cornwall* (Oxford, 1947), p. 167.

73 N. Vincent, *Peter des Roches: an alien in English politics, 1205–1238* (Cambridge, 1996), p. 424.

bestowed upon Ralph FitzNicholas, a former knight of King John's household who later became one of Henry III's stewards (**1234**).[74] Significantly, this grant was made to Ralph in hereditary right. Finborough was assessed at £10 per annum, which made it a fitting award for a man in Ralph's position; the other lands recorded in 1240 varied considerably in importance and value. The half-fee held by Ralph de Iuveny at Cretingham was worth only £5 (**1341**), as was John Lanceleue's whole fee at Brandeston (**1340**), and the estate known as the Soke of Brito in Wangford hundred was assessed at £7 (**1355**), while properties at Sproughton and Acton were valued, as Finborough had been, at £10 per annum (**1392**, **1475**, **1477**). But Wickham Market, then in the King's hands, was said to be worth £12 a year (**1304**), Mutford was assessed at £20 (**1245**), the total value of Combs was reckoned to be £23 16s. 8d. (**1234**), while Hintlesham was sufficiently valuable to be divided into two parts assessed at £16 apiece (**1390**). Only Haughley was worth more.

All these lands, along with others formerly held by Normans, were in the King's gift, providing him with the means of rewarding servants or advancing favourites, and of doing so whenever he chose. This is well demonstrated by the fortunes of Wickham Market in Wilford hundred (**1304**). It was unusual in not coming into the King's hands until 1236, members of the Norman family of Harcourt having contrived to hold on to it long after most of their compatriots had lost their English holdings.[75] In the following year Henry III granted it to a distant kinsman of his, William de Mastac, perhaps a Poitevin or Gascon, with the reservation that he was only to hold it, along with Sherston in Wiltshire, until the King was in a position to give him English lands worth £50 per annum.[76] That moment never came, and by 1240 William was probably back in France, while Wickham Market was back in Henry's hands, to be granted out again a year later first to William de Cumandas, a household knight, who was to hold it during pleasure, and then, only a few months later, to William de Boelles, a soldier who for his good services (he later became seneschal of Gascony) received a life grant of the property.[77]

Some beneficiaries of royal generosity were left undisturbed. The valuable manor of Hintlesham, for instance, forfeited in John's reign by Richard d'Écorchebuef and for a while held by the justiciar Geoffrey FitzPeter, was held jointly in 1240 by William Talbot and William Pipard (**1390**); in 1247 each man obtained a charter granting him his share in fee, after which their descendants retained their Hintlesham lands well into the fourteenth century.[78] But others who held Normans' lands were not always so fortunate. In 1240 the manor of Brandeston, in Loes hundred, was held by John Lanceleue (**1340**). In 1234 John's right in it was challenged on behalf of the King in the court *coram rege*, and when he claimed to hold it by gift from its Norman holder, William de Avranches, transmitted though his uncle, the royal attorney put forward a completely different line of descent for the property. John staved off disaster by vouching William's heirs to warrant the grant, and then having proceedings deferred until they came of age, so that he was still in possession at the time of the eyre.[79] But perhaps the jury's presentment there acted as an

74 *Calendar of Charter Rolls 1226–1257*, p. 1.

75 See F.M. Powicke, *The loss of Normandy, 1189–1204* (2nd edn, Manchester, 1961), pp. 342–3.

76 *Cal. Pat. Rolls 1232–1247*, p. 182.

77 *Ibid.*, pp. 252, 268.

78 T.D. Hardy (ed.), *Rotuli de oblates et finibus ... tempore regis Johannis* (Record Commission, 1835), p. 501; *Calendar of Charter Rolls 1226–1257*, pp. 324–5.

79 *Curia Regis Rolls xv, 1233–1237*, no. 1211 (p. 299).

aide-mémoire to the King's agents, for in the end John lost his case and in 1248 Henry III granted Brandeston to Alan Burnel, a royal serjeant.[80]

Something similar may have happened with lands in Norton, Tostock and Thurston, three vills close together in Thedwestry hundred which seem to have been usually regarded as a unity (**1575**). They had once been held by Renaud de Dammartin, count of Boulogne, and in John's reign had been confiscated when Renaud sided with the French, then returned to him when he returned to John's allegiance, and then granted to a probable kinsman of Renaud's after the count was captured at the battle of Bouvines in 1214, to spend the rest of his life in prison.[81] But by April 1230 the Norton lands were in the hands of Roger de Clare, a younger brother of the fifth earl of Gloucester.[82] In 1240 it was presented that he had held them, the use of the past tense perhaps resulting from his having gone on pilgrimage to the Holy Land, and indeed, he appears to have died on his journey home, some time before August 1241.[83] Again the eyre roll may have helped to alert royal officials to the King's interest in Norton, for on 30 March 1242, Henry III granted it to the courtier Hugh de Vivonne, who held it until his death in 1259.[84] Yet here, too, there was a conditional element in the King's charter, with Henry raising the possibility that even now he might bestow the lands on Count Renaud's 'right heirs'. It was the fact that it lay within his power both to make and revoke grants of the lands of the Normans that made them so valuable to Henry III, and which in turn gave the eyre a particular importance as a means of supervising and controlling them.

The financial issues of the crown pleas

The eyre was not only a means of safeguarding the crown's financial interests; it was also a way of raising money for the King. The same justices who held the Suffolk eyre held similar sessions in Hertfordshire later in the summer, a visitation which doubtless did much to prompt the St Albans chronicler Matthew Paris's bitter account of how in 1240 Henry III 'sent out his itinerant justices, who travelling all over England through the counties pertaining to the King, and punishing the transgressions of many men, under the pretext of justice gathered an infinite amount of money on behalf of the all-squandering King ...'.[85] What Henry did with the money so gathered is something for other historians to analyse. The discussion which follows, made possible by the survival of a record of all the sums due, is concerned with the amounts which the pleas of the crown raised for the King, and their financial impact on the communities and individuals concerned.

The profits of justice came in several forms. Throughout the roll reference is made to the chattels of convicted or suspected felons. Since flight from justice justified their forfeiture, regardless of whether a suspect was guilty or not, a fugitive's belongings could be gathered up by the sheriff as soon as his or her disappearance was known. If he was arrested, he was maintained from them for as long as he remained in prison; if he got away, they became the King's, to be sold and accounted

80 *Calendar of Charter Rolls 1226–1257*, p. 336.

81 T.D. Hardy (ed.), *Rotuli litterarum clausarum i, 1204–1224* (Record Commission, 1833), p. 116; *ii, 1224–1227* (Record Commission, 1834), p. 189; Hardy, *Rotuli chartarum*, p. 186.

82 *Close Rolls of Henry III, 1227–1231*, p. 346.

83 Meekings, *The 1235 Surrey eyre* i, pp. 180–2.

84 *Calendar of Charter Rolls 1226–1257*, p. 268.

85 Matthew Paris, *Chronica Majora*, ed. H.R. Luard, 7 vols (Rolls Series, 1872–83), iv, p. 34.

for at the eyre. Many runaways had no recorded chattels, but the justices were clearly assiduous in their pursuit of such as there were. They caught out the Claydon jurors in an attempt to undervalue the belongings of the abjuror John Unselthe (**1258**), and secured two horses worth 12s. which Reynold Stannard seems to have tried to rescue from sequestration (**1172**), and even 2s. worth of Warin of Stebbings's cloth which had come into the possession of Edmund the fuller (**1196**). They were also concerned to gather up the proceeds of any free land that malefactors had possessed. The practice was for such land to pass into the King's hands for a year and a day, and then to be returned to the wrongdoer's lord, but only after the crown had taken literally everything on it – trees could be cut down, crops reaped and buildings demolished. Some lords negotiated fines with the justices, undertaking to pay rather more than the estimated value of the King's rights in order to avoid such devastation. For example, when Richard the son of Roger of Kettleburgh was hanged for theft at the eyre, forfeiting five acres of land from which 25s. 4d. was due to the King, Richard's lord, Arnold of Kettleburgh, agreed to pay 32s. and thereby recovered his property intact (**1293**).

Forfeited chattels and lands had mostly belonged to men and women who did not come to the eyre. Amercements and fines, by contrast, were financial penalties respectively imposed on and negotiated by those who either attended it or stood surety for people absent from it. To be amerced was to be, in effect, at the King's mercy, which had to be paid for, with sums usually ranging between 6s. 8d. and £2; the exact amount would be assessed in the later stages of the eyre by one or more of the justices, assisted by men of the county competent to advise them as to how much an individual, a tithing or a community could afford to pay.[86] Occasionally the justices may have changed their minds about an amercement. When Stephen the son of Hubert the chaplain failed to attend the eyre, the sureties for his prosecuting Adam the son of Geoffrey Osmund were put in mercy, but their names do not appear in the amercements section – the justices may have decided that since Adam had already been outlawed at his suit, there was no need for Stephen's presence (**1326**). As this case shows, not every amercement imposed at the eyre was collected – in all 118 which were recorded on the roll were not entered in its amercements section. Some may have been pardoned on the grounds of poverty, as, indeed, a few were explicitly in the course of proceedings (**1177**, **1329**, **1454**). Fifty-five men and women nominally in mercy for default, for failing to come to the eyre, are not recorded as having been amerced. John the Butler was absent because his presence elsewhere was demanded by the King (**1506**); others may have obtained writs exempting them from attendance. But overall the imposition and assessment of amercements on mostly minor offenders seems to have been a straightforward business, and one which should have raised a good deal of money.

Fines differed from amercements in that although they were clearly penal in intention, and often followed from their makers' having been put in mercy, they were nonetheless ostensibly negotiated settlements between offenders and the King. As such they had to be paid; the man or woman who made an agreed fine would normally be required to keep to his or her side of the bargain and find the money. The sums involved were seldom much larger than those demanded from people who were amerced, but there were a few noteworthy exceptions. The largest fine of all was not in fact recorded at the eyre, and is known only from its being entered

86 The process is described by Meekings, *The 1235 Surrey eyre* i, pp. 128–40.

on the 1240 pipe roll. The whole county of Suffolk agreed to give the King fifty marks (£33 6s. 8d.) as its 'fine before judgment', a payment conventionally made by every county before an eyre, to cover in advance any collective offences which it might be found to have committed in the course of it.[87] The sum is surprisingly low for a wealthy county, and was paid almost immediately, perhaps helped by a certain sleight of hand on the part of the sheriff's staff – the men of Lothingland later complained that four marks, which they paid to the sheriff's clerk as part of their debt for having their own coroners, had instead been used by him as a contribution towards the county's common fine, from which they claimed to be exempt.[88]

No very large individual fines were made at the Suffolk eyre, and indeed, its issues, from both civil and crown pleas, were almost entirely made up of modest sums. Closest to exceptions to this rule were two £20 fines, one made by Guy de Verdon, a wealthy landowner in both Norfolk and Suffolk, to cover a violent assault made by his men and on his orders (**1192–3**), the other by William le Sauvage, a bailiff of Lothingland, for his unjustified imprisonment of two men and a woman, an abuse of power which had cost one prisoner his life and left the others permanently crippled (**1416**). These payments will have been calculated according to both the offenders' means and – especially in William le Sauvage's case – the seriousness of their misdeeds. The former consideration is likely to have counted for most with regard to the fines made by communities, for example by those of the county's boroughs which chose to pay lump sums to cover infringements of the assizes of cloth and wine by their tradesmen. The largest such payment was one of twenty marks (£13 6s. 8d.) negotiated by Dunwich (**1590**), while Ipswich agreed to pay £10 (**1406**) and Sudbury £5 (**1512**). But the most revealing is that of Orford, which does not seem at first to have intended to make such a fine. The borough's pleas record the amercement of eight drapers and one vintner (**1317–18**). But the amercements section shows that at some point the men of Orford decided, or were persuaded, to strike a deal with the justices, and to pay a total of four marks – £2 13s. 4d. – for all these infringements (**1617**). Had the nine offenders been amerced at the usual rate of 6s. 8d. each, they would have paid £3 all together. The crown lost 6s. 8d. by the fine, but almost certainly gained in terms of certainty and speed of collection, an important consideration at a time when the sheriff, who would presumably have had to raise the money, may have been at odds with the bailiffs of Orford (**1338**).

Not everything relating to the issues of the eyre was as precisely defined as Orford's fine. On a number of occasions where a possible offence or shortcoming was at issue the justices did not impose a penalty, but instead called for discussion, or simply judgment. A fine or amercement can sometimes be seen to have resulted in such cases. The record is silent, for instance, as to what happened after the justices had called for judgment on the bailiffs of Dunwich for allowing a suspected killer to escape from confinement and abjure the realm, but the amercements section shows that they made a two-mark fine (**1595**, **1665**). But more often it is impossible to tell what action, if any, followed in such cases. Uncertainty of a different kind can be associated with the so-called murder fine. It is unclear whether this was introduced or merely re-invigorated after the Norman Conquest, but certain that in the decades after 1066 it was rigorously enforced.[89] In order to deter Anglo-Saxon attacks on

87 *1240 Suffolk Civil Pleas*, citing E 372/84 m. 8d.

88 E 159/21 m. 6.

89 For discussion see J. Hudson, *The Oxford history of the laws of England ii: 871–1216* (Oxford, 2012), pp. 405–9.

William I's Norman followers, it was ordained that communities where men were found anonymously killed were to be subjected to heavy penalties if they could not demonstrate that the victims of murderous attacks were English. As time passed, and the hostility of conquerors and conquered dwindled, the penalties for failing to present Englishry, and so averting payment of the fine, became less onerous, but they did not disappear, essentially because they had become a useful source of revenue for the crown, as was still the case at the time of the 1240 Suffolk eyre.

Every county had its own customs for the presenting of Englishry. An incomplete statement setting out Suffolk's practice was made at the beginning of the crown pleas, declaring that establishing a dead person's Englishness required one kinsman on the father's side and one on the mother's (**1161**), to which a fuller statement from the 1286/7 eyre added that a fine could be incurred regardless of whether the deceased was male or female, or of his or her age, or of whether the cause of death was misadventure or felony.[90] Cases from the 1240 eyre bear out all these possibilities, with murder fines being imposed for the accidental deaths of men, women and children, even for an infant aged eighteen months (**1379**), and also for those of clerics, and thus for both the free and the unfree (**1224**, **1309**, **1469**). In the last of these cases, Polstead vill was put in mercy because it 'falsely presented Englishry'. Other vills (**1515**, **1520**), individuals (**1296**, **1297**) and juries (**1191**, **1226**, **1527**) were similarly penalised. It is impossible to tell if the offence was the same in each case. But since *Bracton* makes it clear that presenting Englishry was a complicated business, with the details given at any initial presentment having to be repeated exactly at the subsequent eyre, and the slightest inconsistency resulting in a murder fine being imposed, it may be that juries, individuals and vills had in different ways simply fallen foul of what had become an over-elaborate rule-book.[91]

This is not to say that Englishry could not be successfully presented. Of the deaths presented by Bosmere's jury, Englishry was presented on five and only two were subjected to murder fines, and Hartismere did almost as well, with four presentments accepted and just one murder fine imposed. As the eyre continued, the number of successful presentments declined, and it is possible that they were not always recorded, but failed attempts and straightforward fines continued to be entered on the roll until almost the end of proceedings. The sums due, however, do not appear to have been assessed with any obvious regard to the number of fines imposed. After Elmham, entered as a quarter of Wangford hundred, which owed 13s. 4d. for a single fine, the smallest amount was 26s. 8d. for three fines due from Stow hundred. Placed in the very centre of Suffolk, one might expect it to have been prosperous enough to pay more, certainly more than Thingoe and Lackford hundreds, in the less fertile north-west of the county, yet the former was assessed at 30s. for three fines and the latter at 40s. for one. Blything, a large hundred at the eastern end of Suffolk, was required to pay £3 6s. 8d. for a single fine, but so was the very small hundred of Exning, at the opposite end of the county, also for a single fine. The same amount was due from Samford, for four fines, while Babergh, next to it in the south of the county, was charged £4 for its three fines, the largest amount due for murder. Hartismere, on Suffolk's northern border with Norfolk, was required to pay 40s. for a single fine, Blackbourn, immediately to the west of it, £2 13s. 4d. for three.

90 JUST 1/833 m. 1.

91 Thorne, *Bracton on the laws and customs of England* ii, pp. 379–82.

These variations doubtless arose largely from differences in size, population and wealth which cannot now be quantified but presumably helped the justices assess the amounts due. But they may also have reflected the other demands made by the eyre on the hundreds concerned. Samford, for instance, may have escaped relatively lightly because three of its vills incurred substantial amercements, together raising a total of £7 6s. 4d. Babergh's issues, on the other hand, apart from £5 due from its jury, were largely made up of modest-sized fines and amercements, and the same was true of Blackbourn, where Thomas de Haya's ten-mark fine was the only considerable debt. It seems possible that in these and other cases the murder fine offered the justices a way to raise some additional money from areas which they had no reason to think had been otherwise overburdened by the eyre, perhaps even as a way of making up for the numerous amercements which were imposed but not collected.

There is a much that is puzzling about the murder fine. Occasionally it is possible to see a rationale for its imposition, notably when neither a person killed nor his or her slayers could be identified (**1383**, **1536**, **1586**) – such circumstances came close to re-creating those in which the fine had originated. But why Englishry was not presented on the many occasions on which, to outward appearances, it could have been, it is impossible to say. Although it may sometimes have been difficult to find suitably qualified people willing to attend a coroner's inquest and there assert both their own Englishness and their kinship to a dead man or woman, the fact that on a number of occasions Englishry was successfully presented, not to mention those on which attempts to present it failed, shows that in certain circumstances it could be avoided. It is those circumstances which constitute the pre-eminent mystery. There is some evidence that the status of a dead person, whether he or she was free or not, was a significant factor,[92] but how such a factor affected the way in which Englishry was or was not presented is impossible to say. There is nothing mysterious about the murder fine's value to the crown, however – it added a total of £48 13s. 2d. to the issues of the eyre.

It was through its financial demands that the eyre made its most immediate impact on Suffolk society as a whole, at every social level. As far as the people of the vills were concerned, there would be amercements and contributions to murder fines to be paid, and also what must have been one of the most tiresome impositions associated with royal justice, namely deodands. These were the material causes of accidental deaths, also known as 'banes', and paradoxically they brought no profit to the King, but instead – as their name indicates – they were given by him to God, in propitiation for the deaths they had brought about. Their value was assessed by the coroner at his inquest, and they were then handed over to the men of the vill where the death occurred, to be sold and the proceeds accounted for at the next eyre. The sums involved were often very small – examples include 2d. for a boat from which a woman drowned (**1585**), 3d. for a ladder from which a man fell (**1495**), 6d. for the oak tree which fell on a child (**1467**) – and altogether deodands raised a total of only £4 12s. 4½d. (how the money was disposed of is unknown). But that did not necessarily make the loss of the things involved less burdensome either to the kindred of a dead man or woman, who may have been ill able to afford the loss of even a cheap horse, or, where objects like the wheels and spindles of mills were concerned, to a whole vill. It is of some interest that no cases were recorded in 1240

92 Meekings, *Crown pleas of the Wiltshire eyre, 1249*, pp. 62–3.

of deodands being concealed or undervalued, as happened at many other eyres; whether this shows that officials were especially watchful, or villagers exceptionally cunning, it is impossible to say.

Deodands were not entered in the amercements section of the roll, which contains a systematic list, under hundreds and boroughs, of all that the justices decided was owing to the crown. The clerk made some mistakes in adding everything up; once these have been corrected, it can be said that if all the money was actually paid, then the Suffolk crown pleas should have raised a total of £411 19s. 2d. – almost double the issues of the civil pleas.[93] Some hundreds paid a good deal more than others, though the amounts due from them could be severely distorted by individual debts. Lothingland was ostensibly the second largest contributor, owing £48 2s. 2d., but if the hundred's fine of twenty marks for having its own coroners and William le Sauvage's £20 fine are subtracted, then it owed less than £15. Hartismere was required to raise even more, a total of £53 11s. 11d., and this sum, too, was distorted by a large fine, Guy de Verdon's of £20, but even without that the hundred would still have been a substantial contributor. Its remaining £33 11s. 11d., along with neighbouring Blackbourn's £23 13s. 6d., may be a pointer to the north of the county's prosperity at this time, just as the total of £44 11s. 4d. due from the hundreds of Bosmere and Claydon (answering separately in 1240, but later administratively linked) may illustrate the advantages arising from being near to Ipswich, and Blything's total debt of £29 13s. 4d. may reflect the benefits of closeness to Dunwich. That has to be speculation, all that is certain, and indeed predictable, is that overall the more heavily populated and productive parts of Suffolk paid more than the less populous ones – the western hundreds of Risbridge, Thedwestry, Thingoe and Lackford contributed less than £10 apiece.

Geography may have dictated how much money was raised by the eyre, but lordship decided where it went, for the King did not receive all the issues of the crown pleas, since the county's two great liberties, those of the abbot of St Edmund's and the prior of Ely, both claimed the right to the profits of justice from their lands. It is not certain that they were claiming exactly the same kind of profits at this time. Henry III's charter for the prior, given in 1233, made no mention of either the chattels or the waste of lands of convicted felons, and it was only in the mid-1250s that he undoubtedly received these.[94] All that can be said with regard to the 1240 eyre is that if the prior obtained the lands and chattels, then the issues of his five and a half hundreds would have enriched him by £33 15s.; without them, by £28 7s. 8d.

The abbot of St Edmund's, by contrast, is recorded as having attended the exchequer in Michaelmas term 1241, and there claimed chattels and lands as among the rights due to him from the Suffolk eyre.[95] In his case, all the recorded issues of his eight and a half hundreds would have brought him £74 3s. 9d., a sum which probably included not only what was due from his own lands but also the twenty marks due from the lands which other lords held within his liberty. In March 1242 Henry III accepted the abbot's claims, backed as they were by the charters of previous kings, and so he ordered the barons of the exchequer to check the abbot's rights and then to make no further demands upon him for the money, which he had clearly

93 *1240 Suffolk Civil Pleas*, pp. lxxviii (the figures given here differ slightly from those presented in the earlier volume).

94 L. Landon (ed.), *The Cartae Antiquae Rolls 1–10*, Pipe Roll Society 55 (1935), no. 14 (pp. 6–7); E. Miller, *The abbey and bishopric of Ely* (Cambridge, 1951), pp. 202–3.

95 E 159/20 m. 7 (two entries).

collected but until then had refused to pay.[96] But the barons ignored the King's command, in line with a recent change in exchequer practice, and for year after year went on trying to obtain the money allegedly due from the liberty of St Edmund, with the abbot each time obtaining a respite from paying it. In Easter term 1245, King Henry granted such a respite 'as the King wishes that judgment be rendered in his own presence whether or not the abbot should rightfully pay those things which are demanded of him',[97] but if he hoped his personal intervention would settle the matter he must have been disappointed, since the abbot had to secure yet another respite at Easter 1247.[98] But despite the exchequer's persistence, the abbot appears to have kept the money, either the full £74 3s. 9d. or the £60 17s. 1d. left after the deduction of twenty marks. The King's receipts from the crown pleas would have been reduced by £107 18s. 9d., or more than a quarter, if all the claims of the two liberties were accepted, by £89 4s. 9d. if they were not.[99]

Of course, it would not have mattered to those who had to pay amercements and fines whether the proceeds went to the King or to some other lord; after the eyre had finished they could still expect officialdom in some form to come in pursuit of their money, and to take distraints for what was due if they had no cash available. Conversation among those who left the eyre when all was over doubtless consisted largely of grumbles about the exactions it entailed. The men and women of Suffolk may also have talked about some of its more unusual or exciting moments. They could have recalled with disapproval the fatal outcome of the quarrel between Henry of Livermere and Thomas de Haya, expressed disappointment that the appeal by Robert the son of William of Peasenhall against Adam the son of Walter of Knodishall had not ended in a fight, savoured the defeat in combat of the approver William Thurbern. They may even have sighed over the terrible death of Sabina of Creeting, and crossed themselves when they thought of Elviva falling lifeless in the road as she went on pilgrimage. That must be speculation, but what may surely be legitimately surmised is that it would never have occurred to them that anything that they saw or heard at the eyre could possibly be of the slightest interest to their descendants nearly 800 years later.

96 E 159/20 m. 14; *Close Rolls of Henry III, 1237–1242*, p. 404.

97 E 159/22 m. 7.

98 E 159/23 m. 4d. For the new regulations see Carpenter, *Henry III*, p. 461.

99 Details of the debts and payments arising from the 1240 Norfolk and Suffolk eyres are set out in *1240 Suffolk Civil Pleas*, pp. lxxix–lxxxvi.

PRESENTMENTS UNDER INDIVIDUAL ARTICLES OF THE EYRE

The numbering is that of Meekings in *Wiltshire Crown Pleas*, 1249, pp. 28–33.

1 Of old crown pleas, heard in the previous eyre but not completed then (*De veteribus placitis coronae*): no specific presentments, but see 1273, 1431.
2 Of new crown pleas, arising since the previous eyre (*De novis placitis coronae*) covering most of the eyre's criminal business.
5 Of ladies in the King's gift (*De dominabus*): 1462, 1476, 1479, 1504, 1555.
6 Of churches in the King's gift (*De ecclesiis*): 1331, 1332, 1350, 1351, 1352, 1389, 1412, 1419.
7 Of the King's escheats (*De eschaetis*): 1234, 1304, 1477. See also 37 below.
8 Of the King's serjeanties (*De serjantiis*): 1178, 1213, 1397, 1420, 1505.
9 Of encroachments (purprestures) made upon the King (*De purpresturis*): 1179, 1311.
11 Of measures [and] cloth sold contrary to the assize (*De mensuris ... De pannis venditis*): 1180, 1187, 1218, 1219, 1251, 1317, 1333, 1422, 1464, 1509.
12 Of wines sold contrary to the assize (*De vinis venditis*): 1188, 1220, 1318, 1421, 1449, 1510.
15 Of [sheriffs and] bailiffs who hold pleas of the crown (*De ballivis qui tenent placita corone*): 1267, 1334. See also 1162.
21 Of malefactors and burglars (*De malefactoribus et burgatoribus*): 1252.
24 Of markets established without the King's consent (*De mercatis levatis*): 1599.
26 Of rapine and seizures (*De prisis factis*): 1357. Perhaps also 1184 and 1559.
27 Of new customs established (*De novis consuetudinibus*): no specific presentments, but possibly 1259, 1339, 1353, 1413.
28 Of defaults … of those who did not come on the first day (*De defaltis*): 1183, 1214, 1240, 1244, 1262, 1305, 1312, 1337, 1354, 1370, 1403, 1429, 1450, 1463, 1465, 1478, 1506, 1526, 1561, 1574.
31 Of poachers in parks and fishponds (*De malefactoribus in parcis et vivariis*): 1239, 1529, 1558, 1562.
32 Of the escape of thieves (*De evasione latronum*): 1284, 1319, 1404, 1451, 1480?
33 Of sea-wreck (*De wrecco maris*): 1426.
35 Of those who do not allow the King's bailiffs to enter their lands (*De illis qui non permittunt ballivos domini Regis*): 1338, 1402, 1404. See also 1460.
37 Of the lands of Normans (*De terris Normannorum*): 1245, 1340, 1341, 1355, 1390, 1391, 1392, 1475, 1575. See also 7 above.
38 Of suits withdrawn (*De sectis subtractis*): 1261, 1356, 1405. See also 1215.

EDITORIAL METHOD

The 1240 Suffolk crown pleas, like the civil pleas before them, are presented in an English translation. They appear as a continuation from the civil pleas and therefore constitute a sequence starting at 1161 and continuing to 1601. Their financial issues follow them in two sequences, 1602–41 and 1665, the numbers being those of blocks consisting of up to twenty entries (numbers 1642 to 1664 are those of the issues of the civil pleas and were published with them).

All the abbreviations in the manuscript except 'etc.' and some terminations of proper names have been extended.

Place-names appear in their modern form, where they can be identified. Unidentified place-names have been italicised; where they are appear as toponyms they are also preceded by 'de' rather than 'of'. Names of French origin, for instance Clarbec, are similarly preceded by 'de', as are some aristocratic names, together with a few that have become too familiar to be plausibly given in any other form. Hubert de Burgh is one example, the sheriff Thomas de Hemmegrave another. Forenames have been modernised where present-day equivalents exist. Occupational names have been translated wherever possible, as have surnames which translate readily into modern forms; Thomas Sarp, for instance, is represented as Thomas Sharp (**1361**).

Marginalia have been italicised and inserted, within round brackets, into the text at the points closest to the phrases to which they refer.

Sums of money are presented in the forms in use in the thirteenth century, when each pound sterling consisted of twenty shillings, themselves made up of twelve pennies. The silver penny was the only coin in general circulation. The mark (13s. 4d.) and half mark (6s. 8d.) which make regular appearances in the text were units of account, not coins.

All translations contain an element of interpretation. This is perhaps especially the case with texts written in medieval Latin, where many words have two meanings and some have several. That the English of the text presented here is a little freer than might once have seemed appropriate is due to the ease with which access can now be had to the original manuscript in The National Archives, thanks to the remarkable digital archive made freely available through the website of the Anglo-American Legal Tradition project, assembled by Robert C. Palmer, Elspeth K. Palmer and Susanne Brand. To facilitate that access, the numbers of the images of every side of every membrane are provided in the text, at the point at which each side begins. Thus equipped, the reader who wishes to check any reading can do so with a minimum of difficulty. But by way of reassurance, a specimen text is offered here, in both Latin and English (the latter as edited), to illustrate both the language in which the crown pleas were recorded, and the translator's response to the challenge presented by a far from straightforward original.

Specimen of an original text – plea 1583 (JUST 1/818 m. 55, AALT IMG_4495)

Willelmus filius Petri Ricardus filius Rogeri et Petrus filius Reginaldi de Ikelingham furati fuerunt tresdecim bidentes in Ikelingham et ibi occiderunt eas et absconderunt sub lecto Katerine de Ikelingham et similiter in presebi vaccarum bidentes non excoriatas. Et predicta Katerina propter hoc capta fuit et ducta ad domum Radulfi de Bayners et ibi imprisonata fuit in custodia Thurstanni Manser et Eudonis le Messer Wolwardi filii Godefridi et Mauricii filii Godefridi. Et Katerina fregit vincula sua et similiter parietem domus in qua fuit et evasit. Et Thurstannus et alii in misericordia. Et Willelmus et omnes alii qui furati fuerunt bidentes fugierunt ideo exigantur et utlagentur. Et Willelmus filius Petri suspensus est. Catalla eius xiiij solidi viij denarii unde Abbas respondeat. Et Ricardus et Petrus fuerunt in decenna Roberti Nuvelhume in Ikelingham ideo in misericordia. Non habuerunt catalla. Catalla Katerine iij solidi unde Abbas respondeat.

William the son of Peter, Richard the son of Roger and Peter the son of Reynold of Icklingham stole thirteen sheep in Icklingham and killed them there and concealed them under the bed of Katherine of Icklingham, and [hid] the sheep they had not skinned in the manger of the cowshed. Katherine was arrested on account of this and taken to the house of Ralph de *Bayners*, where she was imprisoned in the custody of Thurstan Manser and Eudo the hayward, Woolard the son of Godfrey and Maurice the son of Godfrey. She broke her chains, and likewise the wall of the house in which she was, and escaped, so to judgment for the escape. Thurstan and the others are in mercy (*amercement*). William and all the others who stole the sheep have fled, so they are to be exacted and outlawed (*they are to be exacted and outlawed*). William the son of Peter has been hanged. His chattels: fourteen shillings and eight pence, for which the abbot will answer (*14 shillings, 8 pence*). Richard and Peter were in the tithing of Robert Nuvelhume in Icklingham, so it is in mercy. They had no chattels. Katherine's chattels: three shillings, for which the abbot will answer (*3 shillings*).

THE CROWN PLEAS OF THE SUFFOLK EYRE OF 1240

(The National Archives, JUST1/818)

PLEAS OF THE CROWN TAKEN AT IPSWICH BEFORE WILLIAM OF YORK, PROVOST OF BEVERLEY, HENRY OF BATH, AND THEIR FELLOWS, JUSTICES ITINERANT IN THE COUNTY OF SUFFOLK IN THE TWENTY-FOURTH YEAR OF THE REIGN OF KING HENRY THE SON OF KING JOHN IN THREE WEEKS FROM EASTER DAY[1]

1 That is Sunday 6 May 1240, a week after the start of the eyre in Suffolk. See *1240 Suffolk Civil Pleas*, p. 3, n. 1 for the heading.

THE HUNDRED OF BOSMERE COMES BY 12 [JURORS] – BOSMERE[1]

1 The hundred name is repeated three times. Nothing is said about past or present sheriffs and coroners, as is commonly the case in other crown pleas rolls.

1161. William of Eye killed Henry de *Swinedon* at the house of John de *Helles* in Offton vill, and he fled to Offton church and there acknowledged the death and abjured the realm. He was not in a tithing, but he was of the household of William Talebot, who is in mercy (*amercement*).[1] Because Offton vill did not pursue it is in mercy (*amercement*). He had no chattels. Richard Stubbard and Richard Cook, who were with William when he killed him, fled and are not suspected, so they may return if they wish, and are to be under sureties. Richard Cook was not in a tithing, but Richard Stubbard was in the tithing of Gerard Stubbing in Offton, so it is in mercy for his flight (*amercement*). Four near neighbours, attached for that death, come and are not suspected, nor is anyone else. Englishry was presented by two, namely one on the father's side and another on the mother's.

1 *in manupastu* – literally 'mainpast', meaning that he ate the bread of his lord, who was responsible for his good behaviour and was amerced if he committed felony.

1162. Matilda the widow of Nicholas de *Westwode* appealed Adam of Boulogne of the death of William her son, and Adam was arrested and imprisoned in the gaol at Ipswich, and he died there. Godfrey the son of Sephul of Creeting,[1] Roger Aunsel of the same and Nicholas the son of William de Cape, who were with Adam when he killed him are not suspected, nor were they attached, so the sheriff is in mercy, namely Robert de Brywes (*amercement*).[2]

Afterwards it was established by the coroners that William de Cyresy had taken Adam's livestock and detained them against gage and pledge until he [Adam] caused them to be delivered by the King's bailiffs,[3] and afterwards he claimed the King's peace before the same bailiffs in the hundred court, and the peace was given to him. On the following day Adam placed his livestock in his meadow, while at the same time William sent Thomas Makefare, William the son of Nicholas de Westwode and Ralph his brother, and Robert the son of Simon of Stonham, his servants, to take Adam's livestock. And a quarrel having arisen between William's servants and Adam and his men, it happened that Adam killed William[4] and made two wounds on the head of Thomas Makefare. Because the twelve jurors falsely concealed this, so they are all in mercy (*amercements*). Because Robert de Brywes held a plea concerning that death without warrant, so to judgment on him (*to judgment*).[5] William de Cyresy comes and readily grants that he sent his servants to take Adam's livestock, but he firmly denies that he sent them there to do some evil, and the jurors attest the same, so he is acquitted.[6] Because Creeting St Olaves vill did not raise the hue, it is in mercy (*amercement*).[7] Because the twelve jurors attest that no Englishry was presented and it was established by the coroners that it was presented, they are again in mercy (*amercement*). Englishry was not presented, so Murder (*murder*).[8]

1 Identifiable only as one of several Creetings in Bosmere hundred.

2 Robert de Briwes was sheriff from 7 December 1237 to 29 September 1239.

3 When a lord took a distraint from a tenant for services withheld, the tenant could attempt to recover the distraint – usually cattle, as in this case – by offering security – gage and pledge – for proving in the county court that no services were owed. If the lord then refused either to accept the security or surrender the distraint, the tenant could obtain a royal writ directing officials to return the latter to him, as happened in this case.

4 That is, William the son of Nicholas de Westwode.

5 Robert had contravened Magna Carta c. 24, which forbade sheriffs and other officials to hear pleas of the crown.

6 In 1228 either William or his father and namesake was recorded several times as involved in litigation over land in indistinguishable Creetings and Stonhams, including one lawsuit over eight acres in a Creeting in which the unnamed heirs of Walter de Bononia, presumably kinsmen of Adam's, were vouched to warranty. JUST 1/819 m. 27d. This William was at least once a justice of assize in Suffolk. C 66/49 m. 11d. Adam's widow was involved in litigation at the eyre over her dower and the wardship of her son (**522**).

7 What became Creeting St Olave in Bosmere hundred is named 'Cretinge Grestenge' in the roll, from its having belonged to Grestain Abbey in Normandy.

8 The clerk's error on the presentment of Englishry suggests that he was basing his record on the jury's veredictum, and overlooked its correction on this point by the coroner's record.

1163. Margaret, the daughter of Osbert Biscop, was found killed by unknown thieves in the house of her sister Beatrice. They do not know who they were. Alice the wife of Hugh Wynde first found her. She comes and is not suspected, nor is anyone else. Englishry was presented.

1164. Matilda, the daughter of Alan de Bosco, was found drowned in a ditch in Somersham vill. Agnes her mother, the first finder, comes and is not suspected, nor is anyone else. Englishry was not presented, so Murder (*murder*).

1165. Thomas the son of Matilda was found killed in Easton vill in the road facing the church.[1] Adam Myner, the first finder, comes and is not suspected, but the jurors say that Gilbert the smith killed him and fled, so he is to be exacted and outlawed (*he is to be exacted and outlawed*). A certain Alice of Westleton colluded in Thomas's death, and she fled to the church of Easton and acknowledged that Thomas was killed on her account and abjured the realm. Gilbert's chattels: eighteen shillings and two pence in gear[2] for which the sheriff is to answer (*18 shillings and 2 pence*). Alice had no chattels. Gilbert was harboured in Easton vill outside a tithing, so it is in mercy (*amercement*). Sewal of Thorpe, in whose house Thomas was killed, was not attached, and so to judgment on Thomas de Hemmegrave who was then sheriff[3] (*to judgment*). Afterwards, it was established that Gilbert resided for almost five years in Gisleham vill in Mutford half hundred, so it is to be discussed there (*to be discussed during Mutford*).[4]

1 Identified by being entered in the amercements section as 'Eston Gosebek', this vill later lost its Easton prefix and came to be known simply as Gosbeck, from its having been held by members of the Gosbeck family. K. Briggs and K. Kilpatrick, *A dictionary of Suffolk place-names*, English Place-Name Society (Nottingham, 2016), p. 61. See also **1169** below.

2 *in utensilibus.*

3 Thomas de Hemmegrave was sheriff from 22 May 1234 to 21 April 1236.

4 Nothing about this case is found among Mutford's pleas, but there were proceedings relating to it in Thredling hundred, **1269** below.

1166. Clemency the daughter of Geoffrey Smalknyct was found drowned in Creeting All Saints vill. Parnel her mother was the first finder and she comes and is not suspected, nor is anyone else. Englishry was presented and four neighbours attached for the death come.

1167. Robert the son of Reynold the smith was found drowned in a ditch in Stonham vill.[1] Mabel his mother, the first finder, has not come and it was attested that she lies in childbirth, so nothing from her or her sureties. No one is suspected. Judgment: misadventure. Englishry was presented. Four neighbours have come.

1 *Estanham*, which could be Stonham Aspall, Earl Stonham or Little Stonham, all in Bosmere hundred.

1168. John de Hauville, who appealed Robert the son of Gilbert de la More of felony and ham-soken,[1] has not come, and he found sureties for prosecuting, namely Robert Blund of Stonham and Ralph de *Bramham*, so they are in mercy (*amercement*). Robert the son of Gilbert has not come because he is in gaol for an amercement.[2] The jurors attest that Robert entered into John's stable in Creeting St Mary, on land which John had bought from Robert's father Gilbert, and he docked the tails of John's horses and broke up the mews[3] and suchlike, so he is in mercy (*amercement*). Later, Robert comes, whereupon Master Edmund of Walpole, the official[4] of the Bishop of Norwich, comes and claims him as a clerk, and he has him, and he asks that the King's gaol be made available to him, and it is granted. Later Robert came and made fine by half a mark by the surety of William Pudsoft of Creeting and Nicholas Pig de *Darmsden* (*half a mark*).

1 House-breaking.

2 Robert was also amerced in **163** and **166** in the *1240 Suffolk Civil Pleas*, actions clearly related to this appeal.

3 *estruceria*.

4 A bishop's official was his principal judicial officer, who presided in his court and often administered the diocese in his employer's absence. Edmund had been instituted to the church of St Mary, Great Dunham, in Norfolk in 1227, when he was styled 'clerk', so presumably he attended the schools afterwards. He is not otherwise recorded as acting in this capacity, and may have been appointed to represent the newly-installed Bishop William de Raleigh specifically for this eyre. C. Harper-Bill (ed.), *English Episcopal Acta 21: Norwich, 1215–1243* (Oxford, 2000), no. 41.

1169. Henry Fleheye was found drowned in the fish-pond of Hugh of Gosbeck in Easton vill.[1] Richard the son of Hugh, the first finder, comes and is not suspected, nor is anyone else. Judgment: misadventure (*Misadventure*). Four neighbours come. Englishry was presented.

1 Again the future Gosbeck vill – see **1165** above.

1170. Edith the daughter of Stephen Fusedame was found killed in Earl Stonham vill in a house in the courtyard of Simon Curteys. William Brictmer, the first finder, comes and is not suspected, but he says that unknown thieves killed her. Stonham vill did not pursue when the hue was raised, so it is in mercy (*amercement*).

1171. William Aldeth, having falling sickness,[1] was found dead in a marl-pit in Coddenham vill. Emma the wife of William of Reydon, the first finder, comes and is not suspected, nor is any one else. Judgment: misadventure (*Misadventure*).

1 *gutta caduca*, usually translated as epilepsy, though the term seems also to have been applied to other afflictions involving a sudden seizure or collapse. See also nos. **1189**, **1241**, **1460** and **1598** below.

1172. Mabel the widow of Adam of Barking appealed Simon Haliday and Reynold Stannard of the death of Geoffrey Petypas her son. Simon Haliday, suspected of that death, fled to Battisford church, acknowledged the death, and abjured the realm. Reynold Stannard, likewise suspected of the death, has fled. Because Battisford vill did not pursue, it is in mercy (*amercement*). Simon was in the tithing of John Cook of Battisford, so it is in mercy (*amercement*). Reynold was in the tithing of Geoffrey the son of Alan of Battisford, so it is in mercy (*amercement*). Simon's chattels twenty-seven shillings and four pence (*27 shillings, 4 pence*). The same had houses and land from which the King's year and waste is fourteen shillings and four pence, for which the sheriff will answer (*14 shillings, 4 pence*). Reynold's chattels, in corn and other things, are thirty-three shillings, for which the sheriff will answer (*33 shillings*). The same Reynold had two horses, valued at twelve shillings, which the prior of the Hospital of Jerusalem in Battisford[1] received from Reynold, and afterwards handed back to him, so to judgment on him.

1 The Hospitallers had a preceptory at Battisford by around the middle of the twelfth century. *VCH Suffolk* ii, pp. 120–1.

1173. Alice the wife of Gerard Sybrun appealed Gerard the son of Alice of Hemingstone, Walter Draghestre, Walter the son of Roger of Ash and Millicent the wife of the said Gerard of breach of the King's peace, wounding and robbery. Now she comes and prosecutes against them as before. And because a woman cannot have an appeal against anyone except for the deflowering of her body and the death of her husband killed in her arms, it is adjudged that her appeal is invalid, and the trespass is to be inquired into by the country. Gerard and the other appellees, except Millicent, come, and she was attached by William Snod of Hemingstone and Walter the son of Wunerus of the same, so they are in mercy (*amercement*). The jurors attest that all are guilty, and so Walter and Gerard are in mercy.

1174. Geoffrey and Richard the sons of Alexander Costentyn of Claydon were found drowned from a boat on the bank of the river at Bramford.[1] Hugh le Futur, the first finder, comes and is not suspected, nor is anyone else. Judgment: misadventure (*Misadventure*). Price of the boat: 6 pence.[2]

1 Bramford stands on the River Gipping, a few miles downstream from Claydon.
2 The margin, which is very rubbed, contains no visible reference to a deodand or the value of the boat.

[At the foot of the manuscript are the words 'Pleas of the Crown. Pleas' and some indecipherable scrawls.]

Membrane 45d *AALT 4597–8*

STILL BOSMERE

1175. Geoffrey the son of Arnold the merchant was found drowned in a ditch in Badley vill. Margaret his sister, the first finder, comes and is not suspected, nor is anyone else. Judgment: misadventure, and the four neighbours have come.

1176. William the son of Richard Reyner was found drowned in a marsh in Stonham vill. Rose the wife of John Prest, the first finder, comes and is not suspected, but they say that Geoffrey the son of Reinerus of Earl Stonham and Agnes his wife are suspected of that death and have fled,[1] so Geoffrey is to be exacted and outlawed (*he is to be exacted and outlawed*). Geoffrey was in the tithing of Alexander the son of Hugh of Stonham, so it is in mercy (*amercement*). His chattels: 3 shillings.

1 Literally 'he has fled', the clerk having failed to take Agnes's involvement into account.

1177. Edith, the widow of Robert Wighe, appealed Robert the son of Odo of Bramford of breach of the King's peace and wounding, and she appealed Peter de la Tye and Robert's mother Christian of abetment. Edith does not come and she found sureties for prosecuting, namely Robert Wighe and Richard Gurle of Coddenham, so they are in mercy (*amercement*). Robert and the other appellees come and the jurors attest that Peter and Christian are not guilty, nor have they come to an agreement,[1] so they are acquitted thereof, but they say that Robert is guilty, so ---- [unfinished].[2] Afterwards it was ordered that Robert the son of Odo be released because of his poverty.

1 That is, they have not made an out of court settlement without the consent of the justices.
2 Both in the text and the margin the clerk has crossed out the orders for Robert's remand and amercement.

1178. (*Serjeanties*) Concerning Serjeanties, they say that there is a serjeanty in Hemingstone vill, from which Natalia the wife of Edmund de *Brunton* holds a messuage.[1]

The aforesaid Edmund, who held that serjeanty, set out on pilgrimage to the Holy Land, and before his departure he sold 60 acres of land to many in the county, namely more than two thirds to the Prior of the Hospital of Saint John of Jerusalem in England, and he sold a portion to Ralph de Blunville, and a portion to Walter Oldecoren, and he sold a portion to Robert le Wetherwye and a portion to Robert the Butler, but they do not know how much he sold to each of them. They say that in this hundred that serjeanty is worth twenty shillings a year, and there ought to be performed for it a leap, a whistle and a fart.[2]

1 The tenant of Hemingstone held his estate by the service of performing this 'fantastic foolery' before the King on Christmas Day every year. A.L. Poole, *Obligations of society in the XII and XIII centuries* (Oxford, 1946), p. 66. Presumably Edmund sold lands to finance his pilgrimage. In the civil pleas his wife, described as his widow, sued for dower against four men, including two named in this presentment. *1240 Suffolk Civil Pleas*, **328.** She may have done so on the assumption that her husband would not return from the Holy Land, but in fact he seems to have returned, as Edmund was recorded as holding Hemingstone in 1244. *Book of Fees* ii, p. 1154. A presentment at the 1286/7 eyre showed that the alienation of the serjeanty lands continued after 1240. It also recorded that in about 1256 Henry III abolished the service on the grounds that it was unseemly, preferring to receive 26s. 8d. *per annum* instead. JUST 1/833 m. 11.
2 There is a space of 3.9 centimetres between this plea and the next one, presumably left for further information about the serjeanty which was never forthcoming.

1179. Concerning Encroachments, they say that John de *Ofwde* has narrowed a royal highway in Little Bricett, so he is in mercy (*amercement*). The sheriff is ordered to inspect that highway and to have it restored and to be as it ought and is accustomed to be.[1]

1 *Ofwde* or *Offewode* is a lost place-name in Bildeston. Briggs, *Suffolk place-names*, p. 479. Despite the justices' order, John's encroachment was not corrected, but in 1275 was in the possession of Hugh de *Offewode*, perhaps his son. W. Illingworth (ed.), *Rotuli Hundredorum* ii (Record Commission, 1818), p. 193.

1180. Concerning Measures, they say that the men of Ipswich, Bricett and Needham buy by a greater measure than they sell by.

1181. Alexander de *Ulvertoft* charged with the theft of cloths and corn, and of the death of Avelina Stock, comes and denies all and puts himself on the country. Similarly Mabel the wife of the same Alexander comes and denies all, and because it was attested that Mabel is his wife, she is acquitted (*she is acquitted*).[1]

The jurors say that Alexander is guilty of larceny, so etc.[2] Concerning the death they say that they do not know if he is guilty or not. His chattels: five shillings, for which the sheriff will answer (*5 shillings*). The same had 2 acres of land and a messuage, from which the year and waste etc. are three shillings (*3 shillings*).

1 Mabel was here the beneficiary of an outlook that usually treated wives as being so under the control of their husbands that they were unable to disobey their orders, with the result that they were automatically acquitted of crimes committed in their company.

2 There is no marginal note recording Alexander's fate, but the forfeiture of his lands and chattels shows that he was hanged.

1182. Geoffrey Herlepyc, charged with stealing a cow in Earl Stonham, has fled, so he is to be exacted and outlawed (*he is to be exacted and outlawed*). He was in the tithing of Walter Mor of Earl Warenne's Stonham,[1] so it is in mercy (*amercement*). His chattels: five shillings, for which the sheriff will answer (*5 shillings*).

1 Stonham had long been in the possession of the Bigod earls of Norfolk, but in 1240 it formed part of the dower of Maud, countess dowager of Norfolk, who had married Earl William de Warenne as her second husband, and for that reason it was probably regarded as being under his control. M. Morris, *The Bigod earls of Norfolk in the thirteenth century* (Woodbridge, 2005), p. 34.

1183. (*Defaults*) Concerning Defaults, they say that the abbot of Grestain, the abbot of Bernay and the abbot of Bec-Hellouin did not come on the first day, so to judgment (*to judgment*).[1]

1 The Norman abbeys of Grestain and Bernay had dependent cells at Creeting St Olave and Creeting St Mary respectively. Both were in Bosmere hundred, as was Bec-Hellouin's manor of Blakenham. M. Morgan, *The English lands of the Abbey of Bec* (Oxford, 1946), p. 148.

1184. The jurors present that Brother Peter of the Hospital of St John of Jerusalem arrested three men for the inadequate keeping of an ox and put them in the stocks, so to judgment on him (*to judgment*).[1]

1 Peter will have been an inmate of the Hospitaller preceptory at Battisford, as in **1172** above.

1185. A horse struck a boy in Great Bricett so that he quickly died. Price of the horse: half a mark, for which the sheriff will answer (*half a mark*). Because Great Bricett vill did not present this case in the county court, it is in mercy (*amercement*).

THE PRESENTMENT OF THE BOROUGH OF EYE [WHICH] COMES BY 12 [JURORS]

1186. Adam of Worlingworth was found killed in Thrandeston vill.[1] Geoffrey the son of Sarah of Eye and Sarah his mother were arrested for that death and put in Ipswich gaol, and because this happened in Hartismere hundred, let it be more fully inquired into there (*to be inquired into in Hartismere Hundred*). Later Sarah comes and puts herself on the country for good or ill. The jurors attest that she is not guilty, so she is acquitted thereof (*she is acquitted*). Geoffrey comes and says that he is a clerk, and as it is not known if it is true that he has been ordained, so he has been put in gaol again.[2]

1 For this case see also **1208** below.

2 There is a space of 2.8 centimetres between this item and the next, no doubt left to be filled should Geoffrey reappear in court.

1187. Concerning Cloths sold contrary to the assize, they say that John Faukun, William the merchant, Gervase the merchant, Anketill the merchant and Matthew Luvcecok have sold cloth contrary to the assise, so they are in mercy (*amercement*).

1188. Concerning Wines sold contrary to the assize, they say that Alexander of Kettleburgh has sold wine contrary to the assize, so he is in mercy. (*amercement*).

Membrane 46 *AALT 4476–7*

THE PRESENTMENT OF THE HUNDRED OF HARTISMERE [WHICH] COMES BY TWELVE [JURORS]

1189. Baldwin Crachepane, having falling sickness, was found dead in his father's barn in Mellis vill. Agnes, his wife, the first finder, comes and is not suspected, nor is anyone else. Judgment: misadventure. Englishry was presented and the four neighbours have come.

1190. Matilda the daughter of Leofric of Oakley appealed William the son of John of Eleigh that he forcibly lay with her and deflowered her. Matilda does not come and she found no sureties except her oath, so she is to be arrested. William does not come and he was attached by William the son of Gilbert of Stutton and William the son of Margery of Ipswich, so they are in mercy (*amercement*).

1191. Alice the daughter of Richard Dragheswerd was found drowned in a ditch in Finningham vill. Mary, the first finder, has not come because she has died, and she is not suspected nor is anyone else. Judgment: misadventure (*Misadventure*). Englishry was not presented, so murder (*murder*). The twelve jurors falsely presented Englishry, so to judgment on them (*to judgment*).

1192. Robert of Boxted appealed Roger Spurecat of breach of the King's peace and wounding. He appealed Alexander the son of William of Hockham, Theobald the son of William, Matthew Piketheu, Engelram the son of Ellen, Guy Cokerel, and William Copping [of abetment].[1] He appealed Guy de Verdon of giving the order. Robert does not come and he found sureties for prosecuting, Stephen of Boxted, his own brother, and Roger the son of Alice of Grundisburgh. Theobald and Matthew have not come. Theobald was attached by Roger of Cransford and Adam le Moyne de *Stubburg*. Matthew was attached by William de Verdun of Shaddingfield and Roger de la Grene de *Stubburg*. So all the sureties are in mercy (*amercements*). Alexander, Engelram, Guy [Cokerel], William and Guy [de Verdon] come and deny everything. The jurors attest that they have come to an agreement and that Alexander, and all the appellees, did that trespass by the order of Guy de Verdon, and they say that they wounded Robert and badly beat him as he appealed them. So all are to be remanded in custody (*they are to be remanded in custody*).

The same appealed Robert Warenger of a like abetment. He comes, and the jurors attest that he is guilty together with the others. So he is to be remanded in custody (*he is to be remanded in custody*). Later Guy de Verdon came and made fine for himself and his men by twenty pounds, by the surety of Richard the butler of Upton, Robert de Bosco, Hugh Burt, Robert Malet, John de *Curton*, William de Verdun, William of Sproughton, Nicholas of St Edmund's and Robert of Waldingfield (*20 pounds*).[2]

[1] Implicitly, the record does not specify the charge.

2 Guy de Verdon was primarily a Norfolk landowner, as lord of the manor of Bressingham. In Suffolk his family's principal interest was the half-manor of Culpho, and he was also a benefactor to Sibton Abbey. M. Hagger, *The fortunes of a Norman family: the de Verduns in England, Ireland and Wales, 1066–1316* (Dublin, 2001), pp. 244–5; P. Brown (ed.), *Sibton Abbey cartularies and charters* i, Suffolk Charters 7, SRS (1985), pp. 108–9; ii, Suffolk Charters 8, SRS (1986), nos. 271–5.

1193. Godiva the wife of Aylmer Cook appealed Alexander the son of William of Hockham of breach of the King's peace, wounding and beating and she appealed of abetment John the son of Guy de Verdon, Richard Spurecat, Theobald the son of Walter, Guy Cokerel, Engelram the son of Ellen, Matthew Copping. And she appealed Guy de Verdon of giving the order. Godiva does not come because she has died. John, Theobald and Matthew do not come. John was attached by Guy de Verdon and Richard the Butler of Upton. Matthew and Theobald were attached by the same security as in the previous entry. So all the sureties are in mercy (*amercements*). Alexander, Engelram, Guy [Cokerel], William and Guy [de Verdon] have come. The jurors attest that when Richard Spurecat wounded Robert of Boxted he fled to Godiva's house, and Alexander then gave her a wound.[1] All the others appealed were in abetment, and they did this by the order of Guy de Verdon. So all are remanded in custody (*they are remanded in custody*).

1 The wound which Alexander gave Godiva was later suspected of having caused her death, see **1217** below.

1194.[1] William of Risby was found killed in Mellis mere. The first finder has died. Warin of Stebbing is suspected of that death and he has fled, so he is to be exacted and outlawed. He was in the tithing of John Catun in Burgate, so it is in mercy. His chattels: seven pounds eight shillings eight pence, for which John the sheriff will answer. The same Warin had land, wood, and houses from which the King's year and waste are four pounds four shillings four pence (*it is below*).

1 The whole entry has been struck through and all the marginalia deleted except for a solitary 's', which is accompanied by a note indicating that the case may be found below, **1196.**

1195. Roger de Furnaus is suspected of stealing the horse of Richard the Butler, and he has fled, so he is to be exacted and outlawed. Afterwards it was established that he was not in a tithing because he was a free man and held by military service. His chattels eighteen shillings, for which John the sheriff will answer (*18 shillings*).[1] The same had houses and twenty-four acres of land, from which the King's year and waste are four pounds twelve pence, for which John the sheriff will answer (*4 pounds, 12 pence*).[2]

1 Here and elsewhere the 'J' of the text has been extended into 'John', representing John de Ulecote, sheriff at the time of the eyre.

2 This entry is repeated as **1550** below.

1196. William of Risby was found killed in Mellis mere. The first finder has died. Warin of Stebbing[1] is suspected of that death and has fled, so he is to be exacted and outlawed (*he is to be exacted and outlawed*). He was in the tithing of John Catun in Burgate, so it is in mercy (*amercement*). His chattels: seven pounds eight shillings eight pence, from which Thomas de Hemmegrave, then sheriff,[2] will answer for six pounds nineteen shillings eight pence. John de Ulecote, the sheriff, will answer for nine shillings (*7 pounds, 8 shillings, 8 pence*).[3] The same had land, wood and houses, from which the King's year and waste are four pounds four shillings four pence, for which John the sheriff will answer (*4 pounds, 4 shillings, 4 pence*). Afterwards, it was attested[4] that Edmund the fuller was attached for a cloth of Warin's which he carried off, and because he has not come he and his sureties are in mercy, namely: Richard Bern and William the painter of Finningham (*amercement*). Price of the cloth two shillings, for which John the sheriff will answer (*two shillings*).

1 In Hinckford hundred, Essex.

2 This crime appears to have occurred when Thomas was sheriff of Norfolk and Suffolk, between May 1234 and April 1236.

3 The clerk must have crossed out **1194** above on realising that each of the sheriffs was responsible for some of Warin's chattels, John de Ulecote having at first been shown as solely responsible for all of them.

4 The marginalia intrude so far across the membrane that at this point the clerk used his customary symbol for a new entry to separate them from his continuation of the text.

1197. Emma the daughter of Martin of Bacton appealed Simon the son of Robert Woolmer of rape, and she appealed Robert the son of Lambert Grigg of abetment. Emma does not come and she found sureties for prosecuting, Martin of Bacton and Nigel the son of Walter of Haughley. So they are in mercy (*amercement*). Simon was not attached nor was Robert because she did not proceed against them.[1]

1 Emma can have sued only once or twice in the county court.

1198. William of Eleigh[1] killed Philip the son of Cecilia of Brome. He fled, so he is to be exacted and outlawed (*he is to be exacted and outlawed*). He was not in a tithing, so Oakley vill which harboured him outside frankpledge is in mercy (*amercement*). His chattels forty-two shillings, for which John the sheriff will answer (*42 shillings*). The same had land and houses from which the King's year and waste are twenty shillings (*20 shillings*). Later William of Hoo, the lord of the fief, came and made fine by twenty shillings, by the surety of John de Crammaville and William of Stuston (*20 shillings*).[2]

1 Either Monks Eleigh or Brent Eleigh in Babergh hundred.

2 Since it was the usual practice for a lord paying to keep his tenant's lands out of the king's hand to offer rather more than the original assessment, it seems likely that the clerk accidentally entered the same sum twice, and that the property was at first valued at less than 20s.

1199. Peter the son of Ricolf of Westhorpe was found drowned in a ditch in Wyverstone vill. Richard the son of William of Wyverstone, the first finder, comes and is not suspected, nor is anyone else. Judgment: misadventure (*Misadventure*).

1200. Robert the son of William appealed Matthew the son of Richard[1] de Scheyt of breach of the King's peace, and wounding and robbery, and he appealed John de Geraunvile,[2] Adam the son of Thomas of Tivetshall[3] and Martin the son of Roger de Scheyt of abetment, and Matthew de Gerardvile of giving the order. Robert does not come and he found sureties for prosecuting, William Gernun of Thornham and William de Cumpenye his brother. Adam the son of Thomas does not come and he was attached by Alan the son of Richard of Thornham and Sewal the tailor of the same. John and Matthew come and the jurors attest that Matthew the son of Richard is guilty of the deed. They say also that John de Gerardvile and Adam are guilty of abetment, so they are in mercy (*amercement*), let them be remanded in custody (*they are remanded in custody*). They say also that Roger the son of Martin[4] and Matthew de Gerardvile, who were appealed of giving the order, are not guilty, so they are acquitted thereof. Matthew the son of Richard is a clerk and is delivered to the bishop, and John de Gerardvile is a layman and is delivered to the gaol. Later John came and made fine by ten shillings, by the surety of Matthew de Gerardvile and Thomas de Gerardvile (*10 shillings*).

1 Replacing Roger, struck through.

2 *sic* – this toponymic is otherwise spelt Gerardvile throughout the entry.
3 Either Tivetshall St Margaret or Tivetshall St Mary in Diss hundred, Norfolk.
4 Probably a clerical error for Martin the son of Roger.

1201. Mabel the wife of Hubert Kembel was found killed in her house at Cotton by unknown thieves. Mabel the daughter of Joce, the first finder, comes and she is not suspected. It is not known who the evildoers were.

1202. William the son of Burghard appealed Gilbert the son of William de *Caketon* of breach of the King's peace and wounding, and he comes and continues to sue against him. Gilbert does not come and he was attached by Hugh de Blogate and Ralph the son of Eudo of Benningham, so they are in mercy (*amercement*). And William was told that he may sue against him in the county court until he comes to stand trial or is outlawed according to the law of the land.

The same appealed Everard[1] de *Caketon* and Olive his wife of abetment and he says that when the said Gilbert gave him a wound in the right shin, they were with him and aiding him, but because the deed has not yet been proved, the plea against them is respited until it is proved. Later Gilbert came, as appears in the following section.

William Burchard of Suddon[2] appeals Gilbert the son of William de *Kaketon* that on the Sunday next after the Feast of St Gregory three years ago now[3] he came to him when he was at the house of Walter his son in Yaxley, where he gave him a wound in the right shin with a knife, one five inches long and in depth to the bone. And that he did this wickedly and feloniously, against the King's peace, he offers to prove as the court decides, as one who has been maimed and is over age, for he says that he cut two sinews in his shin.[4]

Later William came and withdrew, so he and his sureties for prosecuting are in mercy, namely Hugh the reeve of Occold and Walter the son of William Burchard (*amercement*). The jurors say that they have come to an agreement and that Gilbert is guilty, so both are to be remanded in custody. They say also that Everard de *Caketon* is guilty of abetment, so he is to be remanded in custody. Later, William came and made a fine by half a mark by the surety of Nicholas the son of Emma of Braiseworth and Hugh the reeve of Benningham (*half a mark*). Later Everard came and made fine by one mark by the surety of Hugh de Blogate of Yaxley and Everard Dubber of the same (*one mark*). Later Gilbert came and made fine by two marks by the surety of Hugh de Blogate of Yaxley, John the son of Peter de *Kaketon*, Everard of Sutton and Alexander the son of William of Yaxley (*two marks*).[5]

1 Replacing Robert, struck through.
2 Gilbert's appearance in court leads to William renewing his appeal against him in conventional form. The additional detail shows that he probably came from Suddon in Stow hundred.
3 15 March 1237.
4 Both his alleged injury and his age (over sixty) would have prevented William from offering trial by battle.
5 Some of the words in the margin relating to the later stages of this entry have been rubbed or torn away.

Membrane 46d *AALT 4599–600*

1203. Adam the son of Gerard Sirich was found drowned in a ditch in Barningham vill. Gerard, his father, the first finder, comes and is not suspected, nor is anyone else. Judgment: misadventure (*Misadventure*). Englishry was presented.

1204. Benedict the son of Roger Rolaund was found drowned in a ditch in Wickham Skeith vill. Basilia, his mother, the first finder, comes. No one is suspected. Judgment: misadventure (*Misadventure*).

1205. Robert the son of Thomas of Bacton was found killed in Bacton vill in the house of Peter Sexe. Peter Sexe and his wife Agnes were tied up in the same house. The same Peter and his wife Agnes come and are not suspected. It is not known who the evildoers were. Englishry was presented.

1206. Guy the son of William of Lopham was found killed in Redgrave marsh. Ralph of Oakley, the first finder, comes and is not suspected, but they say that Richard the son of Robert Hare killed him, so he is to be exacted and outlawed (*exacted and outlawed*). He was in the tithing of Roger Spyr of Wortham, so it is in mercy (*amercement*). His chattels: six shilling nine pence, for which the sheriff will answer (*6 shillings, 9 pence*). Richard Stanhard who was with Guy when he was last seen alive comes and denies that death and puts himself on the country for good or ill.

The jurors say that the said Richard is not guilty of that death, so he is acquitted thereof (*he is acquitted*).

1207. Hervey the son of William Foul was found killed near to the mill of Robert Blund. It was attested that he killed himself by misadventure (*Misadventure*).

1208. Adam of Worlingworth was found killed in Goswold meadow. Hugh Wrenne, the first finder, comes and is not suspected. They say that Geoffrey the son of Sarah of Eye killed him, and he was arrested and held in gaol. Englishry was presented.[1]

1 For this case see also **1186** above.

1209. Burghard, who was charged with wounding his brother mortally so that he died, comes and put himself on the country for good or ill. The jurors say that he wounded him mortally so that he quickly died. Judgment: he is to be hanged (*he is to be hanged*). His chattels: eighteen pence, for which John the sheriff will answer (*18 pence*).

1210. Walter the son of Leofric and Edith his sister, charged with stealing clothes and herrings and other larcenies, come and put themselves on the country for good or ill. The jurors and four vills attest that they are guilty, so they are to be hanged (*they are to be hanged*). They had no chattels. Leofric Dyrunt is suspected of harbouring thieves and has fled, so he is to be exacted and outlawed (*he is to be exacted and outlawed*). He was in the tithing of William of Chevington, so it is in mercy (*amercement*).[1] He had no chattels.

1 The amercement appears among those for Eye, which although in Hartismere hundred answered by its own jury (**1604**).

1211. Thomas the son of Thomas Crowe appealed John de *Couele* of breach of the King's peace, wounding and robbery, and Thomas comes and now sues against him. John does not come and he was attached by Alexander Ketel of Stow and William the son of Ralph of Potsford, so they are in mercy (*amercement*). Thomas is told that he may prosecute against him in the county court until he is outlawed or has been attached according to the law of the land.

1212. Matilda the daughter of Celestra and Andrew Dandeler were charged with larceny, and he has fled (*sic*), so Andrew is to be exacted and outlawed. He was in the tithing of Robert the Baker of Wyverstone, so it is in mercy (*amercement*). He had no chattels. Matilda is to be exacted and waived. She had no chattels.

1213. (*Serjeanties*) Concerning Serjeanties, they say that John Cordebof holds one hundred shillings of land in Mendlesham by the service of being in the King's army as a crossbowman for forty days at his own expense, and he will perform this service wherever the King is in the army.

They also say that Richard de Auillyers holds twenty shillings of land in Brome by the service of being in charge of the King's foot-soldiers, so that he is to be their leader in the army for forty days whenever the King is in the army in Wales.[1]

[1] The origins of these serjeanties cannot be dated, but John Cordebof's ancestors had been holding land in East Anglia by service as crossbowmen since at least the reign of Henry I. Richard de Auillyers' presumed father held Brome in 1212, with a serjeanty that may have been created in the early years of the reign of Henry II. Not only did that king make four expeditions to Wales between 1157 and 1165, but he might also have wanted to install reliable men in Suffolk at a time when he was concerned to clip the wings of Hugh Bigod, earl of Norfolk. It was for that reason that he began to build Orford Castle in 1165. *Book of Fees* i, pp. 127, 134. For Richard see also **1397** below.

1214. Concerning Defaults they say that the prior of Broomholm and the prior of Norwich did not come on the first day, so they are in mercy (*amercement*).

1215. They also say that Adam of Stebbing owes three pence per annum of sheriff's aid, and he has withdrawn it.[1]

[1] Sheriff's aid was a customary due, of uncertain origins, paid to the sheriff either annually or six-monthly. By 1240 it had long formed part of the revenues of his shire for which he accounted at the exchequer. See also **1261** below.

1216. William Oslac, charged with stealing a very little corn, and not suspected of other larcenies, may return if he wishes.

1217. Alexander the son of William of Hockham, charged with the death of Godiva the Cook, comes and denies everything and puts himself on the country for good or ill. The jurors say that he is not guilty, so he is acquitted (*he is acquitted*).[1]

[1] For this case see also **1193** above, where Alexander is said to have wounded Godiva.

THE PRESENTMENT OF [THE BOROUGH OF] BECCLES [WHICH] COMES BY TWELVE [JURORS][1]

[1] Not defined in the heading and referred to as a vill in the text below and in the amercements section, Beccles was recorded as a borough in Domesday Book.

1218. Concerning measures they say that Robert Endgar of Beccles and Alan Waghals of the same have sold cloths with false measuring-rods,[1] so they are in mercy (*amercement*).

[1] *cum falsis ulnis.*

1219. Concerning cloths sold contrary to the assize they say that Robert Aalc of Beccles de *Rewa*, Roger of Weston and Alexander of Kessingland have sold cloths contrary to the assize, so they are in mercy (*amercement*).

1220. They say also that Alan the Baker has sold wine contrary to the assize, so he is in mercy (*amercement*).

1221. Adam Talifer, charged with stealing a cow, Alan Olaf, charged with [stealing from] fishponds, and Margery, the widow of William of Barsham, charged with stealing corn and cloths and with harbouring thieves, come and deny everything and they say that they do not put themselves on the vill of Beccles, but on Wangford hundred and on four vills of that hundred. Because they allege and offer proofs that the vill of Beccles has a grudge against them, so it is decided that the country should inquire.

The jurors say that none of them is guilty, so they are acquitted thereof. And because it has been established that Beccles hated Alan because he had taken at farm from a knight a piece of land in which they were accustomed to have common rights; and Adam because his wife was in dispute with their neighbours; and Margery because her husband was at one time bailiff in Beccles, and often quarrelled with the men of Beccles; therefore it is in mercy (*amercement*).

1222. Godfrey the smith appealed Simon Walram, Philip of Ingate, John Maynard, Henry Prat, John Golde, Hugh Margarete, Roger le Seynur, Adam le Macecreur, Robert Bule, Robert Fydekar, Hugh Fideker, Roger de Porta, Alan Kurlefu, John Gunware, William Kokerel, Geoffrey Gernun, William Walram, Walkelin Stoclond, Henry Gyse, William Wrenne, Andrew Syred', Henry of Stoven, Reynold Curlefu, Gerard le Wyte and Edith de la Forde of breach of the King's peace and robbery. Godfrey does not come, and he found sureties for prosecuting, so they are in mercy (*amercement*).

All the appellees come. The jurors say that they have come to an agreement and that they are guilty, so they are in mercy (*amercement*), let them be remanded in custody. Later Simon Walram came and made fine for himself and all the other appellees by sixty shillings, by the surety of Robert the Engineer and Philip the son of -------[1] (*60 shillings*).

1 Illegible here, the amercements section shows him to have been Philip the son of William of Beccles (**1607**).

1223. Roger Ful is suspected of larceny and has fled, so he is to be exacted and outlawed (*he is to be exacted and outlawed*). He was in the tithing of Andrew Talyfer of Beccles, so it is in mercy (*amercement*). He had no chattels, but he had a little house, from which the King's year and waste is twelve pence, for which John the sheriff will answer (*12 pence*).

Membrane 47 *AALT 4478–9*

THE PRESENTMENT OF THE HUNDRED OF STOW [WHICH] COMES BY TWELVE [JURORS]

1224. Robert the chaplain of Buxhall fell down dead in the house of Gerard Cook in Buxhall in the presence of the same Gerard and of many others sitting and drinking[1] there, who have come and are not suspected, nor is anyone else. Englishry was not presented, so murder, and four neighbours have come (*murder*).

1 Literally *bidentibus* (sheep), but clearly a mistake for *bibentibus*.

1225. Robert the son of Walter was found drowned in a ditch in Thorney vill. Walter the son of Robert, the first finder, comes and is not suspected, nor is anyone else. Judgment: misadventure (*Misadventure*). Englishry was presented, and four neighbours have come.

1226. Agnes the widow of Adam Kopenger[1] was found killed in the house of Adam Kopenger in Buxhall. Thomas Copenger, the first finder, comes and is not suspected. Clarice of Buxhall, who was in the same house and was then bound, comes and is not suspected, nor do they know who killed her. Because the vill of Buxhall neither raised the hue nor pursued, it is in mercy (*amercement*). Thomas the son of Ordiner, one of the neighbours, who was attached for that death, does not come and he was attached by John Copenger and Adam Tytemund, so they are in mercy (*amercement*). Because the twelve falsely presented Englishry, they are in mercy (*amercement*).

1 With Thomas and John, Agnes appears to have been an early member of the long-lasting Copinger family of Buxhall. A William Copinger, too, is recorded in *1240 Suffolk Civil Pleas*, **420** and **567**.

1227. Roger Bauce of Rattlesden[1] and Nicholas his son were found killed on the King's highway in Wetherden. Matilda Polle, the first finder, comes and is not suspected. Englishry was not presented, so murder (*murder*). Because Wetherden vill neither pursued nor raised the hue, it is in mercy (*amercement*). Alexander le Cyverer and Roger le Furmager[2] charged with that death have fled. It was attested that they are living in the liberty of St Edmund at Rattlesden, so it is to be more fully inquired into there (*To be discussed*). The jurors attest that they are not guilty, so they are acquitted thereof.

1 Rattlesden replaces 'Wetherden', struck through.
2 A maker or seller of cheese.

1228.[1]

1 A paragraph mark is followed by an empty space, perhaps left by the clerk for more information relating to the preceding plea. The late Lesley Boatwright suggested that when none was forthcoming he may have inserted the paragraph mark to signal that plea's conclusion.

1229. William Hardekin was found dead in Thorney vill. Beatrice, the first finder, comes and is not suspected, nor is anyone else. Judgment: misadventure (*Misadventure*).

1230. Robert the son of Hervey Kokerel and Matilda the daughter of William le Franceis were found burnt in the house of Roger the Miller. Agnes his mother, the first finder, comes and is not suspected, nor is anyone else. Judgment: misadventure (*Misadventure*).

1231. Alexander Maloysel appealed William Putsoft of breach of the King's peace and wounding. Alexander does not come, and he has found sureties for prosecuting, namely John Prichert of Ipswich and Alexander Abwot of Battisford, so they are in mercy (*amercement*). William comes and the jurors attest that they have come to an agreement, and that William gave a wound to Alexander as he appealed him, so he is in mercy, let him be remanded in custody. Afterwards William Putsoft came and made fine by half a mark, by the surety of Stephen le Eyr of Creeting and Alexander de Prato of the same (*half a mark*).

1232. Humphrey Sytte appeals Robert Kokerel that at vespers on Tuesday, the feast of St Laurence in the King's twenty-second year,[1] he came to him when he was in Bricett vill at the end of the market and struck him with a bronze club on the left side of the head. And afterwards he took a pick-axe and gave him two wounds on the top of the head, and that he did this wickedly and feloniously, against the King's peace, he offers to prove against him as the court decides. Robert comes and denies whatever is against the King's peace, wounding and everything, word for word, where and when etc., as one who is over age and not in control of himself.[2]

The same appeals of abetment William Cable, Ralph le Bole, his brother Kebbe, and Roger Hacke, and they all come. Later Humphrey came and withdrew, and he places himself in the King's mercy, and all the others likewise place themselves in the King's mercy, and they made fine by five marks, by the surety of John of Gedding, knight,[3] and Adam Kokerel (*5 marks*).

1 10 August 1238.

2 *non compos sui.*

3 An inquest held early in 1241 recorded John as holding a knight's fee in Buxhall, about eight miles from Bricett. E 159/19 m. 3d.

1233. Sabina of Creeting was charged with killing her son, who was one night old. She came and avowed that her infant was born dead and that she was out of her mind at the time, and that it is so she puts herself on the country. The jurors attest that the boy was born alive, and that at the time she was of good understanding and sound in her mind,[1] so it is adjudged that she should be burnt (*she is to be burnt*).[2]

1 *in bono sensu et bone memorie.*

2 This distressing case, recorded in a smaller than usual hand, has been squeezed into the space between the entries on either side of it. Infanticide was a felony, and men and women were occasionally hanged for it. This seems to be the only occasion on which it was punished with such extreme severity.

1234. (*Escheats*) Concerning Escheats they say that Combs vill is an escheat to the King from the land of the Normans. Bartholomew of Creake holds it at fee farm by the service of twenty-two pounds and half a mark, and he pays thirty shillings each year as scutage whether the scutage is levied or not. And he pays the twenty-two pounds and the thirty shillings at the Exchequer.[1]

They also say that Haughley was an escheat to the King and is worth forty pounds a year, and Earl Richard[2] holds it.

They also say that Finborough was an escheat to the King from the land which was Hugh de Cantilupe's. Ralph FitzNicholas holds it, and it is worth ten pounds a year.[3]

1 Once held by members of the Avenel family, Combs was in the hands of Robert of Creake by 1212, and in those of Bartholomew of Creake by 1236. In 1289 it was in the hands of John of Creake, perhaps Bartholomew's son, who was described as holding the manor 'of the king in chief at fee farm', for a payment well-nigh identical with that recorded nearly fifty years earlier. *Calendars of Inquisitions Post Mortem* ii, no. 715.

2 Henry III's younger brother Richard, who had been earl of Cornwall since 1227, and who was granted the manor in 1234. N. Vincent, *Peter des Roches: an alien in English politics, 1205–1238* (Cambridge, 1996), p. 424. With its honour it had previously passed through several hands, most recently those of Hubert de Burgh. I.J. Sanders, *English baronies: a study of their origin and descent, 1066–1327* (Oxford, 1960), pp. 120–1.

3 Hugh appears to have been hanged in 1225. C 60/23 m. 3; the manor was granted to Ralph, a royal steward, in 1227. *Calendar of Charter Rolls 1226–1257*, p. 1.

1235. William Fyke and Thomas Drumbel are suspected of larceny and have fled, so they are to be exacted and outlawed. William Fyke was in the tithing of Ralph Oky in Wetherden, so it is in mercy (*amercement*). Thomas was in the tithing of John Howard of Shelland, so it is in mercy (*amercement*). William Fyke had no chattels. The chattels of Thomas: three shillings, for which John the sheriff will answer (*3 shillings*).

1236. William del Hill charged with larceny comes and denies everything, and he puts himself on the country for good or ill. The jurors attest that he is not guilty, so he is acquitted thereof (*he is acquitted*).

1237. John the son of Simon, Robert Crowe, William Scut and Vincent of Dagworth are suspected of larceny, so they are to be exacted and outlawed (*they are to be exacted and outlawed*). John was in the tithing of Ranulf Yring of Haughley. Robert was not in a tithing because he is a clerk. William Scut and Vincent were in the tithing of Roger Perdut in Dagworth, so it is in mercy (*amercement*). They had no chattels.

1238. Alan the son of Hugh of Combs and Peter the son of Ailwin, charged with larceny, have fled, so they are to be exacted and outlawed (*they are to be exacted and outlawed*). Alan was in the tithing of Sewal le Noreys in Combs, so it is in mercy. He had no chattels.[1]

Peter was in the tithing of Woolward of Thorney, so it is in mercy. His chattels: two shillings, for which John the sheriff will answer. The same had one messuage, from which the King's year and waste is twelve pence (*12 pence*).

1 Written over an erasure.

1239. Simon the chaplain and Hugh le Porcher of Harpole broke into the park of Ralph de Arderne and there they took one beast,[1] so the sheriff has been ordered to arrest them if they are found.

1 *bestia* – a 'beast of the chase', meaning a deer of some kind. An action among the civil pleas (**423**) may indicate that the park was at Finborough.

1240. (*Defaults*) Concerning Defaults they say that Robert de Mucegros and Ralph FitzNicholas did not come on the first day, so they are in mercy (*amercement*).

1241. An unknown man was found dead in the graveyard of Steeple Creeting.[1] It is not known who he was. Steeple Creeting vill buried him without a coroner's view, and so the twelve jurors are in mercy for concealment and the vill is in mercy for the burial (*amercement, amercement*). No Englishry, so murder (*murder*). Afterwards it was attested that the man was from Creeting vill and had falling sickness, and he was found dead in the church. And the chaplain of the church had him taken out and buried.

1 Identity uncertain, but certainly one of the Creetings recorded before the end of the fourteenth century on either side of the boundary between Stow and Bosmere hundreds. We are grateful to Keith Briggs for advice on this point.

THE PRESENTMENT OF THE HALF HUNDRED OF MUTFORD [WHICH] COMES BY SIX [JURORS]

1242. Richard the son of Warin Hakun was drowned in a spring. Warin his father, the first finder, has died. No one is suspected thereof, nor is anyone else.[1] Judgment: misadventure (*Misadventure*). Englishry was presented and four neighbours have come.

1 A superfluous, presumably automatic, extension on the part of the clerk.

1243. Richard the son of Robert the carpenter was found drowned in a turf pit[1] in Kessingland vill. Lecia his mother, the first finder, has come. No one is suspected thereof. Judgment: misadventure (*Misadventure*). Englishry was presented.

1 *in turbario* – no doubt a digging for peat.

1244. (*Defaults*) Concerning Defaults they say that Roger de Mohaut, William Pimbel de Mohaut, William de Arderne, Ranulf de Moresbarwe, Roger the son of Thomas, the prior of Weybourne, Hugh of Tynemouth and the prior of Broomholm did not come on the first day, so they are in mercy (*amercement*).

1245. Concerning those who hold the lands of Normans they say that Thomas de Hemegrave holds the manor of Mutford by gift of the present King, and it is worth twenty pounds a year. They say that he holds it by the service of one knight, as they believe.[1]

[1] Henry III gave half of Mutford vill to Thomas on 3 June 1232, and followed this with a further grant of land there on 25 March 1233. *Close Rolls 1231–1234*, pp. 67, 204. The lands had belonged to Reginald de Bosco before 1204. T.D. Hardy (ed.), *Rotuli litterarum clausarum i, 1204–1224* (Record Commission, 1833), p. 9.

Membrane 47d *AALT 4601–2*

THE PRESENTMENT OF THE BOROUGH OF BUNGAY [WHICH] COMES BY TWELVE [JURORS]

1246. Agnes the daughter of Ralph Becke de *Boyscote* appealed Robert Bond of Bungay of having forcibly deflowered her, and now she comes and sues against him. Robert was not attached, and so Roger of Attleborough, the bailiff of Wangford hundred, who makes attachments in Bungay vill, is in mercy because he did not attach Robert. Agnes was told that she may sue against him in the county court until he is attached or outlawed according to the law of the land.

1247. Ralph the son of Alice 'at the church'[1] was found killed in the graveyard of Holy Cross church, Bungay.[2] Alice his mother was the first finder, and she is not suspected, nor is it known who killed him. Englishry was presented and four neighbours have come.

[1] *ad ecclesiam.*
[2] The church of Bungay Priory, a house of Benedictine nuns founded about 1160 which was dedicated to the Blessed Virgin and the Holy Cross.

1248. Matilda Cumpanyun appealed Roger Pinchun of Bungay of the death of Seman her son. Roger was outlawed at Matilda's suit for the death, and he was not in a tithing because he is a clerk. Because the vill of Bungay did not pursue, it is in mercy (*amercement*).

1249. Sylvester Hauec appealed Roger Balle of Homersfield that wickedly with his abettors he broke the door of his house and gave him a blow on the head and other dreadful blows. Sylvester does not come and he found sureties: Hugh Heved and Geoffrey Sor of Bungay, so they are in mercy (*amercement*).

The same appealed Roger Leueger, William Puleyn, Geoffrey the cooper, William Kenop, Henry Offe and William Humphrey of abetment. William Puleyn does not come, and he was not attached because he is a clerk. Geoffrey the cooper does not come, and he was attached by Walter le Franceys and Robert le Demur of Elmham, so they are in mercy (*amercement*). William Kenop does not come, and he was attached by Benedict le Mester of Elmham and Robert le Demur, so they are in mercy (*amercement*). Roger Balle, Roger Leuenger, Henry Offe and William Humphrey come, and the jurors attest that they have come to an agreement and that they are guilty as he appealed them, so they are remanded in custody (*they are remanded in custody*).

1250. Benedict Harding appealed Roger Balle and Roger Longer that they broke the door of his house, dragged him out by the hair and badly beat him. Benedict does not come, and he was attached by Reynold the son of Godman and Geoffrey the son of Godman, so they are in mercy (*amercement*). And Roger Balle and Roger Longer have come.

The same appealed Henry Offe, William Kenop, William Humphrey, William Puleyn of abetment. Henry Offe and William Humphrey have come, and William Puleyn, William Kenop and Geoffrey the cooper have not come and they were attached by the sureties recorded in the previous entry, so they are in mercy (*amercement*). The jurors attest that they have come to an agreement and that they are guilty, as he appealed them, so they are in mercy (*amercement*), let them be remanded in custody (*they are remanded in custody*).

1251. Concerning Cloths sold contrary to the assize they say that Walter Floret of Bungay has sold cloths contrary to the assize, so he is in mercy (*amercement*).

1252. Concerning Evildoers[1] they say that Robert Bude of Bungay came by night to the house of Alice Catun and entered it by force. And he forcibly threw out her household, and took her key and opened her chest, and carried off a gallon measure full of money, and her rings and brooches; and because he is a clerk and has a lay fee the sheriff is ordered to take his land into the King's hand, and that he keep it safely until etc.[2]

1 A presentment under the article '*De malefactoribus et burgatoribus*' (Of evildoers and burglars), no. 21 in the list given by Meekings in *1249 Wiltshire Crown Pleas*, p. 29, where it is mistakenly said to have become obsolete in the 1230s. It is noteworthy, however, that Robert was not put in exigent for taking Alice's valuables, suggesting that the jurors were here using this article to draw the attention of the justices to an action which, although apparently unlawful, was not necessarily perceived as felonious.

2 A cleric's lay fee consisted of the lands he held apart from those on which his church was built, if he had one, and any others essential to the performance of his ecclesiastical duties. Robert was not said to be the incumbent of a parish, and probably had no lands which were not held in lay fee.

THE PRESENTMENT OF THE HUNDRED OF CLAYDON [WHICH] COMES BY TWELVE [JURORS] TOGETHER WITH THE HUNDRED OF THREDLING WHICH FOLLOWS IMMEDIATELY AFTER

1253. John the smith of Sharpstone appeals Adam Bullok that on the Saturday next after the Nativity of the Blessed Mary about the hour of Vespers in the twenty-second year[1] when he was in the house of Matilda of Tuddenham, a widow, he came to him there and in premeditated assault gave him a wound on the head with a bar, and that he did this wickedly and feloniously he offers to prove by his body as the court decides.

Adam comes and denies the felony and whatever is against the King's peace, and asks for a ruling on whether the appeal should be valid or not, since he appealed him of giving him a wound with a bar, and does not name any edged weapon.[2] And because he does not name any edged weapon it is adjudged that the appeal is invalid, but for the maintenance of the King's peace the country is to inquire.

The same appealed William Bulloc that on the same day and hour and in the same place he came with Adam and gave him two wounds on the head and broke his right arm with a stick, and that he did this wickedly and in felony he offers to prove as a man maimed, as the court decides. William comes and denies the felony and whatever is against the King's peace, and puts himself on the country.

The same appeals Philip the son of William and Robert Lurdeyn that on the same day and in the same place they badly beat and shamefully treated him there.

The same appealed Robert de Vallibus of abetment, and he has died.

Later John came and withdrew, so all the appellees, except for Robert who has died, come and put themselves in the King's mercy, and they have made fine by four marks, by the surety of Geoffrey of Denton, William of Holbrook, Bartholomew of Tuddenham, Richard de Bosco and Robert of Roding (*4 marks*).[3]

1 11 September 1238.

2 Adam's objection to John's appeal was in line with contemporary practice as laid down in *Bracton* ii, p. 408 – for the purposes of an appeal only edged weapons gave what could be defined as wounds; blunt implements like clubs and stones inflicted nothing more than bruises and contusions.

3 This appeal may have been a product of the dispute which led to Adam Bulloc and his wife suing Matilda of Tuddenham at the eyre for five acres in that village. *1240 Suffolk Civil Pleas*, **1006.**

1254. William the tailor hanged himself in the barn of his mother Felicia who found him first etc., and she is not suspected nor is anyone else. Judgment: felony on himself (*felony*). His chattels: sixteen shillings six pence[1] for which John the sheriff will answer (*sixteen shillings six pence*).

1 There is no mention of these chattels in the amercements section; perhaps the justices decided they were his mother's rather than William's.

1255. Richard le Ko, charged with stealing sheaves in autumn and similarly a bundle of flax, and with stealing a sheep, comes and puts himself on the country for good or ill. The jurors say that he is not guilty, so he is acquitted thereof, but he is to find sureties for the sheriff that in future etc.[1]

1 Richard's escape from the gallows may have been a narrow one, leaving him with a dubious reputation, hence the requirement that he find guarantees for his future good behaviour.

1256. The jurors say that John the fuller stole a foal worth seventeen pence and fled, so he is to be exacted and outlawed (*he is to be exacted and outlawed*). He was in the tithing of Michael Aiward, so it is in mercy. He had no chattels. They also say that Roger the son of Richard Sewine is a thief who stole a cow, and he has fled, so he is to be exacted and outlawed (*he is to be exacted and outlawed*). He was in the tithing of Herbert Pannecake, so it is in mercy. He had no chattels.

1257. An unknown woman was found drowned in one of Tuddenham's marl-pits. John the first finder comes and is not suspected. Judgment: misadventure. No Englishry, so murder (*murder*).

1258. Alan the carpenter was found killed in Wyverstone fields. Agnes, Alan's wife, the first finder, comes and is not suspected. John Unselthe is suspected of that death, and he fled to the church of the Franciscans of Ipswich, and there acknowledged having killed Alan and abjured the realm. Because Ulveston vill did not pursue it is in mercy (*amercement*).[1] He was in the tithing of William Daniel of Thurleston, so it is in mercy (*amercement*). His chattels: four shillings, for which John the sheriff will answer (*4 shillings*). The twelve jurors falsely presented that his chattels were eighteen pence, so they are in mercy.

1 Ulveston, just outside Debenham, is several miles east of Wyverstone, so this amercement could give an idea of the route which John took on his flight towards Ipswich. However, the

amercements section entry for this case (**1611**) names the offending vill as Whitton, which is just north of Ipswich and certainly closer to the direct route to that town from Wyverstone. It is impossible to say for certain which vill was penalised, but since Ulveston was not amerced, Whitton must be the likelier. This case provides one of the earliest references to the presence of the Franciscans in Ipswich.

1259. The jurors say that the prior of Ely has newly put up a tumbrel in Barham vill where none was accustomed to be, so it is to be discussed etc. (*to be discussed*).[1]

1 A tumbrel was an instrument of manorial or urban discipline, seemingly in the form of either a chair or a cart, in which offenders against by-laws were exposed to public ridicule. It was used especially to punish infringements of the assizes of bread and ale, which in the late 1280s the prior claimed to be licensed to penalise through a charter of Edward the Confessor. W. Illingworth (ed.), *Placita de Quo Warranto* (Record Commission, 1818), p. 729.

1260. The jurors say that Adam Shori, William Wiseman, Walter the son of Augustine and Roger his brother are thieves of sheep and they have fled, so they are to be exacted and outlawed (*they are to be exacted and outlawed*). Adam was in the tithing of William Shory, so it is in mercy (*amercement*). William Wiseman was in the tithing of William Panel in Thurleston, so it is in mercy (*amercement*). They had no chattels. Walter and Roger were in the tithing of Justus of Thurleston,[1] so it is in mercy (*amercement*). They have no chattels.

1 The family of Justus of Thurleston was well established in Ipswich in the thirteenth century. Details in D. Allen (ed.), *The Cartulary and Charters of the Priory of Saints Peter and Paul, Ipswich, part 1, The Cartulary*, Suffolk Charters 20, SRS (2018).

1261. Concerning those who have withdrawn suits they say that Stephen the chaplain, Alexander the son of Norman of Helmingham, William the smith, Robert the weaver, Little Emma and her sisters, John the weaver, Warin de Mara, and Roger Carver were accustomed to contribute to sheriff's aid and to other amercements arising within Helmingham vill, and now they have recently withdrawn them.

1262. Concerning Defaults they say that Thomas the son of Aunger did not come on the first day, so he is in mercy (*amercement*).

1263. Henry Kybus was killed in Pettaugh vill. Fulk le Mei of Otley and Simon the serjeant of John of Bocking, charged with the death, are suspected of it and have fled, so they are to be exacted and outlawed (*they are to be exacted and outlawed*). Fulk was in the tithing of his father, Simon of Helmingham, so it is in mercy (*amercement*). He had no chattels. The jurors concealed this, so they are in mercy (*amercement*).[1]
(*Note*) And be it known that this happened in Thredling, in the liberty of St Etheldreda.

1 Pettaugh was in Thredling hundred, and the Claydon jurors may therefore have 'concealed' this case because they regarded presenting it as the responsibility of the Thredling jury.

Membrane 48 *AALT 4480–1*

THE PRESENTMENT OF THREDLING HUNDRED WHICH IS A THIRD OF CLAYDON HUNDRED, RECORDED IMMEDIATELY ABOVE, AND IT ANSWERS WITH THE OTHER [TWO THIRDS], SO THAT THERE ARE ALTOGETHER TWELVE [JURORS] IN NUMBER

1264. William Pepelin killed Alice Osild with an iron fork and fled, so he is to be exacted and outlawed. He was in the household of William de Colville the younger, who has died, so nothing. He had no chattels. Debenham vill did not present this case in the county court, so it is in mercy (*amercement*).[1]

1 William de Colville the younger died in around 1236; his family held the manor of Aspall, in Hartismere hundred but only a short distance from Debenham. C.A.F. Meekings (ed.), *The Surrey eyre of 1235* i, Surrey Record Society 31 (1979), pp. 184–6.

1265. Edric of Debenham, a carpenter, fell over a beam so that he died. Judgment: misadventure. Price of the beam: four pence, for which John the sheriff will answer (*4 pence, deodand*).

1266. Beatrice the daughter of Gilbert Algor complained that William Fish of Cotton, Arnold the cook of Cotton, Robert Dote of the same, Reynold the painter of the same, Robert his brother, William Champanye of the same, Hugh the son of Benedict of the same, and Walter Fikeman of Thorney came by night to her house, knocked it to the ground, and carried off one tunic of brown cloth and another of red, a cloak of blue cloth and two linen sheets. William and all the others come and firmly deny force and injury, knocking her house down and carrying away those things as she says, and on this they put themselves on the country.

The jurors say that one Robert Hayl had a son by this Beatrice and he gave her a rood of land next to his house. Beatrice had it dug up, and planted shoots on its embankment, and afterwards she put up a house there. Afterwards Robert took another woman as his wife, and she whom he married hated Beatrice, because she was living so near her house, and she caused those men to come by night to that house and knock it down; and so it is adjudged that they are all to be remanded in custody (*they are remanded in custody*). Later William came and made fine for himself and his sureties by four marks by the surety of Hubert Gernegan, William of Cotton, Richard the son of Joce of the same, Hugh the son of Richard of Cotton, Richard the son of Anselm of Newton and Hamo le Neve of Thorney (*4 marks*).[1]

1 This action is an example of a plaint, an informal action for the redress of an injury which the appeal of felony was ill-suited to remedy.

1267. Concerning Bailiffs who have held pleas of the Crown, they say that the prior of Ely's bailiff for Thredling held the plea of Robert de Frechney who appealed Simon Sullyard of breach of the King's peace. Whereupon Matthew Crestien, the prior of Ely's bailiff, comes and says that if anyone appeals another man in St Etheldreda's court of breach of the King's peace, before any appeal for it comes to the county court, it will be entirely lawful for the former court to hear that appeal and to decide the case by battle or in another way. And they have used that liberty from the foundation of the house of Ely, and on this he puts himself on the country. So it is to be discussed (*to be discussed*).[1]

1 Another presentment of an infringement of Magna Carta c. 24. See also **1162** and **1334**.

1268. Roger Onhund, charged with harbouring a thief arrested and imprisoned for larceny, and himself imprisoned after the thief escaped, comes and puts himself on a jury for good or ill.

1269. Roger the smith of Debenham, charged with harbouring Gilbert his son after he had killed one Thomas the son of Matilda,[1] comes and similarly puts himself on the country for good or ill.

The jurors say that they are not guilty, but that crime was maliciously imputed to them by John Blackeye and Roger of Winston, so they are remanded in custody, and the others are acquitted thereof (*they are acquitted, amercements*). Later Roger came and made fine by forty shillings by the surety of Roger of Kenton and Walkelin of Kenton (*40 shillings*). John made fine by twenty shillings by the surety of Ranulf Wyghe and Alexander le Moyne (*20 shillings*).

1 The killing of Thomas the son of Matilda by Gilbert the smith was presented in Bosmere hundred, **1165**.

1270. Richard the miller of Brandeston one night bound two women in Framsden vill and carried off their clothes and other goods of theirs and fled, so he is to be exacted and outlawed (*he is to be exacted and outlawed*). Afterwards it was established that through the women's pursuit he was attached until the arrival of the justices by William de Roville, Henry of Barnack, William the son of Henry of Barnack, Thomas Doket, Roger de Roville, William Miller, Robert Motidun, Nicholas Calegrim, William Fide, Warin the son of a clerk, Geoffrey de Bosco, Robert the son of a clerk, Thomas Warin, Gilbert Arum, Roger Belly and Alan Pullehare, so they are all in mercy (*amercement*). Let it be inquired concerning his chattels in Loes hundred. Afterwards it was established that he had no chattels.

THE PRESENTMENT OF THE HUNDRED OF PLOMESGATE [WHICH] COMES BY EIGHTEEN [JURORS], BECAUSE IT IS A HUNDRED AND A HALF, PART OF THE LIBERTY OF THE PRIOR OF ELY

1271. John Ulsy of Sternfield was found dead in the cowshed of Walter the parson of Blaxhall. Walter is suspected of that death and comes. Whereupon the official of the bishop of Norwich comes and claims him as a clerk, and he is handed over to him, and no one else is suspected of that death. It was attested that he has a lay fee.

1272. Matilda, the widow of William Fukelot, appealed Richard Caperun of the death of William her husband in the county court, so that he was outlawed by her suit. She now comes, and does not suspect anyone else.[1] Because Rendham vill did not pursue, it is in mercy (*amercement*). His chattels: four pence for which John the sheriff will answer. He was in the tithing of Fulk de *Musholt*, so it is in mercy (*amercement*).

1 Since her action had been concluded by Richard's outlawry, there was no obvious reason for Matilda's presence in court, which may explain why the justices appear to have asked her if she suspected anyone else of her husband's death, in case she wished to prosecute further.

1273. Richard Wickerman was killed at Blaxhall before the previous eyre. Roger Bretun of Iken, a clerk, is suspected of that death, and he was arrested for it and handed over to Court Christian. But because it was established that no justice was done on him by Court Christian and he has fled, it is adjudged that he is to be exacted and outlawed (*he is to be exacted and outlawed*). Because he was harboured at the house of his father, Robert le Breton, he is in mercy (*amercement, it is void*).[1]

1 No amercement of Robert le Breton is recorded among the issues of the eyre. This appears to be a presentment under the first of the articles of the eyre, concerning pleas begun at the previous eyre and left unfinished.

1274. Roger the son of Hugh of Rendham has been outlawed for the trespass which he did to Nicholas of Lynn.[1] He was in the tithing of William de Brok in Rendham, so it is in mercy (*amercement*). The prior of Ely had his land and house through his liberty, so he says, so let it be discussed (*to be discussed*).

1 Roger had been involved in a dispute between Nicholas, a lawyer active in the Westminster courts, and the East Anglian baron Roger de Cressy, in which Nicholas suffered injuries for which he appealed a number of Cressy's men in Norfolk county court. Seventeen of them had been outlawed by February 1240, when they were licensed to return to the King's peace as long as they stood trial at the Norfolk eyre which was then in progress. Roger son of Hugh was not among them, and remained an outlaw until November 1257, when he received a pardon, in terms which suggest that the trespass done to Nicholas hurt his self-respect more than his person – Roger was said to have forced Nicholas to kiss his own horse's backside, and then thrown him into a latrine. *Close Rolls 1237–1242*, p. 173; *Cal. Pat. Rolls 1247–1258*, p. 605. For Nicholas see P.A. Brand, *The origins of the English legal profession* (Oxford, 1992), pp. 57–8, 61. He appears to have settled his quarrel with Roger de Cressy during this eyre – *1240 Suffolk Civil Pleas*, **587**.

1275. Alice the daughter of Richard was found drowned in the river at Rendham.[1] Richard her father, the first finder, has come. No Englishry, so murder (*murder*).

1 Rendham stands on the River Alde.

1276. Leviva the wife of Roger Kuse appealed John Kucku of the death of Roger her husband, and he was outlawed for the death by Leviva's suit, and he was in the tithing of William Knich of Benhall, so it is in mercy (*amercement*). He had no chattels.

1277. William Maperelenebolle killed Mabel the daughter of Ranulf in the house of Henry Warner and fled, so he is to be exacted and outlawed. He was not in a tithing because he was a foreigner from Flanders, neither had he chattels. Henry Allebon, who was William's master, charged with that death, is suspected of it, so he is to be exacted and outlawed (*he is to be exacted and outlawed*). He had no chattels.

1278. Macelina the daughter of Henry was found killed in a cottage[1] in Farnham. Basilia her daughter, the first finder, comes. It is not known who killed her. Farnham vill neither raised the hue nor pursued when Macelina was found killed, so it is in mercy (*amercement*).

1 *in bordello* – an unusual choice of word.

1279. Jordan the son of Reinerus was found drowned in a water channel. Geoffrey the son of Reinerus, the first finder, comes. Aldeburgh vill did not present this case in the county court, so it is in mercy (*amercement*).

1280. John de *Tulleberghe* was found hanged in his barn in *Batesdene* vill. Robert Burre, the first finder, comes. Judgment: felony on himself (*felony*). He had no chattels.

1281. Michael the miller, arrested through an indictment by a thief, comes and puts himself on the country for good or ill. The jurors say that he is not guilty, so he is acquitted thereof (*he is acquitted*).

1282. William the son of Nicholas burnt the house of Alice le Ko and fled, so he is to be exacted and outlawed (*he is to be exacted and outlawed*). He was in the tithing of Nicholas Brock of Stratford,[1] so it is in mercy (*amercement*). He had no chattels.

1 Probably Stratford St Andrew in this hundred, rather than Stratford St Mary in Samford hundred.

1283. Ranulf Kebbel is suspected of stealing eighteen pence and other thefts, and he has fled, so he is to be exacted and outlawed (*he is to be exacted and outlawed*). He was in the tithing of William Bacun in Great Glemham, so it is in mercy (*amercement*).

1284. (*escape*) Concerning an Escape they say that the bailiff of the liberty of St Etheldreda arrested one Hugh le Marlur on suspicion of theft, and he placed him in the stocks at Kelton and he escaped from there, so to judgment for this (*to judgment*). Concerning this the bailiff of William d'Auberville comes and says that the prison is his, but truly he was put in the stocks there without his knowing, but nevertheless he says that he has a prison there. The bailiff of the liberty says that he so freely holds the five and a half hundreds that no one ought to have a prison in them except the prior of Ely.

The jurors attest that William d'Auberville holds half of this hundred and that William's bailiff and the prior of Ely's bailiff together arrested Hugh. So to judgment on each court.[1]

1 William had claimed half of Plomesgate hundred as his inheritance against the prior of Ely in 1228, in an action settled by the prior's conceding William's right. JUST 1/819 m. 13d. In 1240 William and the prior paid half each of the 100s. amercement imposed for Hugh le Marlur's escape (**1612**).

Membrane 48d *AALT 4603–4*

THE PRESENTMENT OF THE HUNDRED OF CARLFORD [WHICH] COMES BY TWELVE [JURORS], PART OF THE LIBERTY OF THE PRIOR OF ELY

1285. Alice the wife of John Maynard in her madness killed Richard her son, and she comes. The jurors attest that when she did that deed she was mad and without sense, so it was ordered that she be sent to gaol until it is decided what should be done (*to be discussed*).

1286. Roger Page de *Gasenb'* killed Reynold the son of Muriel and fled. He was outlawed for that death by the suit of Muriel his mother. He was in the tithing of Roger le Newou in Foxhall, so it is in mercy (*amercement*). His chattels: four shillings, two pence for which the prior of Ely will answer (*4 shillings, 2 pence*).

1287. William the son of Elviva was found dead on Martlesham heath. No one is suspected thereof. Judgment: misadventure. No Englishry, so murder (*murder*).

1288. Reynold Lolle of Witnesham, Beatrice his wife and Ida his daughter charged with many larcenies, have fled. Reynold is to be exacted and outlawed (*he is to be exacted and outlawed*). Ida is to be exacted and waived (*she is to be exacted and waived*). Reynold was in the tithing of John the son of Reinerus of Witnesham, so it is in mercy (*amercement*). He had no chattels.[1]

1 No sentence of exigent was pronounced against Beatrice, perhaps by negligence, but possibly on the grounds that her association with her husband automatically made her fate the same as his.

1289. Simon Munpel of Kesgrave is suspected of many larcenies, so he is to be exacted and outlawed (*he is to be exacted and outlawed*). He was in the tithing of Peter Lewine in Kesgrave, so it is in mercy (*amercement*). He had no chattels.

1290. John Blast of Tuddenham, charged with larceny, comes and put himself on the jury and four neighbouring vills for good or ill. The jurors say that he is not guilty, so he is acquitted thereof (*he is acquitted*).

1291. Odierna the daughter of Olive of Otley is suspected of stealing sheep and many larcenies and has fled, so she is to be exacted and waived (*she is to be exacted and waived*). She had no chattels.

1292. Luke King is suspected of harbouring thieves, and Margery the wife of Baldwin is suspected of stealing clothes, lambs and other thefts and they have fled, so Luke is to be exacted and outlawed, and Margery is to be exacted and waived (*he is to be exacted and outlawed, she is to be exacted and waived*). Luke was in the tithing of Luke the son of Humphrey of Otley, so it is in mercy (*amercement*). His chattels: five shillings for which the prior of Ely will answer (*5 shillings*). Margery had no chattels.

1293. William Thurbern of Monk Soham appeals Richard the son of Roger of Kettleburgh that he was with him in breaking into Kettleburgh church, and that from the goods of that church which they carried away from it he had three shillings for his share, and that he was his accomplice in this deed; and that he had those three shillings for his share he offers to prove by his body against him as the court decides. Richard comes and denies his complicity in breaking into that church, and that he did not have anything from the goods of the church which were carried away. And he offers to deny this by his body. So it is decided that there should be a combat between them (*Combat*). Richard is to give sureties for denying and William is to give sureties for proving. The prior of Ely's bailiff has gone bail for Richard. William is in the custody of the sheriff.[1]

A day is given them on Wednesday[2] and then let them come armed. On that day they came armed and the combat was fought, and William was beaten, so he etc. is to be hanged (*he is to be hanged*). Richard has not made a sufficient defence, and because he would not put himself on his country, it was decided that he should find sureties to stand trial if anyone wishes to plead against him and that henceforth he will conduct himself faithfully or abjure the realm etc. Later Richard came before the justices, and because he could not find sureties to stand trial, of his own free will he put himself on the country for good or ill. The jurors attest that he is suspected of many larcenies, and so etc. he is to be hanged. His chattels: thirty-six shillings, two pence (*36 shillings, 2 pence*).

The same had five acres of land from which the King's year and waste is twenty-five shillings, four pence, for which the prior of Ely will answer. Afterwards Arnold of Kettleburgh, the lord of that fief, comes and gives thirty-two shillings for having the King's year and day, by the surety of Robert of Roding and Roger of Carlton (*32 shillings*).

1 The clerk made some miscalculations in the distribution of material for the last part of Carlford's pleas. After the first paragraph of the present entry he left a 1.2-centimetre gap before continuing his record. He had already entered its successor, but then found that the extended proceedings involving Richard son of Roger needed more room than he expected, forcing him to squeeze the rest of the case into a limited space. And after **1295** below he left a considerable gap – 4.3 centimetres – before going on to Wilford hundred's pleas.

2 Probably Wednesday 2 May 1240.

1294. William Belly, Richard the merchant of Brandeston, Roger David of the same, Stephen Copping, Robert the miller, Stephen Redekinge and William Gunnore, appealed by the aforesaid William the approver, come and put themselves on the country for good or ill.

The jurors say that William Belly, Richard the merchant, Roger David and Stephen Copping are not guilty of any larceny or harbouring, so they are acquitted thereof (*they are acquitted*). They also attest that Robert the miller, Stephen Redeginge and William Gunnore are not guilty, so they are acquitted thereof (*they are acquitted*).

1295. Matilda Rogerun of Kettleburgh, charged with larceny, is suspected thereof, so she is to be exacted and waived (*she is to be exacted and waived*). She had no chattels.

THE PRESENTMENT OF THE HUNDRED OF WILFORD [WHICH] COMES BY TWELVE [JURORS], PART OF THE LIBERTY OF THE PRIOR OF ELY

1296. (*Misadventure*) William the son of Richard of Ramsholt was found drowned in a ditch in Ramsholt vill. No one is suspected thereof. No Englishry, so murder (*murder*). William the son of Henry falsely presented Englishry, so he is in mercy (*amercement*). He made fine by half a mark by the surety of Gervase of Bredfield (*half a mark*).

1297. Robert the son of Ranulf was found drowned in a ditch in Ramsholt vill. Ranulf his father, the first finder, comes. No one is suspected thereof. Judgment: misadventure. No Englishry, so murder (*murder*). Henry Prat falsely presented Englishry, so he is in mercy (*amercement*). Later he made fine by half a mark by the surety of Robert de Valoynes (*half a mark*).

1298. Matilda and Cecilia of Pettistree were killed in Pettistree vill. It is not known who killed them, so nothing. Pettistree vill neither raised the hue nor pursued, so it is in mercy (*amercement*).

1299. Matilda Bunting hanged herself in her house in Pettistree vill. Judgment: felony on herself (*Felony*). No one is suspected thereof. She had no chattels.

1300. Beatrice the daughter of William the priest was killed in the house of John the carpenter in Loudham vill. John the carpenter, the first finder, comes. No one is suspected thereof. Loudham vill neither pursued nor raised the hue, so it is in mercy (*amercement*).

1301. Ralph the son of Godiva appealed Baldwin Buck of Pettistree of breach of the King's peace and felony. Ranulf[1] does not come, and he found sureties for prosecuting, William Blacsune of Bing and William Kempe of the same, so they are in mercy (*amercement*). Baldwin was attached by Robert the son of Hugh of Pettistree and Roger Copside of the same and Goscelin the son of Osbert of the same, so they are in mercy (*amercement*).

1 Here and elsewhere, the names Ralph and Ranulf seem to have been well-nigh interchangeable. This man appears as Ranulf in the amercements section (**1615**).

1302. Two men of Woodbridge, namely Alexander Wyffin and Roger Wachet, killed Adam the miller at the prior of Butley's mill.[1] They fled and were outlawed by the suit of Adam's wife Agnes. Let their frankpledge be inquired into in Loes hundred (*To be inquired into*). The chattels of Alexander Wyffin: sixteen shillings, six pence, for which the prior of Ely will answer (*16 shillings, 6 pence*).

1 Perhaps at Capel St Andrew, where the priory had property and which is close to the River Tang. *Rotuli Hundredorum* ii, pp. 190–1.

1303. Adam, the servant of Robert of Boyton, appealed John Kene, William the son of Roger and many others, who have not been attached, of breach of the King's peace and wounding. He has not prosecuted, and he found sureties for prosecuting, Richard the son of Edward of Boyton and Robert the son of Alan of the same, so they are in mercy (*amercement*). John and the others were not attached, so nothing.

1304. (*Escheat*) The jurors present that Wickham Market is an escheat to the King from the lands of Normans, and it is worth twelve pounds a year and is in the King's hand.[1]

1 Forfeited in 1236 by the Harcourts, a Norman family which had previously been able to retain its English lands, the manor was granted to William de Mastac in 1237, for him to hold during pleasure. He had clearly ceased to hold it by 1240, and it was granted out again in 1241, and then again in 1242. F.M. Powicke, *The loss of Normandy* (2nd edn, Manchester, 1961), pp. 342–3; *Cal. Pat. Rolls 1232–1247*, pp. 182, 252, 268.

1305. Concerning Defaults they say that William of Bromeswell, Ralph the son of Ranulf the son of Robert Baron, Roger Loty, William Manekin and William of Childrehus[1] did not come on the first day, so they are in mercy (*amercement*).

1 A lost place-name in Kesgrave in the neighbouring hundred of Carlford. Briggs, *Suffolk place-names*, p. 436.

1306. Robert de *Rindewine*, charged with stealing sheep and other larcenies, comes and puts himself on the country for good or ill. The jurors attest that he is not guilty, so he is acquitted (*he is acquitted*).

1307. William Hidegyne and Alexander Toge, charged with many larcenies, come and deny everything[1] and put themselves on the country for good or ill. The jurors attest that they are not guilty, so they are acquitted thereof (*they are acquitted*).

1 There is a very indistinct *totum*; 'everything' is the clear sense.

1308. William Keyloc, charged with larceny, comes and denies everything, and puts himself on the country for good or ill. The jurors attest that he is guilty of stealing clothes and of burglary, and of many other larcenies, so etc. he is to be hanged (*he is to be hanged*). He had no chattels.

Membrane 49 *AALT 4482–3*

THE PRESENTMENT OF THE HUNDRED OF COLNEIS, PART OF THE LIBERTY OF THE PRIOR OF ELY, [WHICH] COMES BY TWELVE [JURORS]

1309. Walter the chaplain of Kembroke was found drowned in Nacton marsh. Simon the son of the chaplain, the first finder, has not come and he was attached by Ralph del Hame of Foxhall and Thomas de Ponte of the same, so they are in mercy (*amercement*). No Englishry, so murder (*murder*). William le Poter of Bixley, Adam le Poter of the same, Hamo of Bixley and William of Bixley, the four neighbours, have not come, so they are in mercy (*amercement*). Because they were not attached by the coroner, namely Robert Malet, he is in mercy (*amercement*).[1]

[1] Robert Malet was a tenant of the Bigods with property at Wenhaston and Walpole in Blything hundred. He served as an assize justice at Thetford in 1227. At the eyre he was convicted of a disseisin at Benacre; it may have been to pay his 10s. amercement for this that he and Thomas le Latimer borrowed £5 from the principal justice, William of York. P. Brown (ed.), *Sibton Abbey cartularies and charters* i, Suffolk Charters 7, SRS (1985), pp. 71–2; *1240 Suffolk Civil Pleas*, **195**, **525**, **1643**.

1310. Walter of Nacton, a miller, was found killed by the wheel of a watermill in Nacton vill. No one is suspected thereof. Judgment: misadventure. Price of the wheel twelve pence, for which John the sheriff will answer (*12 pence, deodand*).

1311. Concerning Encroachments they say that Nigel the smith of Trimley has narrowed a royal highway in Trimley vill, so he is in mercy (*amercement*).

1312. Concerning Defaults they say that Gilbert de Blevile, Brun de *Latguine*, Robert the son of Hugh Jordan and Robert of Kembroke did not come on the first day, so they are in mercy (*amercement*).

1313. Henry Seman, charged with stealing corn and other larcenies, comes and denies everything and puts himself on the country for good or ill. The twelve jurors and four vills attest that he is not guilty, so he is acquitted thereof (*he is acquitted*).

1314. Agnes Kempe is suspected of many larcenies and has fled, so she is to be exacted and waived (*she is to be exacted and waived*). She had no chattels.

1315. William Bule, charged with stealing of two bushels of malt, has fled, and he is not suspected of any other larceny, so he may return if he wishes. He was not in a tithing because he was under age.

1316. Seyna Rute, charged with many larcenies, has fled and is suspected, so she is to be exacted and waived (*she is to be exacted and waived*).

THE PRESENTMENT OF THE BOROUGH OF ORFORD [WHICH] COMES BY TWELVE [JURORS]

1317. Concerning Cloths sold contrary to the assize, they say that Hubert the merchant of Orford, Stephen Leche, Seman Orgor and John his brother, John of Martlesham, William of Parham, John Fundling and Ralph the merchant have sold cloths contrary to the assize, so they are in mercy (*amercement*).

1318. Concerning Wines sold contrary to the assize, they say that Walter the little sold wine contrary to the assize, so he is in mercy (*amercement*).

1319. Reinerus Sanke was arrested for larceny and taken to Orford castle by Thomas of Ingoldisthorpe, then sheriff, and he escaped from there, and so to judgment for the escape (*escape*).[1]

[1] Thomas was sheriff between 21 April 1236 and 7 December 1237.

1320. Baldwin of Glemham and Reynold the son of Gilbert the miller of Orford were seen in Orford mill one day in the evening, and were never seen afterwards. But it was established by the jury that Baldwin was drowned through his own madness and Reynold fled out of fear. Afterwards it was established by the twelve jurors of Loes hundred and by four neighbouring vills that Reynold killed Baldwin, and so the twelve jurors of Orford are in mercy for concealment and Orford vill is in mercy because it did not present this case in the county court (*amercement, amercement*). Reynold is to be exacted and outlawed, let his tithing and chattels be inquired into in Loes hundred. Afterwards it is attested by Loes hundred that he was not in a tithing, so Eye vill is in mercy, because it harboured him outside[1] frankpledge (*amercement*). He had no chattels.

1 *extra*, replacing *sine* (without), struck through.

THE PRESENTMENT OF THE HUNDRED OF LOES, PART OF THE LIBERTY OF THE PRIOR OF ELY, [WHICH] COMES BY TWELVE [JURORS]

1321. Robert Oldsay appeals William the son of Richard Erkembaud of breach of the King's peace and wounding. And he appeals Theobald the clerk of Rendlesham, William the son of the parson of Boyton,[1] Gilbert the goldsmith of Dunwich, Robert and Thomas his brothers, of abetment. Robert Oldsay comes and he does not wish to sue against them, so he is to be remanded in custody, and his sureties for prosecuting are in mercy, namely: William de Clif of Campsey [Ash] and Reynold the son of Alfred of the same (*amercement*). The jurors attest that William the son of Erkembaud and all the others except Gilbert, Robert and Thomas, the brothers, have come to an agreement and they are clerks. The official of the bishop claims them, to have them in Court Christian, and he has them. It is also attested that Gilbert, Robert and Thomas abetted William the son of Richard Erkembaud when he gave him a wound. So they are in mercy (*amercement*).

1 There are Boytons in Plomesgate, Wilford and Risbridge hundreds.

1322. Ranulf the son of John of Wantisden, a child aged eleven, and Norman the son of William, a child aged seven, were found drowned in Framlingham vill. Gillian, the first finder, comes. No one is suspected thereof. Judgment: misadventure. Englishry was presented.

1323. William the son of Robert of Carlton was found drowned in the mere below Framlingham castle. Hugh the son of Roger, the first finder, comes. Peter the chaplain was attached for that death, and he does not come, so he and his sureties are in mercy, namely Roger of Carlton, and Adam Hency, the other surety, has died.

1324. Henry of Barnham, the warrener of Sir Roger le Bigot, earl of Norfolk, struck Richard the son of Gilbert Algar in the chest so that he died immediately. He fled to Eyke church, acknowledged the deed and abjured the realm. He was in the household of the said earl of Norfolk,[1] who is in mercy (*amercement*). Because Eyke vill did not pursue, it is in mercy (*amercement*).

1 The earl had the advowson of Eyke church as one of the appurtenances of his manor of Staverton, which was probably where Henry was employed. *Calendars of Inquisitions Post Mortem* i, no. 744.

1325. William Luvered of Saxmundham was crushed to death by a beam in the barn of the prioress of Campsey Ash.[1] Judgment: misadventure. Price of the beam three and a half pence (*deodand, 3½ pence, deodand*).[2]

1 A house of Augustinian canonesses founded around the end of the twelfth century.
2 The word *deodand* is written twice in the margin.

1326. Stephen the son of Hubert the chaplain and Matilda the daughter of Geoffrey appeal Adam the son of Geoffrey Osmund of burning their houses. Adam has been outlawed by the suit of Matilda and Stephen. He was in the tithing of Andrew the son of Nicholas of Easton, so it is in mercy (*amercement*). His chattels: six shillings, six pence for which the prior of Ely will answer (*6 shillings, 6 pence*). Stephen does not come and he found sureties for prosecuting: Roger the son of Odo of Easton and William Cook of the same, so they are in mercy (*amercement*).[1] Adam had five acres of land, from which the year and day of the King's waste is three shillings and eight pence, for which the prior of Ely will answer (*3 shillings, 8 pence*).

1 The amercement of Stephen and his sureties is surprising in the light of Adam's outlawry, and since there is no reference to any of them in the amercements section, the justices probably decided that no payment was called for.

1327. Estrilda, the widow of Frebern of Kenton, was killed in her own house. Robert Pepelyn is suspected of that death and he fled to Kenton church and abjured the realm. He was in the tithing of Walter Pileroc in Kenton, so it is in mercy (*amercement*). His chattels: four shillings, for which the prior of Ely will answer (*4 shillings*). Because Kenton vill neither raised the hue nor pursued, it is in mercy (*amercement*).

1328. Hugh the son of Basilia appealed William de la Dune of the death of his wife Basilia. William comes and is a clerk, whereupon the official of the bishop comes and claims him, to have him in Court Christian, and he has him.

The same appeals Andrew the serjeant of Margaret la Bigote, William's nephew Roger[1] and Roger's groom Robert of abetment. Roger and Robert do not come, nor were they attached because they were not found. Andrew comes and asks for judgment as to whether he should answer to his appeal, which is one of abetment, until the deed is established.[2] And so he is sent to gaol until the deed is established (*Gaol*). Hugh is told to sue against Roger and Robert once the deed has been established. The jurors attest that William struck Basilia with a stake so that she died. They also say that Roger and Robert and Andrew came with William to her house but they gave her no blow. Later Andrew came and made fine by one mark, by the surety of William of Holbrook (*1 mark*).

1 Corrected from Reginald.

2 Proceedings against alleged abettors could not proceed until the principal accused had been convicted. If he or she was acquitted, the case against abettors lapsed.

1329. Matilda the daughter of Richard del Hill appealed Gilbert the son of Humphrey that on the day of the apostles Simon and Jude[1] he came to her in Orford fields[2] and there ravished her virginity and took eighteen pence from her in robbery. Gilbert comes, and because Matilda neither came to the next county court nor made an immediate pursuit, it is adjudged that the appeal is invalid. The jurors attest that he did not deflower her, but that in truth he took that money from her as she appealed him, so he is in mercy for that trespass (*amercement*). He is to be remanded in custody. Matilda is in mercy for a false claim. She is pardoned because she is poor.

1 28 October. No year is specified, but 1239 seems likely.

2 Loes hundred extends as far east as Butley, about four miles from Orford, which is itself in Plomesgate hundred.

Membrane 49d *AALT 4605–6*

STILL THE HUNDRED OF LOES

1330. William Lanis appealed Robert Oldsay in the court of St Etheldreda of breach of the King's peace and wounding. William does not come and he found sureties for prosecuting, namely William Bricnoth of Ash and Robert del Clif of the same, so they are in mercy. Robert does not come, and he was attached by Roger the son of Alfred of Ash and Robert the son of Reynold of Campsey Ash, so they are in mercy (*amercement*). Because this case was not presented in the county court, let it be discussed.[1]

[1] Because the case had not been presented to the county court, the justices could have found no record of it independent of that of the appeal itself.

1331. Concerning Churches which are in the King's gift, they say that Nicholas of St Albans holds Kettleburgh church, which is in the King's gift (*Churches*).[1]

[1] In 1224 William of St Albans was presented to Kettleburgh church, which was later said to have been in the gift of Guy de Laval, a baron of Maine, until the loss of Normandy. Nicholas may well have been a kinsman of William's, but he was also a royal servant, employed in the exchequer, where in 1248 he was appointed King's remembrancer. *Patent Rolls of Henry III, 1216–1225*, p. 441; *Book of Fees* i, pp. 390–1; E 159/24 m. 5d.

1332. Adam de *Haverton'* holds Easton church, which is in the King's gift through the elect of Valence.[1]

[1] William of Savoy, bishop-elect of Valence in the Rhône valley, was the uncle of Queen Eleanor of Provence and accompanied her to England in 1236, quickly becoming a major figure at court and in government. Easton church, which like Kettleburgh had formerly been in the gift of Guy de Laval, was doubtless granted to him by Henry III, and came back into the latter's hands when William died on 1 November 1239. D. Carpenter, *Henry III: the rise to power and personal rule, 1207–1258* (New Haven, 2020), pp. 187–207; R.C. Stacey, *Politics, policy and finance under Henry III, 1216–1245* (Oxford, 1987), pp. 96–130.

1333. Concerning Cloths sold contrary to the assize, they say that Baldwin of Easton has sold cloths contrary to the assize, so he is in mercy (*amercement*).

1334. Concerning Bailiffs who have held pleas of the Crown, they say that the bailiffs of the five and a half hundreds[1] hold pleas of the Crown, so let this be discussed (*to be discussed*).

[1] The five and a half hundreds constituting the liberty of the prior of Ely.

1335. Hugh Hachard and Robert his brother and Walter the son of William Erneland have fled, and they are suspected of many larcenies, so they are to be exacted and outlawed (*they are to be exacted and outlawed*). Hugh and Robert were in the tithing of Robert the son of the carpenter of Framlingham, so it is in mercy (*amercement*). They had no chattels. Walter was in the tithing of William the serjeant in Framlingham, so it is in mercy (*amercement*). He had no chattels.

1336. Richard the son of Andrew of Easton broke into the house of Roger his brother, and carried off from it about nine marks and fled, so he is to be exacted and outlawed. He was in the tithing of the said Andrew, the son of Nicholas of Easton, so it is in mercy (*amercement*).[1] He had no chattels.

[1] For the outlawry of another member of Andrew's tithing see **1326** above.

1337. (*Defaults*) Concerning Defaults they say that Andrew the tailor[1] and Thomas Godwin did not come on the first day, so they are in mercy (*amercement*).

1 *1240 Suffolk Civil Pleas*, **400**, records Andrew as being sued over land at Framlingham in this hundred.

1338. The jurors present that the King's bailiffs for Orford do not allow the sheriff's bailiffs to take distraints in Gedgrave vill for summonses of the Exchequer, and so let this be discussed.[1]

1 As a royal manor, in 1235 Orford paid at least 20 marks towards the issues of the county accounted for by the sheriff. Until 1256 it was administered by royal bailiffs, who probably competed with the sheriff for control of Gedgrave, about a mile from Orford Castle, itself usually in the sheriff's hands. Early in Edward I's reign the constable of the castle is recorded as asserting his authority in Gedgrave at the expense of other royal officials, when he arrested and imprisoned two men who came there to issue a summons in the King's name. C 60/34 m. 6; *Rotuli Hundredorum* ii, p. 199.

1339. The jurors present that Robert of Roding has put up a tumbrel in Hoo vill where one was never put up before, and this without warrant, so he is in mercy (*amercement*). The sheriff is ordered to have that tumbrel thrown down.[1]

1 Named from one of the several Essex Rodings, Robert also had property in Norfolk as well as Suffolk. In 1249 he was one of several men prosecuted in the bench by Bartholomew de Sakevill, who alleged that they had broken into his house, beaten his men and taken his cattle at Marlesford, like Hoo in Loes hundred. *Curia Regis Rolls xv, 1233–1237*, no. 675; *xix, 1249–1250*, no. 1033.

1340. Item: Brandeston was the land of Normans, and it is worth one hundred shillings a year. John Lanceleue holds it from the heir of William de Avranches by the service of one knight.[1]

1 John Lanceleve was sued by the King in 1234 over his right to Brandeston. He claimed to have inherited from his uncle, whom William de Avranches had enfeoffed with it. This was contradicted by the King's attorney, and though proceedings were then adjourned, John must eventually have lost the manor, which Henry III gave to Alan Burnel in 1248. *Curia Regis Rolls xv, 1233–1237* (1972), no. 1211; *Calendar of Charter Rolls 1226–1257*, p. 336.

1341. Item: Cretingham was the land of Normans, and it is worth one hundred shillings a year. Ralph de Iuveny holds it from Philip de Columbars by the service of half a knight's fee. Because the twelve jurors concealed this, they are in mercy (*amercement*).[1]

1 Cretingham may not have been truly an escheat from the lands of the Normans. Philip de Columbars, principally a Somerset baron, lost his Norman lands in 1204. He temporarily joined the rebels against King John in 1215 and so lost his English lands as well, but soon recovered them. Perhaps Ralph was granted the manor at that time and allowed to continue to hold it afterwards. Powicke, *Loss of Normandy*, pp. 166, 336–7.

THE PRESENTMENT OF THE BOROUGH OF ELMHAM, WHICH IS A QUARTER OF THE HUNDRED OF WANGFORD AND ANSWERS BY ITSELF BY SIX [JURORS]

1342. Cecilia Puleyn was killed in her house in Elmham vill. Benedict the weaver, the first finder, does not come and he was attached by James le King of Elmham and William Blokere, so they are in mercy.[1] It was attested that Benedict is guilty of that death and has fled, so he is to be exacted and outlawed (*he is to be exacted and outlawed*). He was in the tithing of Roger Brun of Elmham, so it is in mercy (*amercement*). His chattels: one mark, for which the bishop of Norwich will answer.

Because the vill of Elmham neither raised the hue nor pursued, it is in mercy (*amercement*).

[1] There is no marginal note for this amercement, but it is recorded in the amercements section, **1619**.

1343. Everard of Chattisham was found drowned in a stream at Elmham.[1] Joan his daughter, the first finder, comes. No one is suspected thereof. Judgment: misadventure. No Englishry, so murder (*murder*).

[1] Presumably a stream flowing into the River Waveney.

1344. John Huyte of Flixton was found killed on the riverbank at Flixton.[1] William his brother, the first finder, comes. Henry the serjeant of Earsham and Reynold King are suspected of that death and have fled, so they are to be exacted and outlawed (*they are to be exacted and outlawed*). The sheriff is ordered to inquire into their chattels and tithings in Norfolk, and to inform the justices at Cattishall (*at Cattishall*).[2]

[1] The river is the Waveney, at this point the boundary between Norfolk and Suffolk. Earsham is a short distance north of it.

[2] The justices remained at Ipswich until 13 May, and began to hear pleas for the liberty of St Edmund on the 21st. There is no record of these two men in the amercements section.

1345. Henry Buscell of Flixton appealed Henry the son of Roger of breach of the King's peace and wounding. He appealed Hervey Crangel of abetment, and William of Flixton, Margery his wife, Gillian the widow of Richard the son of Burchard, and Sarah the sister of Gillian of giving the order and harbouring. Henry [Buscell] does not come, and he was attached by Osbert del Brok of Elmham and Robert the son of the clerk of the same, so they are in mercy (*amercement*). Henry [son of Roger] and all the other appellees come. It was attested by the jurors that they have not come to an agreement, but they say that the said Hervey and Henry gave him a wound, so they are to be taken into custody. They say also that William de Bosco,[1] Margery, Gillian and Sarah are not guilty of harbouring or giving the order, so they are acquitted thereof. Later Henry came and made fine by one mark by the surety of Henry de Bosco and Henry le Sor (*1 mark*).

[1] Presumably another name for William of Flixton.

1346. Robert Pertrich, Robert Bruning and William Brunhege, charged with the death of a man, have fled and are suspected, so they are to be exacted and outlawed (*they are to be exacted and outlawed*). Robert Pertrich was in the household of Walter his father in Elmham, so he is in mercy (*amercement*). He had no chattels. Robert Bruning and William his brother were in the tithing of Gerard the son of Richard in Elmham, so it is in mercy (*amercement*).[1]

[1] For more about this killing see **1437** below.

THE PRESENTMENT OF THE HUNDRED OF WANGFORD [WHICH] COMES BY NINE [JURORS] BECAUSE ELMHAM, WHICH IS A QUARTER, ANSWERS BY ITSELF

1347. Ivetta the daughter of Robert of Bures was found hanged in the brewhouse of Geoffrey Ingelram of Ilketshall.[1] Simon the son of Sparrow, the first finder, comes. It was attested that she hanged herself with a rope. Judgment: felony on herself. Her chattels: twenty shillings for which the sheriff will answer (*20 shillings*).

[1] One of three Ilketshalls in Wangford hundred, named from dedications to Saints Margaret, Andrew and Lawrence.

1348. Robert the Woodward struck Geoffrey the son of Gillian with a wedge so that he died next day. Gillian his mother, the first finder, comes. Robert has fled, so he is to be exacted and outlawed (*he is to be exacted and outlawed*). He was in the household of Beatrice, the widow of Roger le Poure, so she is in mercy (*amercement*). His chattels: two shillings for which the sheriff will answer (*2 shillings*). Avelina the wife of William le Neuman, attached for that death, does not come and she was attached by Nicholas le Neuman of Sotterley and Roger Wlsi of the same, so they are in mercy (*amercement*).

1349. Geoffrey the son of Ralph Garnoyse was found killed below the courtyard of Emma Hakede in Mettingham vill. Millicent Keyl, the first finder, comes. John the son of Henry Hakede is suspected of that death and he has fled, so he is to be exacted and outlawed (*he is to be exacted and outlawed*). He was in the tithing of Geoffrey le Rode in Mettingham, so it is in mercy (*amercement*). He had no chattels. Englishry was presented.

1350. Concerning Churches which are and ought to be in the King's gift etc. they say that Weston church is in the King's gift, and Stephen the clerk of Thanet holds it, and it is worth fifteen marks a year.[1]

1 Stephen was presented to Weston church on 1 October 1229, following the resignation of his presumed kinsman Master Simon of Thanet. *Book of Fees* i, p. 389; *Patent Rolls of Henry III 1225–1232*, p. 272.

1351. They say also that Cove church is in the King's gift. Martin de la Wardrobe holds it, and it is worth twelve marks a year.[1]

1 In 1235 Cove church was held by William of Bodham, who had been presented by King John as long ago as 1201. Following his death or resignation, the presentation of Martin may have been recorded in one of the lost chancery rolls for the years 1238–40. T.D. Hardy (ed.), *Rotuli litterarum patentium, 1201–1216* (Record Commission, 1835), p. 2; *Book of Fees* i, p. 404.

1352. They say also that the church of St Mary of Willingham is in the King's gift. Robert de Saintes[1] holds it and it is worth thirteen marks a year.

1 Robert was holding the church by 1235. He is recorded among the civil pleas as litigating over the status of a number of small properties held of Willingham church. *Book of Fees* i, p. 404; *1240 Suffolk Civil Pleas*, **252**.

1353. The jurors present that Brian of Ringshall put up a tumbrel in the King's holly-wood[1] without warrant; and there did justice on Gilbert Talun. Brian was present and acknowledged that he did justice on his own authority, so to judgment on him (*to judgment*).

1 *in Husseto domini Regis*. This Latin term (or the corresponding French *houce*) referring to a holly-wood occurs in a number of minor and lost Suffolk place-names. It is not known where this wood stood, only that it was substantial, since it was presumably identical with the *Hussetu'* held by ten villeins in 1275, and with the sixty acres of heathland called *Husset'* which nine tenants were said to hold at the 1286/7 eyre; this second presentment suggests that by then the land had been cleared of trees. *Rotuli Hundredorum* ii, p. 179; JUST 1/833 m. 1d. Information about place-names gratefully received from Keith Briggs. For Brian of Ringshall see **1357** below.

Membrane 50 *AALT 4484–5*

STILL WANGFORD

1354. (*Defaults*) Concerning Defaults they say that Roger Bigot, earl of Norfolk, Gilbert the son of Thomas of Ilketshall and Hugh the son of Ralph did not come on the first day, so they are in mercy (*amercement*).

1355. Concerning the lands of the Normans they say that William de Chaeny holds the soke of Brito in Wangford hundred through Philip d'Aubigny, and it is worth seven pounds a year.[1]

[1] The soke of Brito, or of the Breton, consisted principally of the vills of Worlingham, Weston and North Cove. Held by a series of Breton lords from the reign of Henry I onwards, it had been forfeited by the last of them, Olivier de Tinténiac, by 1212. In 1226 it was granted to Philip d'Aubigny, who in 1235 made it over to his kinsman William de Chaeny, at around the time that William accompanied him on crusade. William appears to have been dispossessed of the soke following the 1240 eyre, but had recovered it by July 1242. He eventually gave it back to the King, who in 1257 granted it to William de Valence. *Rotuli Hundredorum* ii, p. 179; *Book of Fees* i, p. 134; *Rotuli litterarum clausarum 1224–1227*, p. 163; *Cal. Pat. Rolls 1232–1247*, pp. 106–7, 313; *Close Rolls 1242–1247*, p. 15; *Calendar of Charter Rolls 1226–1257*, pp. 469–70.

1356. Concerning those who have withdrawn suits from county courts, they say that Roger Elsy, Alan Pye, Gilbert the merchant, Warner Dubbedent, Christian Frost and Robert Bacun, who are from Barsham, have withdrawn the King's suit from Wangford hundred. Whereupon the steward of the prior of Norwich comes and says that they are all villeins of the prior and of his church of Norwich, and that they have never made any suit nor should they do so.

The twelve jurors attest that they should and have been accustomed to make that suit, and for this reason, because one Geoffrey the son of Peter, formerly constable of Melton, assigned three shillings from the rents of those tenants to the church of Norwich, and then all the aforesaid made suit, and so let this be discussed (*To be discussed*).[1]

[1] As recorded, the jurors' statement is less than ideally clear, but appears to say that Geoffrey's tenants at Barsham made suit until he assigned their rents to Norwich Cathedral Priory, which treated this as justification for preventing suits being made in future. The Melton of this entry is Melton Constable in Norfolk, so named by being held by the hereditary captain of some forty knights whose service the bishop of Norwich owed to the crown. It is impossible to identify the grantor in this case, since the names Peter and Geoffrey recur continuously in the sequence of twelfth- and thirteenth-century constables. N. Stacy (ed.), *Cartae Baronum*, Pipe Roll Society new series 62 (2019), pp. 227–8; F. Blomefield, *An essay towards a topographical history of the county of Norfolk* ix (2nd edn, London, 1808), pp. 415–26.

1357. Concerning Seizures made,[1] they say that Brian of Ringshall arrested Hugh of Willingham and imprisoned him in the house of Andrew de Lana, and he detained him in prison until he had given him half a mark, and so to judgment (*to judgment*).

[1] A presentment under the article *De prisis*, which was originally intended to deal with officials who took goods from their owners without paying for them, but is here used by a jury to complain of an abuse of power. Brian of Ringshall was later recorded as having been the bailiff of Peter of Savoy, but as Peter does not appear to have become a major landowner in Suffolk until 1241, Brian may have been acting – or claiming to act – on behalf of Margery de Rivers, whose tenant he was. *Book of Fees* ii, p. 914; *Calendar of Charter Rolls 1226–1257*, p. 259.

1358. Adam Fulekanne charged with stealing a cow and several larcenies, and Alice, the widow of William Derstan, charged with stealing a cow, come and put themselves on a jury of the country and on four neighbouring vills. The jurors and four vills attest that Adam is guilty etc. He is to be hanged (*he is to be hanged*). They also attest that Alice is not guilty, so she is acquitted thereof (*she is acquitted*). Adam had no chattels.

1359. Elyas Biscop, Ralph Tendy and William Pestel, charged with larceny, have fled and are suspected, so they are to be exacted and outlawed (*they are to be exacted and outlawed*). Elyas Biscop was in the tithing of William Garneys in Ilketshall, so it is in mercy (*amercement*). Ralph Tendy was in the tithing of William Leverich of Ilketshall, so it is in mercy (*amercement*). They had no chattels. Inquiry is to be made in Blything hundred concerning the tithing and chattels of William Pestel (*Inquiry in Blything*). Afterwards it was attested by Blything hundred that William Pestel was in the tithing of Geoffrey Crul of Southwold, so it is in mercy (*amercement*). His chattels: five shillings, six pence, for which the sheriff will answer (*5 shillings, 6 pence*).[1]

[1] William Pestel's chattels and the amercement of his tithing are included among the issues of Blything hundred, **1627.**

THE PRESENTMENT OF THE HUNDRED OF HOXNE [WHICH] COMES BY TWELVE [JURORS], PART OF THE LIBERTY OF THE BISHOP OF NORWICH.

1360. Matilda, the widow of William de *Northage*, and Geoffrey her son were killed in the house of Matilda at Stradbroke. Alice the daughter of Matilda, the first finder, comes. It was attested that two unknown thieves killed them, and afterwards they were arrested at Thetford. Englishry was presented and four neighbours come.

1361. Humphrey of Earsham[1] appealed Thomas Sharp, that as he went to Earsham church on St Andrew's day in the peace of the lord King, Thomas came to him in the King's highway and feloniously gave him a wound in his right arm, and he offers to prove this by his body as the court decides.

Thomas comes and denies force and injury, wounding and felony and everything etc., and asks to be allowed that in his appeal he does not name the place where he gave him this wound, nor does he specify the weapons or the year, and he asks for judgment on this. So it is adjudged that the appeal is invalid. And … [unfinished][2]

The same appealed Robert Ters of Hoxne and Thomas's wife Isolda of abetment. Thomas and all the other appellees come. The jurors attest that Thomas did not give him that wound, and so Thomas is acquitted thereof and Humphrey is in mercy (*amercement*). They also attest that Robert gave him that wound and that Isolda abetted him, and so they are remanded in custody. Afterwards Robert and Isolda came and made fine by one mark, by the surety of Adam of Mendham and Thomas Sharp (*1 mark*).

[1] Earsham Street in Wingfield parish, Briggs, *Suffolk Place-Names*, p. 603. In the amercements section Humphrey is recorded as 'de *Criketoft*' (**1621**).

[2] There are traces of erasure at this point.

1362. Walter Nobelet was found wounded in the stomach, so that he died at once, in Laxfield vill. Christian his mother, the first finder, comes. It is not known who killed him. No Englishry, so murder (*murder*). Agnes Litewif was attached for that death. She does not come, and was attached by Ivo the son of Gilbert of Laxfield and Daniel Herre, so they are in mercy (*amercement*). Alice the daughter of Daniel was attached by Walter Carpenter of Laxfield and Geoffrey Eem of the same, so they are in mercy (*amercement*). Because Laxfield vill said before the justices that Agnes and Alice have died, and they have now come, it is in mercy for concealment (*amercement*).[1]

1 The involvement of the vill in providing information to the justices is noteworthy.

1363. Alice the widow of Nicholas Chartres was found killed in her house in Badingham. Robert Silvester, the father of Alice, the first finder, comes. It is not known who killed her. No Englishry, so murder (*murder*).[1]

1 In the amercements section a murder fine is recorded as due from Badingham vill alone, rather than from the hundred (**1621**). This could indicate that Badingham was a privileged community, excused contributing to a murder fine imposed on the whole hundred; but obliged to pay it alone when it was the place where a death incurring a fine occurred. But as there is no evidence that Badingham was in fact so advantaged, it seems just as likely that clerical error was responsible for attributing the fine to the vill rather than the hundred.

1364. Alan Newman was drowned from a horse in a ditch in Wilby. Mabel his wife, the first finder, comes. No one is suspected thereof. Judgment misadventure. The price of the horse is two shillings, for which the sheriff will answer (*deodand, 2 shillings*).

1365. As Robert of Parham led his cart he fell under it into a ditch in Dennington, so that he and the mare which hauled the cart were drowned. The price of the cart and hide of the mare is sixteen pence, for which the sheriff will answer (*deodand, 16 pence*).

1366. Alexander Cockel, Agnes his wife, and Thomas and William their sons were found killed in their house in Weybread. Egelina the daughter of Agnes, the first finder, comes. Miles Sugge, Osbert his son, Bertha the wife of Miles, Alice and Gunnild of Weybread are suspected of those deaths. Miles has died. Osbert, Alice and Gunnild have fled, so Osbert is to be exacted and outlawed (*he is to be exacted and outlawed*). He was not in a tithing because he is a clerk, and was in the household of Miles his father, who has died. Alice and Gunnild have fled, so they are to be exacted and waived (*they are to be exacted and waived*). They had no chattels.[1]

1 For more about this case see **1371** below.

1367. Alexander Innegrenne of Wingfield was found dead in the house of Martin Cook of Whittingham.[1] Henry his son, the first finder, comes. No one is suspected thereof. Alexander of Elveden was attached for that death by Matthew Ele of Whittingham and William Dole of the same and he does not come, and so they are in mercy (*amercement*). Because the twelve jurors concealed that attachment they are in mercy (*amercement*).

1 'Watigham' in the text, but identifiable as Whittingham from the amercements section (**1621**).

1368. William Spekeman of Thetford was found drowned from a cart in a ditch in Hoxne. John of Scoulton,[1] the first finder, comes. No one is suspected thereof. Judgment: misadventure. The price of two horses, the cart and the herrings found in it is twenty-nine shillings, for which the bailiffs of the bishop will answer (*deodand, 29 shillings*).

1 Scoulton is in Wayland hundred, Norfolk.

1369. Muriel the daughter of Gunnulda of Syleham gave birth to a stillborn child, and she put him in a marl-pit and fled out of fear.[1] She is not suspected, so she may return if she wishes. Because Syleham vill did not present this case in the county court, it is in mercy (*amercement*).

[1] The Latin form, *puerum suum*, suggests that the child was male.

1370. (*Defaults*) Concerning Defaults they say that Richard of Fressingfield, knight, Richard Veel of Fressingfield, Nicholas Peche of Mendham, Thomas Pese of Fressingfield, Arnold Grom of the same, Richard Stumpecok, Geoffrey Hume, Eadmer Buylun, Adam de *Sypford*, Hervey the merchant of Horham, and *Harlingham* vill[1] did not come on the first day, so they are in mercy (*amercement*).

[1] Unidentified.

1371.[1] Bertha the wife of Miles Sugge, charged with the death of a man, comes and puts herself on the country for good or ill etc. The jurors attest that she is not guilty, so she is acquitted thereof (*she is acquitted*).

[1] This is a continuation of **1366** above.

1372. Matilda who was the wife of Robert Haghene[1] and Avelina his mother are charged with larceny. They are not suspected of any larceny, so they are acquitted thereof (*they are acquitted*).

[1] For Robert see the following entry. Matilda may have been referred to as formerly his wife because she had been effectively separated from him by his flight and probable outlawry.

1373. Walter Chory, Gerard Rugheved, Ida his wife, Robert Haghene, Richard of Westleton and William the son of Robert, charged with larceny, and Walter [also] with harbouring thieves, are suspected and they have fled. So all except Walter Chory and Ida the wife of Gerard Rugheved, who are not guilty, are to be exacted and outlawed. Walter and Ida may return if they wish. Gerard was in the tithing of William Buck of Tannington, so it is in mercy (*amercement*). He had no chattels. Robert Haghene was in the tithing of William the tailor of Kelsale, so it is in mercy (*amercement*). His chattels: fifteen pence for which John the sheriff will answer (*15 pence*). Richard of Westleton was not in a tithing and he was harboured in Kelsale vill outside a tithing, so it is in mercy (*amercement*). He had no chattels. William the son of Robert was in the tithing of the said William the tailor, so it is in mercy (*amercement*). He had no chattels.

1374. William Tullyhil, Roger Wylceys and William Colt, indicted by William, hanged approver, come and put themselves on the country for good or ill. The jurors say that they are not guilty, so they are acquitted thereof (*they are acquitted*).[1]

[1] The absence of an indefinite article makes it likely that these men had also been accused by William Thurbern (**1293** above). Accusations by an approver who had been hanged did not lapse with his execution, but remained on the charge sheet as indictments and were tried by a jury's verdict.

1375. Adam the son of William Wysterd charged with larceny, is suspected and has fled, so he is to be exacted and outlawed (*he is to be exacted and outlawed*). He was in the tithing of Simon of Banham of Bedfield, so it is in mercy (*amercement*). He had no chattels.

Membrane 50d *AALT 4608–9*

Farewell[1]

[1] *Valete* is written upside down at the head of the membrane.

THE PRESENTMENT OF THE HUNDRED OF SAMFORD [WHICH] COMES BY EIGHTEEN [JURORS], BECAUSE IT IS A HUNDRED AND A HALF

1376. Albreda, the widow of Robert of Holbrook, appealed Geoffrey del Perer of Wherstead and Augustine of Kirkton of the death of Robert her husband. Afterwards they were outlawed by Albreda's suit. Geoffrey and Augustine were in the tithing of Robert de *Saltemede* in Thorington, so it is in mercy (*amercement*). They had no chattels.

1377. Richard the son of Alice of London killed Peter the son of Eustace Bacheler in Sproughton, in the house of Agnes de *Prestleg*, and he took away a horse and valuables of Agnes's and fled, so he is to be exacted and outlawed (*he is to be exacted and outlawed*). Agnes the daughter of Arnold, the first finder, comes. Sproughton vill neither pursued nor raised the hue, so it is in mercy (*amercement*). No Englishry, so murder (*murder*).

1378. Godwin Bullock, who appealed William Bullock of wounding and robbery, and Guy Bullock and Katherine his mother of abetment and giving the order, comes and has withdrawn, so he and his sureties are in mercy. He made fine for himself and his sureties by one mark, by the surety of Roger of Boyland and Michael of Freston (*1 mark*). It was attested by the jury that they[1] have not come to an agreement, nor are they guilty, so they are acquitted thereof (*they are acquitted*).

[1] The litigants.

1379. A boy aged one and a half was drowned in a ditch in Wenham. The first finder has died. No one is suspected thereof. Judgment: misadventure. No Englishry, so murder (*murder*).

1380. Matthew the son of Godfrey killed Hagenilda the wife of Henry Ballard, and he was arrested and hanged at Cattishall. His chattels: seventeen pence for which the sheriff will answer (*17 pence*).

1381. William of Badley appealed Robert Newman, Roger Gile and Emma the daughter of Roger de Ripa that on Sunday before the feast of St Martin two years ago,[1] about the middle of the night, they came to William's home and barn and there took his corn, carrying off five and a half loads of wheat to the house of Roger de Ripa, and that he [*sic*] did this wickedly and in theft he offers etc. And he appeals the said Roger of abetment. William and all the appellees come, and they deny everything etc.

Roger comes and says that he was the executor of his mother, and that he placed the corn in that barn as his mother's legacy and [it was] not William's corn, and the jurors attest this.

So it is decided that the appeal is invalid and that he is in mercy for a false appeal, and Robert and all the others are acquitted thereof. Later William came and made fine by half a mark, by the surety of Hugh of Badley and Geoffrey Richeoud in Sproughton (*half a mark*).[2]

1 7 November 1238.

2 This action is probably related to the assize of novel disseisin which William brought at this eyre against Roger de Ripa and Roger Grubbe (perhaps identical with Roger Gile) for dispossessing him of land in Sproughton (**427**).

1382. Marswet the wife of Thomas the son of Matthew of Wenham, Lettice and Margaret her daughters, and four unknown women were killed in Thomas's house in Sproughton. Roger the son of Matthew, the first finder, comes. It is not known who killed them. No Englishry, so murder (*murder*). Sproughton vill neither raised the hue nor pursued, so it is in mercy (*amercement*).

1383. An unknown man was found killed in Holbrook park. Robert Smech, the first finder, comes. It is not known who killed him. No Englishry, so murder (*murder*). Holbrook vill neither raised the hue nor pursued, so it is in mercy (*amercement*).

1384. Jordan the son of Henry of Dodnash appeals Geoffrey the son of Maurice that on the Sunday next before the feast of St Dunstan three years ago,[1] he came to him and wickedly and in premeditated assault attacked him, and gave him three wounds on the head with a stake, and broke a bone in his right arm, and that he did this wickedly and in felony he offers to prove as one who has been maimed as the court decides. The same appeals Roger the dauber and Robert[2] the miller of abetment.

Geoffrey and all the appellees come except for Roger the Dauber, and Roger was attached by Maurice of Dodnash and Andrew Felhage, so they are in mercy (*amercement*). Later Jordan came and withdrew from his appeal. It was attested that Roger the Dauber gave him a blow on the arm so that he was maimed, and so Roger is to be arrested. They also attest that Geoffrey gave him those wounds on the head and that Robert the Miller abetted him, so they are to be remanded in custody (*they are to be remanded in custody*). Later Geoffrey came and made fine by one mark by the surety of Geoffrey de Bosco and Alexander of Stutton (*1 mark*). It was attested that Robert is poor, so he is acquitted.

1 17 May 1237.

2 Robert's name is squeezed in at the end of the line.

1385. Theda the daughter of Odo appeals Ralph the black of Wenham that on the Sunday next after the feast of St George, against the King's peace and in felony, he gave her a wound on the head with a stick, and that he did this wickedly and in felony she offers etc.

Ralph comes and asks that it be allowed him that she does not name in her appeal either the place or the hour where he made that wound, and moreover that she does not have an appeal against anyone except for her husband killed in her arms or for rape. So it is adjudged that the appeal is invalid.

The same appealed Robert Waleran and Clarice his wife of abetment and she now comes and has withdrawn, and so she and her sureties are in mercy, namely: Richard the son of Richaud and Simon the son of Robert of Little Belstead (*amercement*). Robert and Clarice are acquitted thereof (*they are acquitted*). The jurors attest that they have not come to an agreement and that Ralph gave her that wound, so he is to be remanded in custody (*he is to be remanded in custody*).

1386. Roger the son of Geoffrey the cook was killed by a mill wheel. Richard Ban, the first finder, comes. No one is suspected thereof. Judgment: misadventure. The price of the wheel: twelve pence, for which John the sheriff will answer (*deodand, 12 pence*).

1387. Robert Bunne fell from his cart so that he died at once. Roberta his wife, the first finder, comes. No one is suspected thereof. Judgment: misadventure. The price of the horse and cart: two shillings, six pence, for which the sheriff will answer (*deodand, 2 shillings, 6 pence*).

1388. Unknown evildoers broke into the house of Roger le Daneys and killed Matilda his wife and fled. It is not known who they were. Belstead vill neither raised the hue nor pursued, so it is in mercy (*amercement*).

1389. (*Churches*) Concerning Churches they say that the church of Hintlesham is in the King's gift and Michael Belet holds it, and it is worth thirty marks a year.[1]

They say also that the church of Chelmondiston and the church of Tattingstone are in the King's gift. Alan de Beaufoy holds the church of Chelmondiston and it is worth one hundred shillings a year.[2] The church of Tattingstone is worth ten marks. Afterwards, it was established that one Robert, the dean of Rockland, holds that church by the gift of Ralph de Blumvile, formerly archdeacon of Norfolk, who was presented to the bishop of Norwich and at the presentation etc., and so it is to be discussed.[3] The eighteen jurors concealed this, so they are in mercy (*amercements*).

1 The advowson of Hintlesham had been acquired from Richard I by Michael's father and namesake, a royal justice. He held the living from 1200 until his death in 1246 or 1247. S.D. Church, 'Belet, Michael (d. in or before 1247), royal servant', in H.C.G. Matthew and B. Harrison (eds), *Oxford Dictionary of National Biography*, 60 vols (Oxford, 2004), 4, pp. 887–8.

2 Alan had become parson of Chelmondiston no later than 1228. He probably held the living until around 1244, when Henry of Canterbury, a royal chaplain, was presented to the living. *Book of Fees* i, p. 390; *Cal. Pat. Rolls 1232–1247*, p. 432.

3 Ralph was archdeacon in the late 1230s; similarity of names suggests that he was related to, and appointed by, Thomas de Blundeville, bishop of Norwich 1226–36. Rockland was a large rural deanery in the south of Norfolk, containing the hundreds of Guiltcross and Shropham. Tattingstone church was said to be vacant in 1243, when the King was attempting to present to it, allegedly in the face of obstruction by the archdeacon of Suffolk. C. Harper-Bill (ed.), *English Episcopal Acta 21: Norwich, 1215–1243* (Oxford, 2000), pp. xlviii–xlix; *Curia Regis Rolls xviii, 1243–1245*, no. 983.

1390. (*Lands of the Normans*) Concerning the lands of Normans they say that William Talbot holds half the manor of Hintlesham of the King's gift by the service of one knight, and it is worth sixteen pounds a year. William Pipard holds the other half by the service of an unmewed sparrow-hawk and it is worth sixteen pounds a year.[1]

1 The manor of Hintlesham had been divided no later than 1212, when one moiety was in the hands of the justiciar, Geoffrey FitzPeter, and the other in those of Richard d'Écorchebuef, a Norman who may have remained in the service of King John, since he held it until his death, when John granted it to William Talbot. Within weeks of the death of the justiciar in October 1213 Geoffrey's moiety was granted to William Pipard, who gave five palfreys for it. In 1247 Talbot and Pipard received charters granting them their moieties in fee, so enabling them to pass to their descendants. *Book of Fees* i, p. 134; T.D. Hardy (ed.), *Rotuli de oblates et finibus ... tempore regis Johannis* (Record Commission, 1835), p. 501; *Calendar of Charter Rolls 1226–1257*, pp. 324–5.

1391. The jurors present that the prior of Leighs[1] holds part of the soke of Brito, namely the whole part which is in Samford hundred,[2] and it is worth ten pounds a year.

1 The Augustinian priory of Leighs was in Essex, a few miles north of Chelmsford.

2 In 1237 the prior was recorded as holding lands worth £15 per annum at East Bergholt in this hundred; this seems more likely to be the estate referred to here than the quarter fee which five years later the prior was said to have at Wenham, also in Samford hundred. *Book of Fees*, i, p. 619, ii, p. 915. For the soke of Brito see **1355** above.

1392. William of Ingham holds one knight's fee in Sproughton from the lands of Normans, and it is worth ten pounds a year.[1]

[1] Presumably the fee formerly held by Robert d'Angerville which King John gave to Roger Bigod, second earl of Norfolk. Information from the website of 'The "Lands of the Normans" in England (1204–1244)', project of the University of Sheffield, accessed at www.dhi.ac.uk/normans, 2 October 2020.

Membrane 51 *AALT 4486–7*

STILL SAMFORD

1393. William Bullock appealed Master John of Buxhall of breach of the King's peace and wounding. John comes and is a clerk, whereupon the official of the bishop of Norwich comes and claims him for Court Christian, and has him. The same appealed Walter, John's groom, and Matilda the widow of Laurence de *Harfhagh*, of abetment.

Walter does not come, nor was he attached as he was not found. Matilda comes. The jurors attest that John gave him a wound, and that Walter and Matilda abetted him. So William is ordered to sue against John in Court Christian until the deed is proved.

1394. Walter the carpenter, who appealed John the son of John the chaplain of breach of the King's peace and breaking his arm, has not prosecuted. So he and his sureties for prosecuting are in mercy, namely: Nicholas the clerk of Hintlesham and Thomas the son of Baldwin of the same (*amercement*). The jurors attest that they have come to an agreement and that he gave him a wound as he appealed him. So John is to be remanded in custody (*he is to be remanded in custody*). Later John came and made fine by one mark by the surety of John the son of Richard of Chattisham, Geoffrey the son of John of the same and Thomas Nauke of the same (*1 mark*).

1395. Richard the son of Walter of Bergholt, appealed of the death of Fulk the son of Arnold, was outlawed by the suit of the same Fulk.[1] He was in the tithing of William of Redisham, so it is in mercy (*amercement*). His chattels: forty-three shillings, for which John de Ulecote the sheriff will answer (*43 shillings*). The same had eight acres and a house from which the King's year and waste is one mark, for which the sheriff will answer (*1 mark*).

[1] *sic* – although certainty is impossible, it seems likely that Richard was outlawed for Fulk's death by the suit of his father Arnold.

1396. William Spinc, charged with larceny, is suspected of many larcenies and has fled, so he is to be exacted and outlawed. He was in the tithing of Hamo the son of Emma in Freston, so it is in mercy. He had no chattels, but he had a house and two acres of land, from which the King's year and waste is two shillings, for which the sheriff will answer.

1397. Richard de Avylers holds a piece of land in Erwarton by the service of leading the King's foot-soldiers into Wales, and the twelve jurors concealed this, so they are in mercy (*amercement*).[1]

[1] Although they are a long distance apart, Erwarton and Brome (**1213**) together made up Richard de Avylers' serjeanty – the inquisitions *post mortem* of his son and grandson show them being held by the same service. The presentment above gives no valuation of the Erwarton property, but in

1212 it was said to be worth 40s. per annum. *Calendars of Inquisitions Post Mortem* ii, nos. 627, 676; *Book of Fees* i, p. 134.

1398. Simon the fuller, charged with larceny, has fled and is suspected, so he is to be exacted and outlawed (*he is to be exacted and outlawed*). He was in the tithing of Selicus of Wenham, so it is in mercy (*amercement*). His chattels: twenty shillings, for which John the sheriff will answer (*20 shillings*).

1399. Robert le Clop of Little Wenham has fled for larceny and is suspected, so he is to be exacted and outlawed (*he is to be exacted and outlawed*). He was in the tithing of Henry of Little Wenham, so it is in mercy (*amercement*). His chattels: forty pence, for which John the sheriff will answer (*40 pence*).

1400. Alan the son of Algor has fled for harbouring thieves and is suspected, so he is to be exacted and outlawed (*he is to be exacted and outlawed*). He was in the tithing of Sampson of Boyton, so it is in mercy (*amercement*). He had no chattels.

1401. Walter the son of Hugh of Holbrook has fled and is suspected, so he is to be exacted and outlawed (*he is to be exacted and outlawed*). He was in the tithing of Geoffrey Shadewe of Holbrook, so it is in mercy (*amercement*). He had no chattels.

1402. The jurors present that the bailiffs of Earl Warenne hold a view of frankpledge in Holbrook without the King's bailiff, and this without warrant.[1] The bailiff of Margery de Rivers similarly holds a view of frankpledge in Harkstead without the King's bailiff and without warrant, when the King's bailiff should attend and receive two shillings a year.[2]

1 Holbrook is otherwise recorded as held by a family of that name of the Bigod earls of Norfolk. Its being in Earl Warenne's hands in 1240 suggests that like Earl Stonham it formed part of his wife's dower, see **1182** above.

2 Harkstead is recorded among the fees held of Margery de Rivers in the years on either side of 1240. *Book of Fees* i, p. 608, ii, p. 914.

1403. (*Defaults*) Concerning Defaults they say that Robert of Cattishall, Henry de Merk de *Redeton*, Elyas the keeper of Holton St Mary, part of the land of Hugh de Montchensy, Earl Warenne, William Pipard, the abbot of Aumâle[1] and Elyas de Holenden did not come on the first day, so they are in mercy (*amercement*).

1 The endowment of the Benedictine abbey of Aumâle (Seine-Maritime) in Normandy included Belstead church in this hundred. *Placita de Quo Warranto*, p. 727.

1404. The jurors present that the bailiffs of Earl Warenne do not allow the King's bailiffs to take distraints for the King's debts in Holbrook, nor does Margery de Rivers in Harkstead, so let this be discussed.

They also say that an unknown thief was arrested and imprisoned at Sproughton by the men of that vill, and he escaped from them and fled to the church and abjured the realm. So to judgment for the escape (*Escape*).

1405. The jurors present that Robert of Alwarton withdrew his suit to Samford hundred from Alwarton vill.[1] Peter of Purton, Geoffrey Poogel and Robert Poogel withdrew their suit to Samford hundred from *Torp*, so let this be discussed (*To be discussed*). Walkelin Visdelu withdrew his suit to the county and hundred courts from his land at Shotley. Laurencia of Gedding similarly withdrew her suit to the county and hundred courts from Stutton, so let this be discussed (*To be discussed*).

1 *Alwarton* was a now lost vill in the parish of Erwarton – information gratefully received from Keith Briggs, along with the identification of Purton.

THE PRESENTMENT OF THE BOROUGH OF IPSWICH [WHICH] COMES BY TWELVE [JURORS]

1406. From Ipswich vill, as fine before judgment for drapers and vintners, fifteen marks (*15 marks*).

1407. A man named Germanus was found drowned in Stoke marsh. Geoffrey his brother, the first finder, comes. No one is suspected thereof. Judgment: misadventure.

1408. William the furbisher and Roland the son of Gunnilda beat Nicholas the godson of Reinerus the cook so that he died four days later. They were arrested by the bailiffs of Ipswich and put in their prison, from which they escaped and fled to the church of the Blessed Mary in Ipswich and abjured the realm. So to judgment for the escape (*to judgment, escape*). William the fuller[1] was in the tithing of Hervey Ters in Ipswich, so it is in mercy (*amercement*). His chattels: twelve pence for which Sylvester the son of Walkelin will answer. Roland was not in a tithing because he is a clerk, and he did not belong to anyone's household, so nothing.

1 A furbisher was a repairer or restorer, especially of armour, and certainly had nothing to do with fulling. The amercements section, which names the killer as William the fuller, puts his occupation beyond doubt (**1641**).

1409. John Bude killed Emma his wife and fled to the church of Holy Trinity of Ipswich and abjured the realm. He was in the tithing of Adam de Campo of Ipswich, so it is in mercy (*amercement*). His chattels: three shillings, for which the bailiffs of Ipswich will answer (*3 shillings*).

1410. John Osmund struck Adam the miller with a lance, so that he died four days later, and fled, so he is to be exacted and outlawed (*he is to be exacted and outlawed*). He was in the tithing of Thomas the miller in Ipswich, so it is in mercy (*amercement*). His chattels: twelve pence, for which the prior of Ely will answer (*12 pence*). Because he was killed in Stoke vill, and it neither pursued nor raised the hue, it is in mercy (*amercement*).

1411. Clarice the daughter of John the priest appealed Charles Joye, Richard the dauber and Berard of Ipswich of the death of Letitia her sister. Charles and the others come, and Charles and Richard are clerks, whereupon the bishop's official comes and asks to have them in Court Christian, and he has them.

Berard comes and he is from the liberty of Ipswich, and he has renounced that liberty and puts himself on the jurors of Samford hundred and four neighbouring vills, which attest that neither Berard nor the other appellees are guilty of that death, so they are acquitted thereof (*they are acquitted*).[1]

1 There was nothing obviously relevant to these proceedings in John's charter for Ipswich of 25 May 1200, and Berard was probably objecting to the town's jury on the grounds of its likely bias, insisting instead on trial by a jury from the hundred south of it. Hardy, *Rotuli chartarum*, p. 65.

1412. Robert the parson of Ipswich holds the churches of St Matthew and All Saints of Ipswich by the King's gift. They are worth four marks a year, so let this be discussed (*it is to be discussed*).[1]

1 It is not known when Robert was presented to these churches, which appear to have been customarily held together. Earlier incumbents, on each occasion said to have been presented by the King, are recorded in 1219 and 1224. *Book of Fees* i, p. 283; *Patent Rolls of Henry III, 1216–1225*, p. 434.

1413. The jurors present that the serjeant of the prior of Ely holds a view of frank-pledge in Stoke vill, contrary to its liberty, so let this be discussed (*it is to be discussed*).[1]

1 Stoke, immediately south of Ipswich on the other side of the River Orwell, was granted by King Edgar in 970 to the bishop of Winchester, who subsequently gave it to Ely. It was one of the manors which Bishop Hervey transferred to Ely Cathedral Priory in the early twelfth century. This presentment must represent a stage in a contest for jurisdiction over Stoke between the monks and the town, in which the latter appears to have prevailed, since by the mid-fourteenth century Stoke was one of the 'four hamlets' of Ipswich and was comprehended within a riding of the town's boundaries. J. Fairclough, 'The bounds of Stoke and the hamlets of Ipswich', *PSIAH* 40:3 (2003), pp. 262–77; E. Miller, *The abbey and bishopric of Ely* (Cambridge, 1951), p. 282.

THE PRESENTMENT OF THE HALF HUNDRED OF LOTHINGLAND [WHICH] COMES BY SIX [JURORS]

1414. Benedict the miller and Henry his son from Hobland were found killed in Henry of Hobland's mill. Richard Kue de *Maneford*[1] and Goscelin Kue, Richard's kinsman, are suspected of that death and have fled, so they are to be exacted and outlawed (*they are to be exacted and outlawed*). Richard was in the tithing of Warin Waghe in Somerleyton. His chattels: eighteen pence for which the sheriff will answer (*18 pence*). Goscelin was not in a tithing and had no chattels. No Englishry so murder (*murder*).[2] Hobland vill neither raised the hue nor pursued, so it is in mercy (*amercement*). Nor did it present this case in the county court, so it is in mercy (*amercement*). The six jurors present as finder a man who came and said that he was not the first finder because many found him before he saw him, and the jurors cannot deny this, so they are all in mercy for a false presentment (*amercement*).

1 Probably in Tattingstone, Briggs, *Suffolk Place-Names*, p. 835.
2 The issues of Lothingland hundred do not include a murder fine.

1415. William Gylly the servant of Walter Engaynhe appealed Richard the son of Richard de L'Isle of breach of the King's peace and wounding, and he appealed Simon the chaplain of giving the order, and Andrew the son of Richard, Richard the son of Thomas and Abraham the son of Thomas of abetment. William does not come and he was attached by Oliver the son of Ralph of Burgh Castle and Roger his brother of the same, so they are in mercy.[1] Simon and all the appellees come. The jurors attest that they have not come to an agreement. They also attest that the said Andrew gave him a wound and that all those appealed of abetment aided him, and that Simon the chaplain is not guilty of giving the order as he appealed him. Richard the son of Richard was similarly an abettor, so he is to be remanded in custody.[2] All the others are clerks and they have been handed over to the bishop. Richard made fine by half a mark, by the surety of Master Robert de L'Isle, archdeacon of Colchester (*half a mark*). Abraham has a house in lay fee, and he made fine by half a mark, by the surety of the archdeacon (*half a mark*).

1 There is no corresponding entry in the amercements section.
2 An unusual verdict: Richard, appealed of being the principal in wounding William, is acquitted of that but convicted of abetting Andrew, who had himself been appealed only of abetting Richard but is instead convicted of the actual wounding.

Membrane 51d *AALT 4610–11*

STILL LOTHINGLAND

1416. The jurors present that William le Sauvage the bailiff of Warner Lengaynne arrested two unknown men and a woman and imprisoned them at Gorleston,[1] and he held them in prison until one of them died in prison, and the other man lost a foot and the woman lost both feet from putrefaction. Afterwards he took them to the King's court in Lothingland for them to be judged by that court, and when the court had seen them it was unwilling to judge them, because they were not attached for any theft or wrongdoing for which they could undergo judgment, and so it permitted them to depart. Later William came and made fine by twenty pounds, by the surety of Alexander Alleyn of Yarmouth, Walter of St Etheldreda of Norwich, John de Beaumes of Ipswich, Adam le Sauvage, Richard his brother, John le Sauvage and William de *Leghe* (*20 pounds, so that he may be under surety to stand trial*).[2]

1 The text reads 'Thorlestone', suggesting Thurlestone in Claydon hundred, just outside Ipswich, but Gorleston, now in Norfolk but then in Lothingland hundred, was certainly meant. The same mistake was made in **1419** below with regard to the church, which was unquestionably that of Gorleston. This incident must have taken place between 1235 and 10 December 1237, when Warner (or Walter) Engayne (who is also recorded among the civil pleas as having had custody of Lothingland, **274**) was ordered to hand the manor over to the Balliols – see **1426** below.

2 The phrase about standing trial is so placed in the margin as to leave it less than clear where the clerk intended it to go, and so as to whether William's finding sureties to stand trial was integral to his fine, or whether this was just the clerk's understanding of it.

1417. Emma the wife of John Gos and Richard his son were found killed below Gunton cliff. Stephen Ulfketel the first finder comes. Gilbert of Kessingland, Nicholas and William his sons are suspected of those deaths. Nicholas and William have fled, so they are to be exacted and outlawed. It was attested that Gilbert has fled, so he is to be exacted and outlawed (*They are to be exacted and outlawed*). He was in the tithing of Adam of Corton, so it is in mercy (*amercement*). His chattels: eighteen shillings for which the sheriff will answer (*18 pence*).[1] The same had a house and three roods of land, from which the King's year and waste is one mark, for which John the sheriff will answer (*1 mark*).

1 Clerical carelessness accounts for shillings being entered in the text and pence in the margin. The amercements section shows that the former is correct (**1624**).

1418. Mariota the widow of Ralph Eye of Carlton Colville, charged with the death of Ralph her husband, comes and puts herself on the country for good or ill. The jurors and four vills come and attest that she is not guilty, so she is acquitted thereof (*she is acquitted*). They also attest that three unknown men killed him. It is not known who they were, and so nothing.

1419. (*Churches*) Concerning Churches they say that the churches of Little Yarmouth,[1] Gorleston, Lowestoft and Belton are in the King's gift. The prior of St Bartholomew of Smithfield in London holds them by the gift of the King, and they are worth one hundred marks a year.[2]

1 Little Yarmouth, now Southtown, was in Gorleston parish on the River Yare, opposite Great Yarmouth.

2 The churches could only have been in the King's gift if St Bartholomew's, an Augustinian priory, was vacant at the time of the eyre. They were given to the priory by Henry I, and confirmed to it by Henry II, while both grants were confirmed by Henry III in a charter of 13 September 1229. *Calendar of Charter Rolls 1226–1257*, p. 98. In 1235 a Master Alan de Stok was said to be

holding the churches, which were valued at 100 marks per annum, but paying St Bartholomew's only ten marks yearly. *Book of Fees* i, p. 403.

1420. Concerning Serjeanties they say that Ralph the son of Reynold of Burgh Castle holds the vill of Burgh Castle by the service of [providing] one crossbowman[1] for forty days at his own expense and it is worth one hundred shillings a year. The said Ralph sold that land, so that what remains of it is now worth only five shillings. It was attested that the serjeanty while it was whole was worth fifteen pounds.

1 Domesday Book records Ralph the crossbowman as holding four carucates at Burgh Castle, along with seven other East Anglian estates. Since he was a tenant-in-chief, it may be coincidence that the thirteenth-century serjeanty was held by a crossbowman's service. The purchaser referred to above was Gilbert of Weasenham, who following a legal challenge quitclaimed his rights in the lands to the King, after which Henry III granted them to Broomholm Priory by a charter dated 20 April 1245. Little Domesday Book, fol. 165; *Curia Regis Rolls xvii, 1242–1243*, no. 139, *xviii, 1243–1245*, no. 893; *Calendar of Charter Rolls 1226–1257*, p. 283.

1421. Concerning Wines sold contrary to the assize they say that William le Sauvage and William Pepudros[1] of Little Yarmouth have sold wine contrary to the assize, so they are in mercy (*amercement*).

1 The name means 'dusty foot', and was also applied to the 'piepowder' courts which did justice at fairs and markets on disputes between travelling merchants, of whom William was probably one.

1422. Concerning Cloths sold contrary to the assize they say that Thomas le Lythere, Simon Ashman, Robert de *Cudinton* and Thomas of Lowestoft, who are all from Little Yarmouth, have sold cloths contrary to the assize, so they are in mercy.

1423. John the son of the parson of Somerleyton imprisoned John de Stert of Fritton in the house of Matilda his mother in the vill of Fritton vill for a day and a night and accused him of being a thief. It was established that he arrested him because of his sister with whom he was sleeping, and so he is in mercy (*amercement*).[1]

1 The syntax of this entry is not ideally clear, but the distribution of possessive pronouns shows that the house in which John was imprisoned was that of the mother of his captor, who arrested him ostensibly as a suspected thief but in reality out of resentment against John de Stert for his affair with his sister. It was therefore John the parson's son who was amerced, **1624.**

1424. Herbert of Raveningham[1] fled to the church of St Botolph of Norwich[2] for the death of William Anketil and abjured the realm. He was in the tithing of William of Thurlton in Little Yarmouth, so it is in mercy (*amercement*). His chattels: thirty shillings for which the sheriff will answer (*30 shillings*). The same had a house and three acres of land, from which the King's year, day and waste is forty shillings, for which John the sheriff will answer (*40 shillings*).

1 Both Raveningham and Thurlton are in Clavering hundred in Norfolk, immediately over the border with Suffolk.

2 St Botolph's church stood just to the north of Stump Cross in Norwich; it was demolished in 1548.

1425. Walter le Blund of London, convicted and hanged at London for forged money, had a horse and chattels worth sixteen shillings, for which the sheriff will answer (*16 shillings*).

1426. Concerning Sea-wreck they say that John de Balliol has sea-wreck with the manor of Lothingland by gift from the King, so let this be discussed (*it is to be discussed*).[1]

1 On 10 December 1237 Henry III ordered Warner Engayne to put John de Balliol and his wife Devorguilla in possession of the manor of Lothingland, as a temporary substitute for lands to which Devorguilla was entitled after she had agreed to convey to Henry III her share of the

earldom of Chester, to which she was one of the co-heirs. In the event, Lothingland remained in the hands of the Balliols until 1295. *Close Rolls 1237–1242*, p. 10. Wreck was a royal right unless specifically granted to the lord of a stretch of coastline. It was defined in 1238, in an order to the sheriff of Norfolk and Suffolk concerning the cargo of a ship which had foundered off Yarmouth, as due from any such vessel 'from which no man escaped alive who can claim any of those goods …'. E 159/17 m. 4.

1427. Alan Godrich and Stephen de *Lanthorp*, indicted for larceny, come and put themselves on the country for good or ill. The jurors attest that they are not guilty, so they are acquitted thereof (*they are acquitted*).

1428. Joss Stute, arrested for associating with thieves, comes and puts himself on the country for good or ill. The jurors attest that he is guilty, so etc. He is to be hanged (*he is to be hanged*).

1429. Concerning Defaults they say that Gorleston, Corton, Blundeston, Bradwell, Burgh Castle and Little Yarmouth vills[1] did not come on the first day, so they are in mercy (*amercement*).

1 In the amercements section, Lothingland's amercements for default are distributed among eight groups of two or three men (**1625**).

1430. Henry of Caldecott and Roger of Gunton are the coroners for Lothingland and have taken oath.[1]

1 The men of Lothingland negotiated the right to have their own coroners at this eyre, agreeing to pay twenty marks for the privilege – the money was paid in the next two years. E 372/85 m. 10d, E 372/86 m. 10d. The nomination of these two men was later recorded in the hundred rolls. *Rotuli Hundredorum* ii, p. 169.

THE PRESENTMENT OF THE HUNDRED OF BLYTHING [WHICH] COMES BY TWELVE [JURORS]

1431. Leviva la Wyte appealed Philip the Scot of rape and so far sued against him that Philip was outlawed by her suit, and this was concluded before the previous justices.

The same appealed William Choure of abetment. Leviva does not come and it was attested that she is in childbirth. William Choure does not come and he was attached by Elyas the son of Geoffrey of Middleton and Geoffrey Geldecrowe of Westleton, so they are in mercy (*amercement*).[1]

1 There is no reference to either William or his sureties in the amercement section.

1432. Rose Roffa appealed Robert del Heth that on the night of Palm Sunday three years ago[1] he came to her in Benacre fields and forcibly lay with her and deflowered her. Robert comes. And because she neither raised the hue nor made any pursuit, whereby he can lose life or member, it is decided that the appeal is invalid, but let inquiry be made by the country. The jurors say that he did not lie forcibly with her or deflower her, but he did this at her wish, and so Robert is acquitted thereof, and Rose is in mercy (*amercement*). She is to be remanded in custody.

1 12 April 1237.

1433. An unknown man was found killed in Bulcamp vill.[1] The jurors did not know who killed him. No Englishry, so murder (*murder*). The jurors attest that Nicholas de Monay in Eastbridge, Robert de Monay in Stonham, Alan Iambel of Blythburgh, Geoffrey the son of William the parson of *Stouele* and Absalom the miller of Wenhaston charged with that death, have fled, and they are not suspected of that death, but they suspect all the aforesaid, except for Geoffrey the son of William the parson, of the death of William the son of John de Wicklaw[2] so they are all, except Geoffrey, to be exacted and outlawed (*they are to be exacted and outlawed*). Geoffrey may return if he wishes. Nicholas was harboured in Eastbridge vill, so it is in mercy (*amercement*). He had no chattels. The same had six acres of land, from which the King's year, day and waste is three shillings, for which the sheriff will answer (*3 shillings*). Alan was harboured in Blythburgh vill outside frankpledge, so it is in mercy (*amercement*). His chattels: sixteen pence, for which the sheriff will answer (*16 pence*). Absalom was not in a tithing because he was living in Dunwich vill, so let that be discussed, and likewise his chattels (*to be discussed at Dunwich*). Robert de Monay was in the tithing of Roger Coleman in Stonham, so it is in mercy (*amercement*). His chattels: twenty-three shillings six pence for which the sheriff will answer (*23 shillings, 6 pence*). And because the twelve jurors presented the above as charged with the death of the unknown man, they are all in mercy (*amercement*).

1 It is not clear how many deaths this entry records. It seems possible that the jurors at first presented the slaying of an unknown man, and named five men as suspected of it, but later identified him as William son of John, and charged the same five men, with a single exception, with having killed him. Nicholas de Monay surrendered to the King's peace soon after the eyre, order being given for his release to bail on 16 August 1240. *Close Rolls 1237–1242*, p. 235.

2 Wicklaw, now lost, was the meeting place for the five and a half hundreds making up the liberty in Suffolk of the prior of Ely. It is believed to have been in or near Hacheston, north-east of Wickham Market. K. Briggs, 'Where in Suffolk was Wicklow?', *Journal of the English Place-Name Society* 50 (2018), pp. 11–15.

1434. Alice de *Hendeseye* appealed Matilda the wife of Warin Gebe, Richard the son of Bartholomew of Cove and Christian his wife, Bartholomew of Cove, William the son of Seman and Margery his wife and Matilda the daughter of Seman of burning her house, so that Matilda the daughter of Seman was waived by Alice's suit. Alice comes and continues to sue against them, and Matilda the wife of Warin and all the others come and deny etc., and put themselves on the country for good or ill. Matilda the wife of Warin and all the other appellees give the King forty shillings for having an inquest, by the surety of Walter the son of Sibert of Northales,[1] William of Childrehus of the same, Thorald Herman of the same and Bartholomew the son of Ralph of the same (*40 shillings*). The jurors attest that they are not guilty, so they are acquitted thereof, and Alice is in mercy (*amercement*).[2]

1 The old name for Covehithe.

2 Nothing is said of Alice in the amercements section.

Membrane 52 *AALT 4488–9*

STILL THE PRESENTMENT OF BLYTHING

1435. Alice the widow of Alexander Calver was found hanged in a house in Cove vill. Geoffrey the son of Reynold found her first and comes. No one is suspected thereof. Judgment: felony on herself. Her chattels: two shillings, for which the sheriff will answer (*2 shillings*).

1436. William the son of Ralph the miller was struck dead by a millwheel in Henham vill. Arthur of Henham the first finder comes. No one is suspected thereof. Judgment: misadventure. The price of the wheel: half a mark, for which the sheriff will answer (*deodand, half a mark*). Thomas the son of Walter, one of the four neighbours, does not come and he was attached by Geoffrey Prudekin of Henham and Adam Lefwen of the same, so they are in mercy (*amercement*). Robert de Suzleboys presented that Thomas was dead, so he is in mercy. Later Robert de Sudleboys came and made fine by half a mark by the surety of Richard Champeneys of Sotherton and Thomas de Sudleboys of the same (*half a mark*).

1437. Robert Brunhege, William his brother, and Robert Partrich beat Geoffrey the miller of *Brenham* so that he died, and they have fled. This plea was presented in Wangford hundred, so nothing.[1]

[1] It was presented by the jury for Elmham vill, which, however, was part of Wangford hundred (**1346**).

1438. Alfred the son of Geoffrey of Haverhill was found killed by a cart in *Enethurne* vill.[1] No one is suspected thereof. Judgment: misadventure. The price of the cart and of the horse which was with it: fifteen shillings, for which the sheriff will answer (*deodand, 15 shillings*).

[1] This is the lost vill of *Alneterne* near Walberswick in Blything hundred, recorded under that name in Domesday Book. Briggs, *Suffolk Place-Names*, pp. 289–90.

1439. Baldwin the reeve of Thorington appealed Ralph of Dam[1] and Richard his son of breach of the King's peace etc. and wounding. Baldwin does not come and he found sureties for prosecuting: Stephen Joseph of Thorington and John Russel of the same, so they are in mercy (*amercement*). Ralph and Richard come. The jurors attest that they have come to an agreement, and that Ralph and Richard gave him two wounds, and so they are remanded in custody (*they are remanded in custody*). Later Ralph and Richard came and made fine by one mark by the surety of Walter of Dufford[2] and John the son of John of Cove (*1 mark*).

[1] A lost place-name in Huntingfield. Briggs, *Suffolk place-names*, p. 309.

[2] 'Duffeud', without much doubt representing the lost Dufford in this hundred, but distorted by a scribal error; in the amercements section it appears as 'Duffod' (**1626**). See Briggs, *Suffolk place-names*, p. 288.

1440. A woman named Swaneve was found killed by the wheel of a cart. No one is suspected thereof. Judgment: misadventure. The price of the cart and of the horse which was with it: eight shillings, for which the sheriff will answer (*deodand, 8 shillings*).

1441. John the son of Geoffrey appealed Elyas de Prato that on the Friday next after the feast of St Ambrose in the twenty-third year of the reign of King Henry[1] he beat his sister Sabina, the wife of Elyas, and so ill-treated her when she was quick with child that she died as a result and he offers to prove this by his body as the court decides. Elyas comes and denies everything etc. Because the coroners attest that she neither had a wound nor pursued him immediately afterwards, it is decided that the appeal is invalid and let it be inquired into by the country. The jurors attest that Elyas is not guilty, so he is acquitted thereof, and John is to be remanded into custody (*He is acquitted, he is to be remanded into custody*). Later John came and made fine by one mark by the surety of Elyas of Middleton and John Gunnore of Westleton (*1 mark*).

[1] 8 April 1239.

1442. Thomas the son of Richard of Kelsale killed Robert the son of Roger of Middleton with an arrow and fled, so he is to be exacted and outlawed (*he is to be exacted and outlawed*). He was not in a tithing because he was not living in this hundred, nor had he chattels. The vill of Middleton neither pursued nor raised the hue, so it is in mercy (*amercement*). Afterwards it was found that Thomas was in the tithing of Richer Ailnod of Kelsale, so it is in mercy (*amercement*).[1]

[1] Kelsale is in Hoxne hundred.

1443. Gilbert the son of Walter was found killed in the chapel of the Blessed Mary of Leiston.[1] John the son of Goda of Theberton is suspected of that death and has fled, so he is to be exacted and outlawed. He was not in a tithing because he was under age, being seven years old. He had no chattels. Afterwards it was established that John was only seven when he did that deed, and so let it be discussed (*it is to be discussed*).[2] Leiston vill is in mercy because it neither pursued nor raised the hue (*amercement*).

[1] Most likely a chapel dedicated to the Virgin in Leiston parish church, which has itself always been dedicated to St Margaret of Antioch, though it is also possible that a chapel in Leiston Abbey, which was dedicated to St Mary, was meant.

[2] By the thirteenth century it was generally accepted that children aged twelve or under should not be punished for offences for which adults were liable to be hanged or outlawed.

1444. Walter the son of Richard Peysun appealed Walter Dade of breach of the King's peace and wounding, and he appealed Richard Dade and Roger his son of abetment. Walter the son of Richard does not come, and he found sureties for prosecuting, Richard Peyssun, his brother, and Norman de *Gudeston*,[1] so they are in mercy (*amercement*). Walter Dade does not come, and he was attached by William Hole of Sizewell and Robert Anketil of the same, so they are in mercy (*amercement*). Roger does not come, and he was attached by Reynold Beyser of Sizewell and Robert Kempe of the same, so they are in mercy (*amercement*). The jurors attest that they have not come to an agreement, and that Walter Dade gave him a wound, and that Richard Dade, who has come, abetted him, so Richard is to be remanded in custody. He made fine by half a mark by the surety of Adam the son of Walter of Knodishall and Philip le Rus of Leiston (*half a mark*).

[1] Possibly the lost village of *Guthestuna* recorded in Colneis hundred in the south of the county, Briggs, *Suffolk Place-Names*, pp. 474–5.

1445. Robert the son of William of Peasenhall appeals Adam the son of Walter of Knodishall that together with many other men, whom he names, he came to his house in Knodishall on the night of the Sunday next after the feast of St Dunstan in [Henry III's] twenty-third year,[1] and with his followers broke the doors of his house and robbed him of five loads of barley, two loads of barley malt, two surcoats, five linen cloths, a table cloth, two towels, four sacks, a woman's coat, five wimples, two chemises, a basin, a bronze pot, two pairs of linen sheets and other chattels to the value etc. of fifty shillings, and that this he did evilly and in breach of the King's peace he offers to prove against him by his body as the court decides.

Adam comes and denies breach of the peace, robbery and everything word for word, and he says that in truth he impleaded one Hamo of Felsham concerning a house with common land pertaining to it. And afterwards an agreement was at length made between them in the King's court,[2] whereby Hamo granted him the land with the house upon it, the land being held of Hamo by villein tenure, and he remained in seisin for some time. Afterwards Robert came and ejected him. And Adam returned and ejected Robert, and that he did that robbery wickedly and in felony, against the King's peace, he offers to prove by his body as the court shall decide.[3]

The same appealed William the son of the same Adam, Henry the son of Stephen the carpenter, Seman Hildecrek, William Brun, William the son of Adam, Hubert Birtwald, Godfrey his brother, Hubert Knotte, Richard Bruys, Thomas the charcoal-burner, Geoffrey the servant of the abbot of Leiston, Walter le Curtel', Thomas Ruffus, Robert his son and William the son of Edina of abetment. All the appellees come except for Geoffrey the abbot's servant, who has been outlawed for that deed. Walter the son of Osbert of Knodishall went bail for producing the said Geoffrey in court, so he is in mercy (*amercement*). Geoffrey was not in a tithing, but was in the household of the abbot of Leiston, who is in mercy (*amercement*). He had no chattels.

Because it was established by the coroners and by the country that when that robbery was done the hue was raised and pursuit sufficiently made, it is decided that there be a duel between them (*Duel*). And Adam is to give sureties for defending and Robert is to give sureties for proving. The sureties of Adam: Richard Bern, Peter the son of Walter, Walter de Prato of Theberton, Richard Gripun, Hamo the son of William of Theberton, Ranulf his brother, Robert Botewine and Thomas de Sutleboys of Theberton.

Sureties of Robert the son of Gunnora:[4] Alexander Page of Westleton, John Osegot of the same, Walter the son of Godwin of the same, Hervey Sotel and Elyas of Middleton.

A day was given on Thursday and then they are to come armed. On that day they both came armed and put themselves in the King's mercy, and so they are to be committed to gaol and their sureties are in mercy. Later Robert came and made fine by two marks, by the surety of Godfrey of Brundish and Baldwin Champeneys de *Bonhill* (*2 marks*). Later Adam came and made fine by half a mark, by the surety of Adam Fikelyn of Leiston and Thomas Bulsy of the same (*half a mark*).[5]

1 22 May 1239.

2 The court is said only to be the Lord's – *Domini* – but that the King's was meant is suggested by the agreement recorded among the civil pleas (albeit without details) as having been made at the eyre between Adam son of Walter and Hamo of Felsham, **498**, **499**.

3 This sentence suggests that the clerk was working from notes, either his own or another man's, and that in compiling the final record from them he overlooked the end of Adam's response to Robert's appeal, and the beginning of a rejoinder to it. Robert probably claimed that he had in some way recovered the land whose transfer had been negotiated between Hamo of Felsham and Adam, only for Adam to throw him off it again and take his goods as well, and ended by repeating his readiness to prove his case by combat.

4 A further example of clerical inattention. No such person as Robert son of Gunnora is mentioned elsewhere in this entry. Comparisons with the amercements section suggest that two names have been accidentally telescoped into one, that the clerk began to write 'Sureties of Robert son of William', but mistakenly added 'Gunnora' after omitting both Robert's patronymic and the Christian name of his first surety, John Gunnore – the latter is named in **1441** above, as well as in **1627**.

5 Errors in its record apart, this is a typical example of an appeal in which all the necessary preparations were made for the action's being decided by battle between the parties, but which was concluded without any fighting.

1446. Henry the son of Ranulf of Beckling[1] appealed Richard Sup of Leiston of breach of the King's peace and wounding. And he appealed Elyas the cook of Leiston, William Dreng of Leiston, Walter Calinthewde, Walter Evermund, Patrick de *Bouton*, Laurence Purdeu, William the son of Hamo, John Chaldecok, Walter Sade and Henry de *Boulton* of abetment. Henry the son of Ranulf does not come and he found sureties for prosecuting, Ralph de *Ketling'*, knight, and Walter Glanville of Sternfield, so they are in mercy (*amercement*). All the appellees come except for Richard Sup, who was not attached. The jurors attest that they have come to an agreement, that Richard Sup gave him a wound and that all the others abetted him, so they are remanded in custody. And Elyas and all the others appealed of abetment made fine by forty shillings, by the surety of Philip Ruffus of Leiston, Robert Lutewine of Aldringham, Richard Gripun of Knodishall and Roger le Poer of Theberton (*40 shillings*).

1 A lost place-name in Snape in the neighbouring Plomesgate hundred. Although Henry appears among the civil pleas as 'de Blicling' (**612**) it seems unlikely that he came from Blickling, about fourteen miles north of Norwich. See Briggs, *Suffolk place-names*, p. 723.

1447. Isabel the daughter of John was found drowned in Darsham vill. Gillian her mother the first finder does not come, and she was attached by Walter Kyterel of Darsham and Walter the son of Adam of the same, so they are in mercy (*amercement*). No one is suspected thereof. Judgment: misadventure. William the son of Albreda of Darsham, John the son of Richard of the same, Robert the son of Walter of the same and Robert the son of Elfric of the same, the four neighbours, do not come, and they were attached by William the son of Alexander of Darsham and Robert de Brock of the same, so they are in mercy (*amercement*).

1448. Robert Temprenoyse appealed William the son of Geoffrey Gikel of breach of the King's peace and wounding. He appealed Adam Gykel, Reynold the son of Oliver and William the son of Roger the smith of abetment, and Geoffrey Gykel of counselling and harbouring them. Robert comes and he is a clerk, and says that he does not wish to sue against him except in Court Christian, so he and his sureties are in mercy (*amercement*).[1] Later Robert came and made fine for himself and his sureties by twenty shillings, by the surety of William the son of Hubert of Brampton and Alan Jordan of the same (*20 shillings*). William the son of Geoffrey comes and he is a clerk, and he is handed over to the bishop. Adam comes and he is a layman. The jurors attest that William is guilty of the deed and Adam of abetment. Later Adam came and made fine by twenty shillings, by the surety of Geoffrey Gykel of Westhall and Richard Heyne (*20 shillings*). They say also that none of the others is guilty, so they are acquitted thereof (*they are acquitted*).

1 As a cleric suing against another cleric, it may have seemed reasonable to Robert that he should wish to confine his action to a church court. But his having alleged breach of the King's peace made that impossible.

Membrane 52d *AALT 4612–13*

STILL BLYTHING

1449. Concerning Wines sold contrary to the assize they say that Walter Burchard of Wissett has sold wine contrary to the assize, so he is in mercy (*amercement*).

1450. (*Defaults*) Concerning Defaults they say that John de Veluynes, Thomas de *Pirho*, Simon of Cockfield, Thomas de Fornivaus and the prior of St Neots did not come on the first day, so they are in mercy (*amercement*).

1451. (*Escape*) Concerning an Escape they say that William of Stratton, the bailiff of the earl of Norfolk, arrested an unknown clerk from Ireland on suspicion of theft and imprisoned him in the earl's residence at Peasenhall, and the clerk escaped from there, so to judgment for the escape (*to judgment*).[1]

1 Roger Bigod, fourth earl of Norfolk, had bought the manor of Peasenhall in 1232. Morris, *The Bigod earls of Norfolk*, p. 7 n. 33.

1452. Geoffrey of Henham and Matilda his wife and Agnes their daughter, charged with the deaths of John de *Wygeleghe* and Richard the son of Geoffrey of Blythburgh, come and deny everything and put themselves on the country for good or ill. The jurors say that they are not guilty, so they are acquitted thereof (*they are acquitted*).

1453. Alan the miller, Odo of Eastbridge, Henry Aleyn of Southwold, Roger de *Halle*, charged with harbouring, come and deny everything and they put themselves on the country for good or ill and on four neighbouring vills. The jurors and the four neighbouring vills attest that they are not guilty, so they are acquitted thereof.

1454. Geoffrey of Henham appealed Henry the son of the parson of Stoven[1] of breach of the King's peace and wounding, and he appealed Henry's father William of harbouring him. Geoffrey comes and does not wish to prosecute against them, so he and his sureties are in mercy, namely: Thomas de Gap of Henham and Thomas Oldering. Henry and William come, and the jurors attest that they have not come to an agreement, and that Henry gave him a wound. Henry is a clerk and is handed over to the bishop. They also say that William is not guilty, so he is acquitted thereof. Geoffrey is very poor.[2]

1 *Stovere* in the text, but given the closeness of Stoven to Henham, and the clerk's proneness to error, it seems reasonable to assume that Stoven was the place meant.

2 Geoffrey was presumably identical with the man of that name acquitted of homicide in **1452** above.

1455. Gillian the daughter of Matilda Lauerke and Matilda her mother complain that Richard Cobbe, William Norman, Geoffrey Bolle, Peter Chevre, Robert Temprenoyse and John the son of Ralph came to them on the Sunday next before the feast of the Invention of the Holy Cross two years ago,[1] and seized and led them into Westhall wood and there hung them up and mistreated them. Richard and all the others come and put themselves on the country. The jurors attest that they[2] broke the enclosure of John the son of Ranulf's park, and William the park-keeper took a gage from them, and they did them no wrong, so Richard and all the other appellees[3] are acquitted thereof and Gillian and Matilda are remanded in custody. Later Gillian and Matilda came and made fine by half a mark by the surety of John Sprowyt of Halesworth and Hugh the reeve of the same (*half a mark*).

1 2 May 1238.

2 That is, the plaintiffs.

3 This action is another plaint (see **1266** above). Its informal nature meant that it was not bound by the protocols of the appeal of felony, but perhaps the clerk, who here refers to the defendants as appellees, was unfamiliar with it, or simply did not understand the difference.

1456. Geoffrey Pepper appeals Hugh the son of Camilla of Henham that on the Thursday next after the feast of the Translation of the blessed Thomas the Martyr two years ago[1] he gave him a wound on the head with a stake. And because he does not offer to prove against him by his body, nor specifies felony, it is decided that the appeal is invalid, and let it be inquired into by the country. The jurors attest that Hugh gave him that wound as he appealed him. So Hugh is to be remanded in custody. Similarly Geoffrey is to be remanded in custody. Later Hugh came and made fine by two marks, by the surety of Robert of Layham and Hamo Chevre (*2 marks*). Later Geoffrey came and made fine by half a mark, by the surety of Richard de *Gosemere* and Jordan de *Kinghawe* of Blythburgh (*half a mark*).

1 8 July 1238.

1457. Thomas Stulpard is suspected of larceny and has fled, so he is to be exacted and outlawed. He was in the tithing of Richard de Bruera in Reydon, so it is in mercy (*amercement*). He had no chattels.

1458. Beatrice the daughter of Robert de Blok is suspected of burning houses and has fled, so she is to be exacted and waived. She had no chattels.

1459. Arnold Kinchaut is suspected of larceny and has fled, so he is to be exacted and outlawed. He was in the tithing of John Halyday in Blythburgh, so it is in mercy (*amercement*). His chattels: sixteen pence for which the sheriff will answer (*16 pence*).

THE PRESENTMENT OF THE HALF HUNDRED OF EXNING [WHICH] COMES BY SIX [JURORS].

1460. Isabel the wife of Roger Betel was found dead from falling sickness in Newmarket field. No one is suspected thereof. Judgment: misadventure. Englishry was not presented, so murder (*murder*). The coroners attest that they are unable to enter into that half hundred to make summonses and distraints, so let this be discussed (*to be discussed*). Later it was attested that she was buried without a coroner's view, so Exning vill is in mercy (*amercement*).[1]

[1] The exclusion of the coroners from Exning appears to have been a usurpation extrapolated from Henry III's charter of 1227 granting Richard de Argentein view of frankpledge for his manor of Newmarket, along with a weekly market and yearly fair (a grant which explains Exning's being categorised as a vill or borough in the amercements section). *Calendar of Charter Rolls 1226–1257*, p. 12. Its being presented in 1240 may have prevented its continuance, since no right to exclude the coroners was claimed at the 1286/7 eyre. JUST 1/383 mm. 25, 25d.

1461. Martin the son of Eudo appealed Alexander Cheppe of breach of the King's peace and robbery. And he appealed Adam the brother of Alexander of abetment. Martin does not come and he found sureties for prosecuting, Geoffrey Bule of Newmarket and Gerard the son of Adam of Exning, so they are in mercy (*amercement*). Alexander and Adam come. The jurors attest that they have not come to an agreement and that Alexander gave him a wound as he appealed him and Adam instigated it, so they are remanded in custody. Later Alexander and Adam came and made fine by ten shillings by the surety ...[1] (*10 shillings*).

[1] The sureties, omitted here, are identified in the amercements section as Henry de Cumpenye in Exning and Ralph Cook of the same, **1629**. No doubt clerical carelessness accounts for Alexander and Adam being recorded as appealed of robbery but convicted of wounding.

1462. Concerning Ladies they say that Margery the widow of Henry de Kemesec is in the King's gift and marriageable, and her land in Exning is worth twenty marks.[1]

[1] Henry de Kemesec died some time after 1236. The land in Exning constituted the dower for which Margery is recorded as suing in the civil pleas, **224–5**. Among the defendants was her son Edmund, against whom Margery sued in the bench in 1242, alleging breach of a covenant made concerning her dower before justices itinerant at Cambridge; the record shows that Henry had also held the manors of Tilbury in Essex and Fordham in Cambridgeshire. *Book of Fees* i, p. 590; *Curia Regis Rolls xvi, 1237–1242*, no. 2119.

1463. (*Defaults*) Concerning Defaults they say that William del Acre, Walter del Acre, Geoffrey Chanterel de *Burewde* and Nicholas But did not come on the first day, so they are in mercy (*amercement*).

1464. Concerning Cloths sold contrary to the assize they say that Geoffrey the merchant has sold cloths contrary to the assize, so he is in mercy (*amercement*). The jurors concealed this, so they are in mercy (*amercement*).

Membrane 53 *AALT 4490–1*

THE LIBERTY OF ST EDMUND AT CATTISHALL[1]

1 Having completed their sessions at Ipswich on 13 May, the justices began to hear pleas at Cattishall on the 21st.

THE PRESENTMENT OF THE HUNDRED OF BABERGH [WHICH] COMES BY TWENTY-FOUR [JURORS]

1465. Walter the son of Robert de *Orkelee*, one of the jurors, is in mercy because he has not come.

1466. The jurors of this hundred present that Englishry is presented in the court of St Edmund on every dead man as the men of the county outside present it to the county court. And Englishry so presented comes before the justices on their arrival, and murder is incurred in the liberty as it is elsewhere. If anyone has appealed someone of breach of the King's peace in the court of St Edmund, and appellor and appellee are both from the liberty, that case should be decided in the court of St Edmund, by a duel or in another way.

1467. Henry of Barrow, a two-year-old boy, was struck dead by an oak in Barrow wood. Richard Creek the first finder comes. No one is suspected thereof. Judgment: misadventure. The price of the oak: six pence, for which the steward of St Edmund's will answer (*deodand, 6 pence*).

1468. John the son of the smith of Boxford was killed in Boxford fields. Roger the son of Nigel and Gilbert Heved are suspected of that death. They fled and were outlawed for the death by the suit of William the smith the father of John. Roger was in the tithing of Richard the son of Ralph in Boxford, so it is in mercy (*amercement*). His chattels: four shillings, for which the abbot of St Edmund's will answer (*4 shillings*). Gilbert was not in a tithing because he was living at *Cheleshunte* in Essex, and was never harboured in Boxford except for one night, on which he lodged at the house of John le Chinnere, who is similarly suspected of having connived in John's death on account of disputes at one time between them.[1] John has fled, so he is to be exacted and outlawed and he was in the tithing of Robert Atteforde, so it is in mercy (*he is to be exacted and outlawed*). His chattels: eleven shillings, for which the abbot of St Edmund's will answer (*11 shillings*). Roger the son of Nigel had two acres of land, from which the King's year is six shillings, for which the abbot of St Edmund's will answer (*6 shillings*).

1 *Cheleshunte* is without much doubt a clerical error, misrepresenting one of three Tolleshunts in the Essex hundred of Thurstable, north-east of Maldon, distinguished by their suffixes of d'Arcy, Knights and Major. Gilbert's lodging for one night with John le Chinnere suggests he was complying with the 1233 peace-keeping regulations described in the Introduction, p. xxv.

1469. Adam the priest of Lindsey was found drowned in the fishpond of Polstead. No Englishry, so murder (*murder*). Polstead vill falsely presented Englishry, so it is in mercy (*amercement*).

1470. Nicholas the son of Hugh of Polstead was found drowned from a horse in a marl-pit. No one is suspected thereof. The price of the horse: two shillings, for which the steward of St Edmund will answer (*deodand, 2 shillings*). The jurors did not present the finder, so they are in mercy (*amercement*).

1471. A lad was found drowned in Richard Maskel's[1] fishpond in Cavendish vill. No Englishry, so murder (*murder*). Alice the daughter of Robert, the first finder, comes. No one is suspected thereof.

1 Almost certainly another clerical error – the omission of a suspension mark has resulted in the misspelling of the name Maskerel, a family often recorded as owning property in Cavendish, e.g. CP 25/1/214/15 no. 7.

1472. Anselm the son of William Creek was struck dead by a horse in Lawshall vill. No one is suspected thereof. Judgment: misadventure. The price of the horse: four shillings, for which the steward of St Edmund will answer (*deodand, 4 shillings*).[1]

1 For some 7.5 centimetres from this point the clerk has carefully written round a stitched-up tear in the membrane.

1473. Alan the son of Ralph Galyot was struck dead by a horse in Eleigh vill. No one is suspected thereof. Judgment: misadventure. The price of the horse: five shillings, for which the steward will answer (*deodand, 5 shillings*).

1474. Robert le Franceys, charged with the death of Alan the servant of Walter Wild, comes and denies everything and puts himself on the country for good or ill. The jurors and the four neighbouring vills attest that he is not guilty, so he is acquitted thereof (*he is acquitted*). Fulk Chamberleng and Geoffrey Hunning, who indicted him out of hatred, are committed to gaol. Lawshall vill neither raised the hue nor pursued, so it is in mercy (*amercement*). No Englishry, so murder (*murder*).[1] Later Fulk came and made fine by one mark, by the surety of Roger de Rivers and John de Cramavile (*1 mark*).

1 No individual murder fine is entered in the amercements section, but the whole hundred is recorded there as owing six marks (£4) for murder (**1630**).

1475. Concerning the lands of Normans they say that the land of Hamo de Clarbec in Acton is worth ten pounds. His heir is in the King's wardship, and Paulinus, the King's purchaser, has it from the King.[1]

1 The wardship of Hamo de Clarbec's heir, with his lands and marriage, was granted to Master Paulinus, a purchaser for the King's kitchen, on 6 August 1237. Although Clarbec is a village in the *département* of Calvados in Normandy, there is no evidence that the family named from it suffered any forfeitures in John's reign or later – this was a conventional escheat. Hamo was the heir to a quarter of a large estate at Acton, granted by Henry II to his illegitimate son William Longespée and later subdivided. He was still in wardship in 1242. *Cal. Pat. Rolls 1232–1247*, p. 192; *Book of Fees* i, 391, ii, p. 917.

1476. Concerning Ladies they say that Lauretta de Pontibus is in the King's gift and she is a widow. Her land is worth ten pounds in Withermarsh.[1]

1 Lauretta or Laurencia was the widow of Reginald de Pontibus (Pons, in Saintonge), who was seneschal of Gascony from 1206 until around 1217. Her husband probably died around 1235, not long after his estate at Withermarsh had been assessed at half a knight's fee. Hardy, *Rotili litterarum patentium, 1201–1216*, p. 198; *Rotuli litterarum clausarum i, 1204–1224*, p. 303; *Book of Fees* i, p. 404, ii, p. 1463; *Close Rolls 1234–1237*, p. 330.

1477. (*Escheats*) Concerning Escheats they say that William de Clarbec holds ten poundsworth of land in Acton vill from Norman lands, and William gave them to Peter de Leonibus who has died. Afterwards the King gave that land to Hugh Talemaske.[1]

[1] William de Clarbec held another quarter of the Acton estate which was once William Longespée's, as in **1475** above. Unlike Hamo de Clarbec, William may as a Norman have forfeited English lands. In 1205 King John granted his Acton estate to Peter de Leonibus, 'our clerk', and then in 1213 gave it to Hugh Talemaske. The latter is probably to be identified with the man appointed a keeper of the King's escheats in Suffolk on 8 February 1232; he still held the Acton property in 1242. Hardy, *Rotuli chartarum*, pp. 144, 193; *Close Rolls, 1231–1234*, p. 129; *Book of Fees* ii, p. 917.

1478. (*Defaults*) Concerning Defaults they say that Hubert de Burgh, earl of Kent, Peter Branche, William of Hanningfield, Geoffrey de Capeles, Geoffrey Sank, Richard le Poer, Alan le Chasteleyn, the abbot of St Osyth, Robert of Shelton and John de Beauchamp did not come on the first day, so they are in mercy (*amercements*).

1479. They say that Katherine of Eleigh is in the King's gift and is not married, and she held three knight's fees in Brent Eleigh[1] from the King, and handed over that land in an exchange to Robert her son.[2]

[1] 'Burnt' – so-called to distinguish it from the adjacent Monks Eleigh. The prefix here shows that the disaster it presumably commemorates had occurred by 1240.

[2] Katherine was the daughter of Henry of Eleigh, from whom she inherited the three fees referred to. In 1226, after Henry's death, she and her husband, Randolf of Shelton, gave fifteen marks for possession of her inheritance. Randolf must have been dead by 1236, when Robert was recorded as holding the Brent Eleigh lands; he also inherited three Norfolk manors from his father. C 60/10 m. 7; *Book of Fees* i, p. 600; *Calendars of Inquisitions Post Mortem* i, no. 762.

1480. Robert Twoforhen, the bishop of Ely's bailiff for Glemsford, arrested one John le Waleys in the bishop's granary in Glemsford. He placed him in custody from which he escaped, fled to Somerton church and abjured the realm, so to judgment concerning the escape.[1] He was not in a tithing and he was harboured in the vill of Glemsford outside frankpledge, so it is in mercy (*amercements*). His chattels: five shillings, for which the steward will answer (*5 shillings*).

[1] Somerton is about five miles north of Glemsford.

1481. John Buffet, William Buffet, Robert Frankelyn and John Thoraud charged with breaking into the house of John Griche of Stoke[1] have fled and are suspected, so they are to be exacted and outlawed (*they are to be exacted and outlawed*). John Buffet and William Buffet were in the tithing of Robert the blanket-maker in Stoke, so it is in mercy (*amercements*). They had no chattels. Robert Frankelyn was in the tithing of Sweyn le Berker, so it is in mercy (*amercements*). John Thoraud was not in a tithing because he held his land by knight's service. His chattels: sixteen shillings, for which the steward will answer (*16 shillings*). The same had a house and sixteen acres of land from which the King's year, day and waste is two marks, for which the steward will answer (*2 marks*).

[1] This is Stoke-by-Nayland in Babergh hundred.

1482. Richard the smith of Wissington and Hugh his brother, charged with burgling the house of the aforesaid John, are not suspected, so they may return if they wish.

1483. Eustace the miller and Alan his brother, charged with the death of Leviva the wife of Eustace, fled and are suspected, so they are to be exacted and outlawed. Both were in the tithing of Robert Peper in Little Cornard, so it is in mercy (*amercements*). They had no chattels. Later Eustace came and brought Leviva his wife, alive and in good health. So the sheriff is ordered to receive them to the King's peace, etc., and [to do] nothing about outlawry.[1]

[1] This is one of a small number of cases recorded at eyres in which a suspected killer proved his innocence by presenting himself in court in the company of his alleged victim, e.g. *1238 Devon eyre*, 174, pp. 35–6.

1484. William Stuttemere is suspected of larceny and has fled, so he is to be exacted and outlawed (*he is to be exacted and outlawed*). He was not in a tithing but he was living in Newton vill, so it is in mercy. He had no chattels.

1485. William Fant of Monks Eleigh is suspected of larceny and has fled, so he is to be exacted and outlawed (*he is to be exacted and outlawed*). He was in the tithing of Roger Priur of Monks Eleigh, so it is in mercy. His chattels: four shillings, for which the abbot[1] will answer (*4 shillings*).

[1] Although Monks Eleigh was so called from having been in the possession of Canterbury Cathedral Priory, its head never had the title of abbot, despite his eminence, and the reference is to the abbot of St Edmund's, as lord of the hundred.

1486. Adam of Wix of Preston St Mary and Odo the son of Henry the weaver, charged with larceny, have fled, so they are to be exacted and outlawed (*they are to be exacted and outlawed*). Odo was in the tithing of Edric Fayrman in Preston St Mary, so it is in mercy. He had no chattels. Adam was in the household of the prioress of Wix,[1] who is in mercy. He had no chattels.

[1] Wix was a Benedictine nunnery in Essex, north-east of Colchester. The prioress was recorded as involved in litigation over property at Preston St Mary at the 1228 Suffolk eyre. JUST 1/819 mm. 17d, 24d.

1487. Thomas Aumfrey is suspected and has fled, so he is to be exacted and outlawed (*he is to be exacted and outlawed*). He was in the tithing of Geoffrey Aumfrey, his brother, in Preston, so it is in mercy. His chattels: six shillings, for which the abbot of St Edmund's will answer.

1488. Thomas the son of Roger Mauvessune is suspected of larceny, so he is to be exacted and outlawed. He was in the tithing of Alexander Lewine, so it is in mercy. He had no chattels.[1]

[1] From this point to the end of the membrane the margin has been rubbed into illegibility.

1489. Walter the son of John le Waleys is suspected of larceny and has fled, so he is to be exacted and outlawed. He was not in a tithing. He was harboured in Cavendish vill, so it is in mercy. He had no chattels. Afterwards it was established that Walter fled to Somerton church and abjured the realm, so nothing about outlawry.[1]

[1] Walter was probably the son of the John le Waleys whose abjuration, also from Somerton church, is recorded in **1480** above.

1490. Walter Prat is suspected of burning houses and has fled, so he is to be exacted and outlawed. He was in the tithing of Robert the son of Walter in Glemsford, so it is in mercy. He had no chattels.

1491. William Goche of Long Melford, charged with harbouring thieves, has fled and is suspected, so he is to be exacted and outlawed. He was in the tithing of Roger his brother in Long Melford, so it is in mercy. His chattels: ten shillings, for which the abbot will answer.

1492. Aubrey of Glemsford, Aumfrida, the widow of Peter of Rushbrooke, and Richolda Swinder, charged with harbouring thieves, come and put themselves on the country for good or ill. The jurors attest that they are not guilty, so they are acquitted thereof.

Membrane 53d *AALT 4613–14*

STILL BABERGH

1493. John le Noreys appealed William de *Criketoft'*, Ralph the son of John Marshal and William Blundus of breach of the King's peace and wounding. And he appealed Walter of Stoke of abetment. John does not come and he found sureties for prosecuting, namely: Walter the son of Roger de *Culverston'*[1] and Geoffrey Selet of Stratton, so they are in mercy (*amercement*). William and all the other appellees come. The jurors attest that they have not come to an agreement and that none of the appellees is guilty either of the deed or of the abetment of which they were appealed, and so they are acquitted thereof and John is to be arrested.

1 Probably Domesday Book's *Culverdestuna* in Colneis hundred, Briggs, *Suffolk Place-Names*, pp. 479–80.

THE PRESENTMENT OF THE HUNDRED OF RISBRIDGE [WHICH] COMES BY TWELVE [JURORS]

1494. Two unknown women were found killed in Hawkedon vill. Margery the daughter of William, the first finder, comes. It is not known who killed them. No Englishry, so murder (*murders*).[1]

1 The use of the plural in the marginal note implies that the justices imposed a murder fine for each death. But the amercements section shows that ultimately this hundred, like Babergh, paid a lump sum to cover all its liabilities in this respect (**1630**).

1495. Geoffrey the shepherd of Thomas of Hanchett fell from a ladder with the result that he lived for fifteen days and afterwards died.[1] No one is suspected thereof. Judgment: misadventure. The price of the ladder: three pence, for which the steward will answer (*3 pence*). Walter the cook and Hugh the carpenter, servants, were in Thomas's courtyard and for that reason they were attached. They do not come and were attached by Reynold the son of Ralph and Thomas of Alby, so they are in mercy (*amercements*).

1 In 1242 Thomas of Henchett was recorded in a lawsuit as holding land in Cowlinge in this hundred. *Curia Regis Rolls xvii, 1242–1243*, no. 862.

1496. A certain Hawise was found drowned in a ditch in Great Bradley. Ralph the son of Wicart, the first finder, comes. No Englishry, so murder (*Murder*).

1497. An unknown vagrant lad passed through Dalham, and was suspected of stealing a linen sheet. He fled to Dalham church, acknowledged larceny and abjured the realm. That happened in the time of H. of Hastings, who is the coroner of the liberty, and because he has nothing in his roll and was not at that abjuration, to judgment (*to judgment*).[1]

1 By 1240 the stewardship of the liberty of St Edmund had long been hereditary in the Hastings family, of which the coroner was doubtless a member. A. Green, 'The stewardship of the liberty of the eight and a half hundreds', *PSIA* 30:3 (1966), pp. 255–62.

1498. John the Butler is in mercy for the trespass he did to John Pecok his man in his house at *Relleghe*[1] (*amercements*).

1 Unidentified.

1499. Reynold the shepherd stole twelve sheep in Dalham vill, and fled to Snailwell church and acknowledged larceny and abjured the realm.[1] He was in the tithing of Humphrey Strut in Moulton, so it is in mercy (*amercement*). His chattels: ten shillings, for which the abbot will answer (*10 shillings*).

1 Snailwell is in Cambridgeshire, two or three miles north of Newmarket.

1500. Alexander of Bradley was crushed to death by a beam. No one is suspected thereof. Judgment: misadventure. The price of the beam: four pence, for which the steward will answer (*deodand, 4 pence*).

1501. Gilbert Pot killed Alard of Wratting because he was a poacher in his lord's wood, and he has fled, so he is to be exacted and outlawed (*he is to be exacted and outlawed*). He was in the tithing of Elyas Kent in Great Wratting,[1] so it is in mercy (*amercement*). He had no chattels. Wratting vill is in mercy because it buried him without a view by the coroners (*amercements*).

1 Referred to as 'Wrottinge talewrthe' in this entry from its tenure by the Talworth family – theirs may have been the wood in which Alard went poaching.

1502.[1] Clarice the daughter of Geoffrey Sprot appealed William the son of Ralph the son of Lettice of rape in the court of St Edmund, and she does not come. Whereupon the steward of the liberty of St Edmund comes and says that that plea is in the court of St Edmund and ought to be determined there, notwithstanding the justices' hearing the pleas of the liberty, so let this be discussed (*it is to be discussed*).[2]

1 As on the recto side of the membrane, there is a large stitched-up tear in the membrane, extending through this and the next three entries, which the clerk has had to write around.

2 Nothing further is recorded of this action, so either Clarice abandoned her appeal or the steward carried his point; the former seems more likely.

1503. Ralph the son of Richard of Chedburgh stole two bullocks and two cows and has fled, so he is to be exacted and outlawed (*he is to be exacted and outlawed*). He was in the tithing of William Hodierne in Chedburgh, so it is in mercy (*amercement*). He had no chattels.

1504. Concerning Ladies they say that Hillary Trussebut is in the King's gift. Her land of Badmondisfield is worth fifteen pounds.[1] Similarly Alice de Helyun is in the King's gift and her land in Haverhill is worth forty shillings a year.[2]

1 Hilary Trussebut was a co-heir to the Yorkshire barony of Hunsingore, but Badmondisfield came to her as part of her dower following the death of her husband Robert de Boullers in 1203. She then paid 300 marks and two palfreys not to be compelled to marry again. She probably died early in 1241. *Curia Regis Rolls xvi, 1237–1242*, no. 1611. S.L. Waugh, *The lordship of England: royal wardships and marriages in English society and politics, 1217–1327* (Princeton, 1988), p. 34; J.C. Holt, *The Northerners: a study in the reign of King John* (Oxford, 1961), pp. 63–4 and note.

2 The Helyuns were lords of the barony of Helion Bumpstead, in Essex but only a short distance from Haverhill. Alice, who married Andrew de Helyun, the first of at least three successive generations bearing that Christian name, was a widow by 1235. Sanders, *English baronies*, pp. 121–2; *Book of Fees* i, p. 400.

1505. (*Serjeanties*) Concerning Serjeanties they say that Walter Pichard holds ten shillings worth of land in Wratting vill by the serjeanty of furnishing one man with a bow and five arrows for the King's army in Wales for eight days at the King's expense.[1]

[1] Walter was presumably the son of the Gilbert Pichard recorded as holding the serjeanty in 1219; he had succeeded to it no later than 1228. The land was variously described as consisting of one virgate and of 100 acres; Walter later sold it to Gilbert Peche, a minor baron. *Book of Fees* i, pp. 283, 391, 601; *Rotuli Hundredorum* ii, p. 151.

1506. (*Defaults*) Concerning Defaults they say that John the Butler did not come on the first day. And be it known that he withdrew by licence of Lord William of York by reason of a royal writ by which he was summoned to come to Wales.[1]

[1] The summons was presumably part of Henry III's response to the death of Llywelyn ap Iorwerth, prince of Gwynedd, on 11 April 1240.

1507. William le Champeneys de *Nod* and William Sleg, charged with larceny and with associating with thieves, come and deny everything and put themselves on the country for good or ill. The jurors attest that William Sleg is not guilty, so he is acquitted thereof. They also attest that William Champeneys is a thief of many thefts, so etc., he is to be hanged (*he is to be hanged*).

THE PRESENTMENT OF THE BOROUGH OF CLARE [WHICH] COMES BY TWELVE [JURORS]

1508. From Clare vill as its fine before judgment for murder, drapers and vintners excepted, two marks (*2 marks*).

1509. Concerning Cloths sold contrary to the assize they say that William the son of Thomas of Clare, Laurence the draper of the same, Little William, merchant of the same, Geoffrey Pye, Reynold his associate and Henry of Hawkedon have sold cloths contrary to the assize, so they are in mercy (*amercements*).

1510. Concerning Vintners they say that William Ruffus, Reynold the tailor, William the clerk and Richard de Petrino have sold wine contrary to the assize, so they are in mercy (*amercements*).

1511. Ralph the son of Roger of Clare struck Richard the son of the chaplain of Clare on the head with a cowl-staff and badly wounded him. The jurors attest that he died from that wound. And Ralph was arrested by Clare vill and handed over to Peter the clerk who was then the constable of Clare castle, and he was released by Peter who has died. Ralph is suspected of Richard's death, so he is to be exacted and outlawed (*he is to be exacted and outlawed*). He was not in a tithing because he is a clerk, but he was of the household of Roger the son of Richard, his father, who is in mercy (*amercement*). He had no chattels, but he had a house, from which the King's waste is forty shillings (*40 shillings*).[1] Later Ralph came and was handed over to the bishop of Norwich's official.

[1] The money was to be accounted for by the abbot of St Edmund's (**1633**).

THE PRESENTMENT OF THE BOROUGH OF SUDBURY [WHICH] COMES BY TWELVE [JURORS]

1512. From Sudbury vill as its fine before judgment for drapers and vintners, one hundred shillings (*100 shillings*).[1]

[1] The fine represented a kind of payment in advance for inevitable infringements of the assizes of cloth and wine, which therefore went unrecorded, and may not even have been presented, at the eyre.

1513. Gunnild the wife of John the carter was found drowned in a spring in Sudbury vill. Emma her [?daughter] the first finder comes. No one is suspected thereof. Judgment: misadventure. Englishry was presented and four neighbours come.[1]

[1] The right-hand edge of the membrane is very worn from this point, and a few words are either illegible or call for a measure of speculation.

THE PRESENTMENT OF THE HUNDRED OF THINGOE [WHICH] COMES BY TWELVE [JURORS]

1514. Erneburga of Barton Mills was found dead in Risby fields. Walter the son of William, the first finder, comes and is not suspected. No Englishry, so murder (*murders*).[1]

[1] *Sic* – for some reason the noun was entered in the plural.

1515. Alan the son of Geoffrey Sparke was found drowned in a ditch in Hengrave vill. Robert of Hengrave, the first finder, comes. No one is suspected thereof. Englishry was not presented, so murder (*murder*). Hengrave vill falsely presented Englishry, so it is in mercy (*amercement*).

1516. John the miller of Rede struck Stephen of Hawkedon with a knife in the left thigh and he died on the following day. John fled, so he is to be exacted and outlawed (*he is to be exacted and outlawed*). He was not in a tithing and was harboured in Brockley vill[1] outside frankpledge, so it is in mercy (*amercement*). His chattels: nineteen shillings and three pence, for which the abbot will answer (*19 shillings, 3 pence*).

[1] Illegible here, but identified in the amercements section (**1635**).

Membrane 54 *AALT 4492–3*

STILL THINGOE

1517. William Tunbe of Hawkedon charged with burgling houses, and Walter Buche charged with the same and Humphrey the son of Joscelin charged with the same and with stealing cows have fled. The jurors attest that William is not guilty, so he may return if he wishes. They also attest that Walter and Humphrey are suspected of many larcenies, so they are to be exacted and outlawed (*they are to be exacted and outlawed*). Walter was in the tithing of Reynold the beadle in Chevington, so it is in mercy (*amercement*). He had no chattels. Humphrey was in the tithing of Godfrey Irich in Lackford, so it is in mercy (*amercement*). His chattels: two shillings, for which the abbot will answer (*2 shillings*).

1518. Aylwin Punche of Lackford charged with harbouring thieves has fled and is suspected, so he is to be exacted and outlawed (*he is to be exacted and outlawed*). He was in the tithing of Gilbert Sumer in Lackford, so it is in mercy (*amercement*). He had no chattels. Later Aylwin comes before the justices and denies everything and puts himself on the country for good or ill. The jurors and four vills attest that he is not guilty, so he is acquitted thereof.

1519. Agnes the wife of Robert Horen of Horningsheath and Isabella her sister were found wounded within the liberty and vill of St Edmund, so that they died soon afterwards. It is not known who killed them.

1520. Agnes the daughter of Nicholas le Mervellyus was crushed to death by the beam of a press. Judgment: misadventure. The price of the beam: four pence, for which the steward will answer (*deodand, 4 pence*). Rede vill falsely presented Englishry on Agnes, so it is in mercy (*amercement*).

THE PRESENTMENT OF THE HALF HUNDRED OF COSFORD [WHICH] COMES BY SIX [JURORS]

1521. A woman named Elviva was with William her husband on a pilgrimage towards St Antony's when she suddenly fell dead in the road.[1] William her husband, who was then with her, does not come nor was he attached. The coroners attest that they ordered Geoffrey of Long Melford to attach him, and he did nothing about it, so to judgment (*to judgment*). No Englishry, so murder (*murder*). Because Kersey vill did not arrest Elviva's husband William, to judgment (*to judgment*).

1 It is possible that William and Elviva were on their way to Saint-Antoine-l'Abbaye in south-east France, to venerate the relics of St Antony of Egypt. But it seems much more likely that they intended to visit the shrine of St Antony of Padua, who had died in 1231 and was canonised the following year, drawn by reports of the many miracles which occurred there. Perhaps Elviva hoped to be healed of the disease which struck her down on the road.

1522. The house of Agnes of Cosford was burnt in Hadleigh vill. Robert of Lindsey is suspected and has fled, so he is to be exacted and outlawed (*he is to be exacted and outlawed*). He was not in a tithing because he is a clerk, neither had he chattels.

1523. Wyot of Kettlebaston, charged with stealing sheep, was imprisoned in his own house at Kettlebaston, and he was released by Geoffrey of Long Melford, the serjeant of the hundred, who handed him over to his tithing and the following sureties, namely: Gilbert of Manton and Andrew the carpenter of the same, so they are in mercy (*amercement*). Wyot fled and is suspected of many larcenies, so he is to be exacted and outlawed.[1] He was in the tithing of Robert Chip of Kettlebaston, so it is in mercy (*amercements*). He had no chattels.

1 No marginalia for the exigent of the fugitive.

1524. Richard Kebben is suspected and has fled, so he is to be exacted and outlawed. He was in the tithing of Thomas of Chilton in Hitcham, so it is in mercy. He had no chattels.[1]

1 There are no marginalia for this or the following entry. The roll does not say what Richard was suspected of, but larceny can be assumed.

1525. Peter Hane killed a man in Bentley in Essex and has fled, so he is to be exacted and outlawed. He was in the tithing of Roger Eylwy in Aldham, so it is in mercy. He had no chattels.

1526. (*Defaults*) Concerning Defaults they say that John de Nevile and Ralph Kempe did not come on the first day, so they are in mercy (*amercement*).

THE PRESENTMENT OF THE HUNDRED OF BLACKBOURN [WHICH] COMES BY TWENTY-FOUR [JURORS]

1527. A boy named Robert the son of Lecelina was found killed in Knettishall field. Lecelina his mother, the first finder, comes. It is not known who killed him. No Englishry, so murder (*murder*). Knettishall vill neither raised the hue nor pursued, so it is in mercy (*amercement*). The twelve jurors falsely presented Englishry, so they are in mercy (*amercement*).

1528. William Welshapen of Thorpe Morieux[1] is suspected of larceny and has fled, so he is to be exacted and outlawed (*he is to be exacted and outlawed*). He was not in a tithing but was in the household of Richard de *Langetot*, who is in mercy (*amercement*). He had no chattels.

1 *Gutherestorpe* in the text. It had acquired its suffix by the end of the thirteenth century, after the manor had come into the possession of the Murious family. Briggs and Kilpatrick, *A dictionary of Suffolk place-names*, p. 140.

1529. Sir William de *Wauton'* and Robert his brother, Sampson the servant of Roger de Clare, John de Danmartin and Martin le Sumeter are suspected of breaking into Richard de *Langetoft*'s park, taking his beasts and carrying them away, so they are in mercy (*amercement*). The steward of St Edmund's is ordered to arrest them if he finds them in the liberty of St Edmund. The same order is given to the sheriff if he finds them in the body of the county.[1]

1 This appears to have been a poaching party whose members were linked through the marriages of Alice de Danmartin. Her first husband was John de Wauton, her second Roger de Clare. C.A.F. Meekings, *Studies in 13th-century justice and administration* (London, 1981), chapter 16. A fine made at this eyre records the settlement of differences between Richard de *Langetoft* and his son Robert over property at Stowlangtoft, Walsham-le-Willows, Troston and the unidentified 'Beuchamp', the first three, at least, being in Blackbourn hundred. It is not known where Richard's park was, but Stowlangtoft, bearing the family's name, is perhaps the likeliest. *Curia Regis Rolls xvi, 1237–1242*, no. 830; *1240 Suffolk Civil Pleas*, **1094**; CP 25/1/213/16 no. 57.

1530. Roger the shepherd of Hunston killed a man in Norfolk and fled, so he is to be exacted and outlawed (*he is to be exacted and outlawed*). He was in the tithing of Alexander le Barun of Hunston, so it is in mercy (*amercement*). He had no chattels.

1531. Ralph Godbarlich struck his wife with a hammer on the head and fled because of this. The jurors say that her wound was fully healed and that she did not die from it. They say that she lived for about eight days and afterwards died of the palsy[1] by which she was previously afflicted. So Ralph may return if he wishes.

1 Literally paralysis.

1532. Anselm the son of Albreda Horen is suspected of larceny and has fled, so he is to be exacted and outlawed (*he is to be exacted and outlawed*). He was harboured in Langham vill outside frankpledge, so it is in mercy (*amercement*). He had no chattels.

1533. Philip the chaplain of Battisford fell from a horse in Norton so that he died. No one is suspected thereof. Judgment: misadventure. Price of the horse: half a mark, for which the steward will answer (*deodand, half a mark*).

1534. William Gosetunghe was found killed in Little Ashfield vill. It is not known who killed him. No Englishry, so murder (*murder*). Ashfield vill neither raised the hue nor pursued, so it is in mercy (*amercement*).

1535. Ralph the son of Edward, Peter his brother and Gillian their sister and Stephen the weaver, charged with larceny, come and deny everything and put themselves on the country for good or ill. The jurors and four neighbouring vills attest that they are guilty of larceny, burglary and burning houses, and so etc., they are to be hanged (*they are to be hanged*). Ralph's chattels: three shillings, for which the abbot will answer (*3 shillings*). Peter's chattels: three shillings, for which the abbot will answer (*3 shillings*). Gillian's chattels: three shillings, for which the abbot will answer (*3* *shillings*). Stephen's chattels: four shillings, for which the abbot will answer (*4 shillings*).

1536. An unknown woman was found killed in Euston field. It is not known who killed her. No Englishry, so murder (*murder*).

1537. Henry the smith of West Stow is suspected of burning the house of Robert the smith of West Stow and has fled, so he is to be exacted and outlawed (*he is to be exacted and outlawed*). He was in the tithing of Robert le Totere, so it is in mercy (*amercement*). His chattels: two shillings, two pence, for which the abbot will answer (*2 shillings, 2 pence*).

1538. Walter the son of Ralph was found dead between *Westwode* and Fornham vills. Adam the son of Amice, the first finder, does not come and he was attached by John Uprich of Fornham and Robert Totere of the same, so they are in mercy.[1] No one is suspected thereof. Judgment: misadventure.

1 No amercement is noted in the margin, but as the tithing of Robert le Totere, of which John Uprich may well have been a member, was amerced of half a mark for the deficiency recorded in the previous entry (**1637**), a second amercement was probably thought unwarranted.

1539. Geoffrey the chaplain was killed in Livermere vill. Peter de *Goudingham* is suspected of that death, and he fled to Great Livermere church and acknowledged the death and abjured the realm. It is attested that Robert the parson of Livermere forcibly took Peter to the church and prevented his being arrested. The bishop's official comes and claims him for Court Christian, and he has been handed over to him. The jurors attest that in truth there was a dispute between Thomas de Haya and Henry of Livermere, and one day Peter came, together with two Flemings, one named James Trusse and the other named Boydin, who together were of the household of Thomas de Haya, and they got into a boat and fished in the lake, because of which there was a quarrel between Thomas and Henry. When Geoffrey, who was Henry's chaplain, had noticed this he went to those parts, and then Peter returned to land with the two Flemings and wanted to go against Henry, and Geoffrey the chaplain grasped him, and he then gave him a wound in one arm and another wound in the other arm. And when Geoffrey did not let him go he struck him to the heart with a knife and killed him, and he fled to the church as aforesaid. They say that the said two Flemings abetted him, and so they are to be exacted and outlawed (*they are to be exacted and outlawed*). They were not in a tithing because they were strangers neither did they have chattels. Thomas de Haya is in mercy as they were of his household (*amercement*).

Later Thomas de Haya came and made fine by ten marks, by the surety of Adam the Fleming of Exning, Thomas Kenesman of the same, Geoffrey the merchant of Newmarket, John the son of Laurence of Livermere, Richard Malet of Exning and Peter the son of William of the same (*10 marks*).[1]

1 Actions among the civil pleas show Henry of Livermere and Thomas de Haya litigating over property in Livermere (**765–6**), and a note on a 1241 Curia Regis Roll reveals that they were at odds over a fishery. *Curia Regis Rolls xvi*, no. 2745. The clerk's compressed style is such as potentially to obscure what happened in this affray. It would appear that some of Thomas's men, perhaps in a deliberately provocative way, went fishing in the disputed lake, now known as Broad Water, which gave Livermere its name. Geoffrey the chaplain intervened on his master's behalf and laid hold of Peter, who wounded him in both arms, and then, when Geoffrey still would not let go, stabbed him to the heart. Henry of Livermere seems to have been a quarrelsome man. See also **1540** and **1589** below.

Half[1]

[1] *Dim'* is written at the bottom of the membrane. What it signifies, other than 'half', is impossible to say.

Membrane 54d *AALT 4615–16*

STILL BLACKBOURN

1540. William of Toftes[1] appealed Robert the brother of the dean of Thrandeston[2] of breach of the King's peace and wounding. He appealed Master William of Thrandeston of abetment, and Henry the son of Peter of Livermere of giving the order.[3] William does not come and he found sureties for prosecuting, Sir Thomas de Haya, and Robert de *Predes* of Copdock, so they are in mercy (*amercement*). Robert and all the other appellees come. The jurors attest that they have not come to an agreement, and that Robert did not give him a wound, that Master William did not abet him, and that Henry is not guilty of giving the order, so they are all acquitted thereof (*they are acquitted*), and let William be arrested.

[1] A lost place-name in Ixworth Thorpe. Briggs, *Suffolk place-names*, p. 251.

[2] Neither the person nor the office have been identified, but the latter may have been an alternative title for the dean of Hartismere. B. Dodwell (ed.), *Charters of Norwich Cathedral Priory* i, Pipe Roll Society new series 40 (1974 for 1965–6), no. 253.

[3] The clerk mistakenly wrote *recepto* instead of *precepto*, the offence of which Henry was subsequently acquitted.

1541. Robert the son of Robert de Furnaus appealed Theobald the son of Alan de *Berle* of breach of the King's peace and wounding. He appealed Roger the brother of Theobald and Ralph Sorel of abetment, and Eustace of Barningham of giving the order. Robert does not come and he found sureties for prosecuting: Adam the son of Robert of Horringer and John the son of Hamo of Thorney, so they are in mercy (*amercement*). Theobald and all the appellees come. Theobald and Roger are clerks and are handed over to the bishop. The jurors attest that they have come to an agreement and that Ralph and Eustace are guilty, so they are remanded in custody (*they are remanded in custody*). Later Ralph Sorel came and made fine by half a mark by the surety of Adam de *Hylleye* (*half a mark*).

1542. A boy, a man and his wife were tied up in their house in Stanton vill. Two men were found killed in the same vill. The first finder was Ralph Theraut. He comes and is not suspected. The jurors attest that Ralph the son of Edward, Peter his brother, Gillian their sister and Stephen the weaver, who have been hanged, are suspected of that death, and Stanton vill did not pursue, so it is in mercy (*amercement*).[1]

[1] The hanging of Ralph and the others is recorded in **1535** above. The first offence in this entry may have been one of the burglaries of which they were convicted.

1543. Mabel de Osevil was found killed in Stanton vill. John de *Gatel'*[1] is suspected of that death and he has died. Stanton vill did not raise the hue, so it is in mercy (*amercement*).

[1] Perhaps Gately in Launditch hundred in Norfolk.

1544. Henry Pelehaste and William Pelehaste, charged with larceny and burgling houses, come and deny everything and put themselves on the country. The jurors say that they are not guilty of burgling houses, but they are poachers in the fishponds of the abbot of St Edmund's at Babwell and Thomas de Hemmegrave in Hengrave, and so they are remanded in custody (*they are remanded in custody*).

1545. A house was burnt in Thorpe vill.[1] Hugh le Seyte of Thorpe is suspected of that burning and has fled, as he brought strangers with him who burnt that house.

1 Possibly Ixworth Thorpe.

1546. Geoffrey of Holbeach was found killed in Ixworth vill. Matilda his wife, the first finder, comes. And Geoffrey Baldwin and Ralph Grethant were wounded by the unknown thieves who killed Geoffrey.

1547. William Brun and David the cobbler, charged with larceny, come and put themselves on the country and four neighbouring vills. The jurors attest that they are not guilty, so they are acquitted thereof (*they are acquitted*).

1548. Basilia the maidservant of Roger of Brancaster[1] was crushed to death by the stack of corn which fell on her. No one is suspected thereof. Judgment: misadventure. Price of the corn: three shillings, for which the steward will answer (*deodand, 3 shillings*).

1 In Docking hundred in Norfolk.

1549. Agnes the wife of Richard the Butler struck herself with a lance in the leg so that she died at once.[1] Simon the chaplain of Badwell Ash was attached on account of this. He does not come and was attached by Adam Hovel of Hunston and Andrew the son of the clerk of Ashfield, so they are in mercy (*amercement*).

1 There is nothing to indicate that Agnes's death was other than accidental. Presumably she was the wife of Richard the Butler mentioned in the following entry.

1550. (*The deed was in this hundred and the chattels are in Hartismere*)[1] Roger de Furnaus is suspected of stealing the horse of Richard the Butler and has fled so he is to be exacted and outlawed. Afterwards it was established by Hartismere hundred that he was not in a tithing because he was a free man and held by military service. His chattels: eighteen shillings, for which John de Ulecote the sheriff will answer. And he had houses and twenty-four acres of land from which the King's year and waste is four pounds, twelve pence, for which the sheriff will answer.

1 This entry is well-nigh identical with **1195** above. It is only this marginal note that indicates that the horse was stolen in Blackbourn hundred. Richard the Butler was perhaps identical with the Richard the Butler of Rougham (in the neighbouring hundred of Thedwestry) who served several times as a knight of the grand assize during this eyre. *1240 Suffolk Civil Pleas*, **144**, **369**, **533**, **774**, **776**, **980**, **1019**. He may have been the man of this name recorded in 1244 as royal bailiff for the Suffolk fees of the honour of Lancaster. E 159/22 m. 7d.

1551. John the son of Ranulf, Alice the wife of Robert Palmer and Alice the daughter of Geoffrey Panel were found killed in Barnham vill. Robert the son of John, the first finder, comes. It is not known who killed them. Barnham vill neither raised the hue nor pursued, so it is in mercy (*amercement*).

1552. An unknown man and his wife lodged in the house of Robert Ordrich in Barnham vill, and on the morrow the man departed and left a horse there, and his wife at once fled to the church, acknowledged the theft and abjured the realm. It is not known who that thief was. Price of the horse: three shillings, for which the abbot will answer (*3 shillings*).

1553. Basilia the daughter of Gilbert Aylwin fell into a ditch and Stephen the son of William Threin ran after her and fell on her so that with her neck broken she fell dead in the ditch. The jurors attest that Stephen is guilty of that death and has fled, so he is to be exacted and outlawed. He was in the tithing of Walter the merchant in Great Ashfield, so it is in mercy. His chattels: two shilling, for which the abbot will answer (*2 shillings*).[1]

[1] The record is ambiguous as to whether Stephen chased Basilia into the ditch and killed her by throwing himself on top of her, or whether he accidentally fell on her when trying to rescue her. It was far from uncommon for people to be put in exigent after they fled for causing deaths in plainly accidental circumstances.

1554. Ralph the son of Hugh was found drowned from a horse in the river at Fakenham.[1] Gilbert the son of Edith, the first finder, comes. No one is suspected thereof. Judgment: misadventure. Price of the horse: two shillings, for which the steward of St Edmund will answer (*deodand, 2 shillings*).

[1] This is either Great or Little Fakenham in Blackbourn hundred. The river is the Black Bourn.

1555. Concerning Ladies they say that Margery de Rivers is in the King's gift and her land in Little Fakenham is worth ten pounds a year and she is marriageable.[1]

[1] Margery or Margaret de Rivers was a great landowner, with estates in many counties, both through inheritance, as co-heir to the Somerset lordship of Stogursey, and through her endowment as the widow of Baldwin de Rivers, who died in 1216 as heir to the earldom of Devon. After Baldwin's death, King John gave her in marriage to the soldier Falkes de Bréauté, who died in 1226. The Blackbourn jurors may have been unaware that in 1229 she paid 200 marks for freedom from marriage. Sanders, *English baronies*, pp. 137–8, 143–4; *Book of Fees* iii, p. 510; C 60/28 m. 4.

1556. A boy was found drowned in the river at Euston.[1] He was buried without a view by the coroners, so Euston vill is in mercy (*amercement*).

[1] Again, the Black Bourn.

1557. Maurice the son of the chaplain of Ingham made off for larceny. The jurors attest that he is guilty only of stealing fish, so he may return if he wishes.

1558. Robert the nephew of the dean of Norton is suspected of stealing fish in fishponds, so he is to be remanded in custody (*he is to be remanded in custody*).[1]

[1] A presentment under number 31 of the articles of the eyre; Robert's offence was poaching rather than larceny.

1559. John the son of John of Stanton arrested Thomas the hayward of Stanton, and having tied his feet and hands he held him in prison until he made fine with him by one mark. So to judgment (*to judgment*).

1560. Godwin the miller, charged with the death of his wife, has fled. The jurors attest that he is not guilty, so he may return if he wishes.

1561. (*Defaults*) Concerning Defaults they say that Adam of Otley and Ralph of Cookley did not come on the first day, so they are in mercy (*amercement*).

1562. John the smith, Maurice the son of the chaplain of Fornham,[1] Thomas Chaldot, Peter Bredeye and Martin Manning, charged with stealing fish in fishponds, come and deny everything and put themselves on the country. The jurors say that except for Maurice the son of the chaplain of Fornham they are all guilty, so they are to be remanded in custody and committed to gaol, and Maurice is acquitted thereof (*remand in custody, gaol, acquitted*). They also say that one Maurice, the son of

William the chaplain of Ingham, is similarly suspected of stealing fish, so he is to be arrested (*he is to be arrested*).

[1] This could be one of three Fornhams – Fornham All Saints, Fornham St Genevieve or Fornham St Martin.

1563. Walter Chaym, charged with harbouring thieves, comes and puts himself on the country for good or ill. The jurors and four vills attest that he is not guilty, so he is acquitted thereof.

1564. Robert Kindel, charged with burgling houses, has fled and is suspected, so he is to be exacted and outlawed (*he is to be exacted and outlawed*). He was not in a tithing, but was harboured in Bardwell vill outside frankpledge, so it is in mercy (*amercement*). He had no chattels.

Membrane 55 *AALT 4494–5*

THE PRESENTMENT OF THE HUNDRED OF THEDWESTRY [WHICH] COMES BY TWELVE [JURORS]

1565. John the miller of Drinkstone was crushed to death by an iron mill-spindle[1] at Drinkstone. Alexander the son of Hugh the first finder comes. No one is suspected thereof. No Englishry, so murder (*murder*). The price of the spindle: four pence, for which the steward will answer (*deodand, 4 pence*).

[1] The spindle was the vertical shaft, the rotation of which turned the upper, or runner, stone of a mill.

1566. Matilda the daughter of Ralph of Thurston fell into a marl-pit so that she was drowned. No one is suspected thereof. No Englishry, so murder (*murder*).

1567. Stephen Becolt and Isabella his wife were found killed in [Great] Barton vill. It is not known who killed them. No Englishry, so murder (*murder*). Barton vill neither raised the hue nor pursued, so it is in mercy (*amercement*).

1568. Warin the son of Alexander of Whelnetham was found killed in a ditch in Whelnetham. William the son of Robert, the first finder, comes. It is not known who killed him. Little Whelnetham vill neither raised the hue nor pursued, so it is in mercy (*amercement*).

1569. William the son of Roger de Torpe and William Heved, charged with larceny, have fled. The jurors attest that William the son of Roger is a thief, so he is to be exacted and outlawed.[1] He was not in a tithing because he was living in Norfolk. He had no chattels. They also say that William Heved is not suspected of any larceny, so he may return when he wishes.

[1] There is no marginal note to this effect, perhaps because it was inappropriate to go through the process of outlawry in Suffolk against a man who lived in Norfolk.

1570. William Thwosogod was imprisoned at St Edmund's on suspicion of larceny. The coroners attest that in truth he was imprisoned in the prison of the vill of St Edmund's. Because the vill does not have him, nor can they answer as to how he departed, to judgment (*to judgment*).

1571. Godfrey the son of Peter was arrested at St Edmund's for the death of John de *Ambir'*, and an inquest having been held into that death it was established that he was not guilty, so he was delivered to Richard the son of Hugh his chief pledge and his tithing,[1] and similarly to the following sureties, namely to Adam de *Bicke*, Freche the son of Eustace, Henry the smith and Thurkyl the son of Leviva. Because they do not have him before the justices, they are all in mercy (*amercement*). The jurors say that he is not guilty, so he may return if he wishes.

1 A clumsy phrase meaning that Godfrey was bailed by his tithing, of which Richard the son of Hugh was the head, and by the four other men named.

1572. Stephen Legat and Robert de *Peudes* broke into the granary of Adam of Whelnetham and have fled, so they are to be exacted and outlawed (*they are to be exacted and outlawed*). They know nothing about their tithing because they were living in Thingoe hundred.

1573. Robert Kaym is suspected of larceny and has fled, so he is to be exacted and outlawed (*he is to be exacted and outlawed*). He was in the tithing of Walter Kaym his father in Fornham St Genevieve, so it is in mercy (*amercement*). He had no chattels but he had three acres of land, of which half were sown this year, from which the King's year is half a mark. Later Ralph the son of Hugh came and made fine by one mark for the year, because the land is part of his fee, by the surety of Ralph le Estrange (*1 mark*).

1574. (*Defaults*) Concerning Defaults they say that John de *Presseny*, Geoffrey de *Tynemere*, Robert of Felsham, Roger his son, Geoffrey of Hoo and Hamo of Rushbrooke did not come on the first day.[1]

1 There is no marginal note to suggest that they were amerced, and their names do not occur in the amercements section.

1575. (*Land of the Normans*) Concerning lands of Normans they say that Roger de Clare held twenty poundsworth of land in Thurston, Tostock and Norton.[1]

1 The three vills, close together on either side of the boundary between Blackbourn and Thedwestry hundreds, are usually referred to under Norton. Forfeited in 1202 by Renaud de Dammartin, count of Boulogne, when he allied himself with the French king, they were returned to him in 1212 when he switched allegiance to King John. His imprisonment after his capture in 1214 at the battle of Bouvines, from which he was never released, led to their becoming again at the English king's disposal. By 1230 they had been granted to Roger de Clare, a brother of the earl of Gloucester, who held them until his death in 1241. A year later Henry III gave them to the courtier Hugh de Vivonne. Hardy, *Rotuli litterarum clausarum i, 1204–1224*, p. 116; Hardy, *Rotuli chartarum*, p. 186; *Close Rolls of Henry III, 1227–1231*, p. 346; Meekings, *Surrey eyre of 1235*, i, pp. 180–1; *Close Rolls of Henry III, 1237–1242*, p. 403.

1576. Richard the son of Ranulf, arrested for the death of Roger le Furmager, comes and denies everything and puts himself on the country for good or ill. The jurors attest that he is not guilty, so he is acquitted thereof (*he is acquitted*).

1577. Alan Baril is suspected of many larcenies and has fled, so he is to be exacted and outlawed (*he is to be exacted and outlawed*). He was in the tithing of Nicholas de Spina in Little Bradley, so it is in mercy (*amercement*).[1] He had no chattels.

1 Little Bradley is almost certainly a mistake for Little Bradfield, or Bradfield Combust, where Nicholas's tithing is placed in the amercements section (**1639**). The latter is in Thedwestry hundred, whereas Little Bradley is in Risbridge hundred some fifteen miles away.

1578. Matilda the daughter of Adam of Hessett appealed Robert of Bildeston of rape, and she does not come. And she found sureties for prosecuting, namely: Rery the son of Adam of Hessett and Rery the clerk of the same, so they are in mercy (*amercement*). Robert does not come, and he was not attached because of her insufficient suit.[1]

[1] Matilda would have had to find sureties when she began her appeal, but she might then have needed to continue her action at two or three county courts to ensure that Robert also found sureties for his appearance at the next eyre. Probably she abandoned her action too soon.

THE PRESENTMENT OF THE HUNDRED OF LACKFORD [WHICH] COMES BY TWELVE [JURORS]

1579. Robert the son of Peter of Tuddenham was struck by a stone in the pasture between Tuddenham and Herringswell so that he died as a result. John the carpenter is suspected of giving him that blow and he has fled, so he is to be exacted and outlawed. He was in the tithing of Richard Puttok in Herringswell, so it is in mercy. He had no chattels. Matilda, the mother of Robert, who appealed John, Geoffrey of Shimpling and Elyas the son of Walter of it, does not sue against the appellees, so she and her sureties for prosecuting are in mercy, namely: Peter Newman of Tuddenham and Rogan the palmer of the same (*amercement*). Geoffrey and Elyas were acquitted in the court of St Edmund.

1580. Andrew Chyp was drowned from a cart in Worlington marsh. No one is suspected thereof. Judgment: misadventure. Price of the cart and of the hide of the horse, which was drowned: twelve pence, for which the steward will answer (*deodand, 12 pence*).

1581. Henry the son of William of Hingham was found dead under the wheel of Worlington mill. Alice the daughter of the shepherd of Worlington, the first finder, comes. No one is suspected thereof. Judgment: misadventure. Price of the wheel: four pence, for which the steward will answer (*deodand, 4 pence*).

1582. Parnel the widow of Ralph Hereward hanged herself in her house. Heloise the daughter of Ralph, the first finder, comes. Judgment: felony on herself. Her chattels: six shillings, for which the abbot will answer (*6 shillings*).

1583. William the son of Peter, Richard the son of Roger and Peter the son of Reynold of Icklingham stole thirteen sheep in Icklingham and killed them there and concealed them under the bed of Katherine of Icklingham, and [hid] the sheep they had not skinned in the manger of the cowshed.[1] Katherine was arrested on account of this and taken to the house of Ralph de *Bayners*,[2] where she was imprisoned in the custody of Thurstan Manser and Eudo the hayward, Woolard the son of Godfrey and Maurice the son of Godfrey. She broke her chains, and likewise the wall of the house in which she was, and escaped, so to judgment for the escape. Thurstan and the others are in mercy (*amercement*). William and all the others who stole the sheep have fled, so they are to be exacted and outlawed (*they are to be exacted and outlawed*). William the son of Peter has been hanged. His chattels: fourteen shillings and eight pence, for which the abbot will answer (*14 shillings, 8 pence*). Richard and Peter were in the tithing of Robert Nuvelhume in Icklingham, so it is in mercy.[3] They had no chattels. Katherine's chattels: three shillings, for which the abbot will answer (*3 shillings*).

[1] Not for the first time, the clerk's account of events (given in full on p.lxx) is so condensed as to leave it unclear what had happened. In all probability the thieves killed the sheep, skinned some and hid their skins under Katherine's bed, while putting the unskinned carcasses of the rest in the cowshed.

2 Presumably grandfather or father of the Ralph de Berners who died around the end of 1296 as lord of the manor of Icklingham. *Calendars of Inquisitions Post Mortem* iii, no. 411.
3 There is no marginal note for this, but the tithing was amerced, **1640**.

1584. Agnes the daughter of Stephen was struck dead by a sail-yard of a mill in Herringswell. No one is suspected thereof. Judgment: misadventure. Price of the sail-yard: two pence, for which the steward will answer (*deodand, 2 pence*).

1585. Margaret the daughter of Robert was drowned from a boat in [Santon] Downham marsh.[1] No one is suspected thereof. Judgment: misadventure. Price of the boat: two pence, for which the steward will answer (*deodand, 2 pence*).

1 Santon Downham's position on the Little Ouse river explains the existence of a marsh there.

1586. An unknown woman was found dead at Brandon bridge. It is not known who killed her. No Englishry, so murder (*murder*).[1]

1 Brandon, too, stands on the Little Ouse river. This bridge will have been the wooden one which replaced the ferry which gave the town its former name of 'Brandonferry'; in the 1330s it was itself replaced by a stone bridge. Bailey, *Medieval Suffolk*, pp. 165–6.

1587. William Pompe of [Santon] Downham and Silvester Basse, charged with larceny, come and deny everything and put themselves on the jury for good or ill. The jurors attest that they are not guilty, so they are acquitted thereof (*they are acquitted*).

1588. Richard Bactun of Cavenham, Robert the son of Gilbert of Mildenhall and Hugh Ernald of Icklingham are suspected of larceny and have fled, so they are to be exacted and outlawed (*they are to be exacted and outlawed*). Richard was in the tithing of Stephen the merchant in Cavenham, so it is in mercy (*amercement*). He had no chattels. Robert was in the tithing of William the smith in Mildenhall, so it is in mercy (*amercement*). He had no chattels. Hugh was in the tithing of Peter de Stangno of Icklingham,[1] so it is in mercy (*amercement*). He had no chattels.

1 The clerk wrote *Ikelesham*, certainly a mistake. The amercement for this entry (**1640**) names Icklingham.

1589. Peter the son of Henry of Livermere, charged with larceny, comes and puts himself on the country for good or ill. The jurors attest that he is not guilty, so he is acquitted thereof (*he is acquitted*). They also attest that it was through the hatred in which he was held by Henry of Livermere his father for certain land that he was indicted and arrested.[1]

1 For another of Henry of Livermere's quarrels see **1539** above.

Membrane 55d *AALT 4617–18*

THE BOROUGH OF DUNWICH COMES BY TWELVE [JURORS][1]

1 The right to have its pleas heard before the King's justices at Dunwich itself was one of the privileges granted to the town in King John's charter of 6 July 1215. Hardy, *Rotuli chartarum*, 211. This brief session was held on 11 June 1240.

1590. From the same vill for its fine before judgment for vintners and drapers, twenty marks (*20 marks*).

1591. Seman Rufus (nothing)[1] appealed Robert le Angle of breach of the King's peace and robbery, and he does not come and he found sureties for prosecuting, namely: Burchard Gikel and Gilbert Morefe, so they are in mercy. And be it known that Robert has died, so nothing of him.

[1] The word 'nothing' above the appellor's name should indicate that no amercement was due from him because the appellee had died. But although there is nothing about Seman in the amercements section, both his sureties were amerced, raising the possibility that he was too poor to pay anything (**1665**).

1592. Edmund the son of Robert of Dunwich appealed Robert Aungle, who has died, of breach of the King's peace.

The same appeals Augustine le Aungle of abetment. He does not come and he was attached by Robert the son of Hubert Goce and John Frost, so they are in mercy. The jurors attest that they have not come to an agreement. Augustine's amercement[1] is half a mark by the surety of Gerard the Scot.[1]

[1] The fact that the amount of the amercement is entered here, as well as in the amercements section, probably indicates that Augustine after all came to the eyre.

1593. Philip the son of Robert appealed Roger le Aungle of breach of the King's peace etc. He did not sue, and he found sureties for prosecuting, namely: John the brother of the same Philip and Mathew the son of Robert, so they are all in mercy (*amercements*). Later Roger came and made fine by ten shillings by the surety of Andrew the son of Augustine (*10 shillings*).

The same appealed Stephen Frese and Richard Frese of abetment. All the appellees come. The jurors attest that they have not come to an agreement. They attest also that the said Roger gave him a wound as he appealed him and that Stephen and Richard abetted him. So all are to be remanded in custody. Later Stephen and Richard came and made fine by ten shillings by the surety of ... (*10 shillings*).[1]

[1] The sureties are named in the amercements section as Gerard of Hazelwood and William Wetecake (**1665**).

1594. Cecilia the widow of Alexander Eyol was found drowned in the pit in front of the gate of John the son of Robert in Dunwich. No one is suspected thereof. Judgment: misadventure. John Le Envoyse found her first and has died. Walter de Gynes[1] and Thomas de Fonte, two of the neighbours attached for that death, do not come. They were attached by William Bernard and William Qwacke, John le Pesuner and Alexander the son of William, so they are in mercy.

[1] Perhaps Guînes near Calais, a pointer to the port of Dunwich's cross-Channel connections.

1595. Matilda the widow of Osbert Scamund (nothing) appealed Amisius Schamund of the death of Osbert her husband. She has not prosecuted, and she found a surety for prosecuting, namely: William Pulleko, so he is in mercy. Amisius does not come and he was arrested and committed to Peter Rokelin and Hubert Ringolf, who were then the bailiffs of the vill. He fled to the church of All Saints in Dunwich and abjured the realm, so to judgment on them for the escape. He was in the leet in the North Gate suburb, so the leet is in mercy.[1] He had no chattels.

The same appealed John Burgeys and Alice his wife of abetment. They come and the jurors attest that they are not guilty of the death, so they are acquitted thereof.

[1] Leets, which were seemingly peculiar to East Anglia, originated before 1066 as subdivisions of hundreds, with fiscal and judicial functions. In Dunwich they survived as the basis for a system of mutual responsibility akin to frankpledge, with their adult male inhabitants being responsible for one another's good behaviour. A North leet appears in **1601** below, and a St Martin's leet was referred to at the 1251 Suffolk eyre. JUST 1/1177B m. 12. J. Campbell, 'Hundreds and leets: a survey with suggestions', in C. Harper-Bill (ed.), *Medieval East Anglia* (Woodbridge, 2005), pp. 153–67.

1596. Walter the mason fell from the top of the Temple building of Dunwich[1] and died at once. Bernard the son of Ralph (he has died) found him first and he does not come and he was attached by William de *Mullegos* (he has died) and Simon the son of Lece (he has nothing), so all are in mercy. No one is suspected thereof. Judgment: misadventure (*misadventure*). The four neighbours have come.

1 There was a Templar preceptory in Dunwich no later than 1199, when it received confirmation in a charter from King John, itself confirmed by Henry III in 1227. Hardy, *Rotuli chartarum*, p. 3; *Calendar of Charter Rolls 1226–1257*, p. 8.

1597. Richard Frese,[1] mentioned above, appeals Thomas the son of Robert and Philip his brother of breach of the King's peace etc. Richard came and has withdrawn, so he and his sureties for prosecuting are in mercy, namely: Richard Peculf and Stephen Frese,[2] and Richard is to be remanded in custody. Thomas comes and the jurors attest that they have made an agreement, so he is to be remanded in custody. Philip does not come, and he was attached by Michael the son of Walter and Alexander the son of Gerard, so they are in mercy. Later Thomas came and made fine by half a mark (*half a mark*).[3]

1 See **1593** above, where Philip son of Robert is recorded as having appealed Richard Frese of abetting an assault but did not come to court to prosecute his action.
2 In the amercements section these men are said to have been the sureties of Richard son of Robert (**1665**).
3 This sentence is written in a different hand from the rest of the entry.

1598. Anketil of Framlingham, having falling sickness, was found drowned in a watercourse below Dunwich ditch. Alfred the miller found him first and he comes. No one is suspected thereof. Judgment: misadventure, and the four neighbours come (*misadventure*).

1599. The jurors present that a market has been newly set up at Southwold on Thursdays without warrant, to the detriment of the merchants of Dunwich, so let this be discussed (*it is to be discussed*).[1]

1 The abbot of St Edmund's had first obtained a grant of a Thursday market at Southwold in 1221; it was confirmed by Henry III on 5 April 1227, soon after he came of age. C 60/14 m. 4; *Calendar of Charter Rolls 1226–1257*, p. 30.

1600. (*Blything*) Thomas of Creake (he has nothing) appealed Peter the son of Robert of Dunwich and Andrew the son of Augustine of breach of the peace and robbery etc. Thomas does not come, and he found sureties for prosecuting, namely: Robert Snow of Dunwich and William the son of Hugh of Holton, so they are in mercy. Peter has not come, and he was attached by Robert the clerk of Dunwich and Thomas the son of Robert of the same (nothing), so they are in mercy. Andrew comes. The jurors attest that they have not come to an agreement, nor is he guilty, so he is acquitted thereof (*he is to be acquitted*).

1601. Nicholas the son of Matthew appeals Simon the son of Warin, Peter the son of Robert, Nicholas Speny, Arnold Hillerheyl and Walter del Ars of breach of the King's peace and robbery. Peter the son of Robert, Nicholas Speny and Walter del Ars come. Simon and Arnold were outlawed in the county court by Nicholas's suit. They were in the North Leet of Dunwich, so it is in mercy. They had no chattels.

The same appeals Adam Childerfader, John Aubin, Robert le Mordan and Gilbert the son of Nicholas of abetment, and they come. Later Nicholas comes, and he does not wish to prosecute, so he and his sureties for prosecuting are in mercy.[1] He made fine for himself and his sureties by one mark, by the surety of John the son of Augustine and Lambert de *Holming* (*1 mark*). The jurors attest that they are not guilty, so they are acquitted thereof.

[1] There is no marginal note for this amercement, but it is entered in the amercements section, **1665**.

AMERCEMENTS OF THE CROWN FROM THE COUNTY OF SUFFOLK BEFORE WILLIAM OF YORK AND HIS FELLOWS

Membrane 56 *AALT 4496–7*

The Hundred of Bosmere

1602.	*£*	*s.*	*d.*
From that hundred for murder, the liberties excepted, five marks. [**1162** and **1164**]	3	6	8
From Offton vill because it did not pursue, one mark. [**1161**]	0	13	4
From the tithing of Gerard Stubbing in Offton for the flight of Richard Stubbard, half a mark. [**1161**]	0	6	8
From Creeting St Olaves vill because it did not raise the hue, half a mark. [**1162**]	0	6	8
From John de Ulecote, sheriff, for the chattels of Gilbert the smith, fugitive, eighteen shillings and two pence. [**1165**]	0	18	2
From [Easton] Gosbeck vill for harbouring Gilbert outside a tithing, one mark. [**1165**]	0	13	4
From Robert the son of Gilbert de Mora for trespass, half a mark, by the surety of William Putsoft of Creeting and Nicholas Pik of Darmsden. [**1168**][1]	0	6	8
From Earl Stonham vill because it did not pursue, two marks. [**1170**]	1	6	8
From Battisford vill because it did not pursue, ten shillings. [**1172**]	0	10	0
From the tithings of John Cook and Geoffrey the son of Alan of Battisford for the flight of Simon Aliday and Reynold of Stonham,[2] half a mark. [**1172**]	0	6	8
From the same sheriff for Simon's chattels, twenty-seven shillings and four pence. [**1172**]	1	7	4
From the same sheriff for the year and a day's waste of [the land of] Simon, fourteen shillings and four pence. [**1172**]	0	14	4
From the same sheriff for Reynold's chattels, twenty-three shillings.[3] [**1172**]	1	3	0

From the Prior of the Hospital of Jerusalem in England for Reynold's chattels, twelve shillings. **[1172]**	0	12	0
From Gerard the son of Alice of Hemingstone and Walter Dragestraw of the same for trespass, half a mark. **[1173]**	0	6	8
From the tithing of Alexander the son of Hugh in Earl Stonham for the flight of Geoffrey the son of Reinerus, half a mark. **[1176]**	0	6	8
From the same sheriff, for Geoffrey's chattels, three shillings. **[1176]**	0	3	0
From Robert Wighe of Bramford and Richard Curke of Coddenham because they did not have [Edith the wife of Robert Wighe] for whom they stood surety, half a mark. **[1177]**	0	6	8
From John de *Offewde* for trespass, one mark. **[1179]**	0	13	4
From John the sheriff for the chattels of Alexander de *Ulvertoft* and the year, day and waste of his land, eight shillings. **[1181]**	0	8	0

1 The same sureties guaranteed the amercement which Robert incurred in the civil plea which accompanied this action. *Suffolk Civil Pleas*, **166, 1642**.

2 Reynold Stannard in the text.

3 In the text the value of Reynold's chattels is given as 33 shillings.

1603.

From the tithing of Walter Mor in Earl Stonham for the flight of Geoffrey Herlepik, half a mark. **[1182]**	0	6	8
From John the sheriff for Geoffrey's chattels, five shillings. **[1182]**	0	5	0
From the abbot of Grestain for default, twenty shillings. **[1183]**	1	0	0
From the abbot of Bernay for the same, twenty shillings. **[1183]**	1	0	0
From the abbot of Bec-Hellouin for the same, forty shillings.[1] **[1183]**	2	0	0
From Philip of Winston for a false presentment and concealment, ten shillings.[2] **[1162]**	0	10	0
From Robert Lenveyse and Robert le Blund for the same, half a mark. **[1162]**	0	6	8
From Robert of Olden for the same, half a mark. **[1162]**	0	6	8
From Ranulf Wigghe for the same, one mark. **[1162]**	0	13	4
From Ralph of Mickfield for the same, half a mark. **[1162]**	0	6	8
From Augustine of Blakenham for the same, half a mark. **[1162]**	0	6	8
From Sewal of Ringshall for the same, half a mark. **[1162]**	0	6	8
From John the son of Baldwin of Offton for the same, half a mark. **[1162]**	0	6	8
From Bartholomew of Stonham for the same, half a mark. **[1162]**	0	6	8

From Robert of Bickerwick[3] for the same, half a mark. **[1162]**	0	6	8
From Great Bricett vill for concealment, half a mark. **[1185]**	0	6	8

1 The abbot of Bec's larger amercement reflects the greater wealth of his house, rather than his failure to attend the eyre having been somehow more culpable than that of the other Norman abbots.

2 This and the following nine amercements constitute the first of a number of instances in which the record of the eyre's financial issues helps to make up for the absence of a jury kalendar by identifying some or all of a hundred's jurors.

3 A lost place-name in Ashbocking. See Briggs, *Suffolk place-names*, p. 358.

Total for the Hundred of Bosmere [36 amercements]	**23**	**17**	**6**

The Borough of Eye by twelve

1604.

From the tithing of William of Chevington for the flight of Leofric, half a mark.[1] **[1210]**	0	6	8
From John Faukun of Eye for selling cloth contrary to the assize, one mark. **[1187]**	0	13	4
From William the merchant of the same for the same, half a mark. **[1187]**	0	6	8
From Gervase the merchant of the same for the same, one mark. **[1187]**	0	13	4
From Anketill the merchant of the same for the same, half a mark. **[1187]**	0	6	8
From Matthew Luvcecok of the same for the same, half a mark. **[1187]**	0	6	8
From Alexander of Kettleburgh for selling wine contrary to the assize, one mark. **[1188]**	0	13	4

1 Leofric Dyrunt is in the text.

Total for the Borough of Eye [7 amercements]	**3**	**6**	**8**

The Hundred of Hartismere

1605.

From that hundred for murder, the liberties excepted, forty shillings. **[1191]**	2	0	0
From John the sheriff for the chattels of Burghard, hanged, eighteen pence. **[1209]**	0	1	6

From Guy de Verdon, fine for the trespass of his men, twenty pounds, by the surety of Richard the Butler, Hugh Burt, Robert de Bosco, Robert Malet, John de *Curton'*, William de Verdon, William of Sproughton and Nicholas of St Edmund's.[1] **[1192]**	20	0	0
From Robert of Boxted because he did not prosecute his appeal, half a mark. **[1192]**	0	6	8
From William de Verdun because he did not have [Matthew Piketheu] for whom he stood surety, ten shillings. **[1192]**	0	10	0
From Richard the Butler of Upton for the same, one mark. **[1193]**	0	13	4
From the tithing of John Catum in Burgate for the flight of Warin of Stebbing, half a mark. **[1196]**	0	6	8
From Thomas de Hemmegrave for Warin's chattels, six pounds, nineteen shillings and eight pence. **[1196]**	6	19	8
From John the sheriff for the same man's chattels, nine shillings. **[1196]**	0	9	0
From the same sheriff for the year, day and waste of Warin's land, four pounds, four shillings and four pence. **[1196]**	4	4	4
From John the sheriff for Warin's chattels, two shillings. **[1196]**	0	2	0
From Richard Bern and William the painter of Eye[2] because they did not have [Edmund the fuller] for whom they stood surety, half a mark. **[1196]**.	0	6	8
From Martin of Bacton and Nigel the son of Walter of Haughley for the same,[3] half a mark. **[1197]**	0	6	8
From Oakley vill for harbouring William of Eleigh, one mark. **[1198]**	0	13	4
From John the sheriff for William's chattels, forty-two shillings. **[1198]**	2	2	0
From William of Hoo for having the land and waste of the same man's land, twenty shillings, by the surety of John de Crammaville and William Godwin.[4] **[1198]**	1	0	0
From John de Crammaville[5] for trespass, ten shillings, by the surety of Matthew de Gerardvile. **[1200]**	0	10	0
From William Gernun because he did not have [Robert the son of William] for whom he stood surety, half a mark. **[1200]**	0	6	8
From Alan the son of Richard the parson of Thornham for the same, half a mark.[6] **[1200]**	0	6	8
From William de Cumpenye of Cotton because he did not have [Robert the son of William] for whom he stood surety, half a mark. **[1200]**	0	6	8

1 Robert of Waldingfield is also named as a surety in the text.

2 In the text he is recorded as coming from Finningham, a little over five miles south-west of Eye.

3 *Sic* – they failed to produce Emma the daughter of Martin of Bicton in court.

4 William of Stuston in the text.

5 John de Gerardvile in the text.

6 Alan stood surety for Adam the son of Thomas, as did Sewal the tailor, not mentioned here.

1606.

From Henry[1] de Blogate of Yaxley for the same, half a mark. **[1202]**	0	6	8
From William Burghard, fine because he withdrew, half a mark by the surety of Nicholas the son of Emma of Braiseworth and Hugh the reeve of Benningham. **[1202]**	0	6	8
From Everard de *Catton*, fine for trespass, one mark, by the surety of Hugh de Blogate. **[1202]**	0	13	4
From Gilbert the son of William de *Kaketon* for the same, two marks, by the surety of Hugh de Blogate, John the son of Peter de *Kaketon*, Everard of Sutton and Alexander the son of William of Yaxley. **[1202]**	1	6	8
From the tithing of Roger Spir of Wortham for the flight of Richard the son of Robert Hare, half a mark. **[1206]**	0	6	8
From John the sheriff for Richard's chattels, six shillings and nine pence. **[1206]**	0	6	9
From John the sheriff for the chattels of Roger de Furnaus, fugitive, and for the year, day and waste of his land, four pounds nineteen shillings. **[1195** and **1550]**	4	19	0
From Alexander Ketel of Stow and William the son of Ralph of Potsford[2] because they did not have [John de Couele] for whom they stood surety, half a mark. **[1211]**	0	6	8
From the tithing of Robert the baker of Wyverstone for the flight of Andrew Dandeler, half a mark. **[1212]**	0	6	8
From Hubert of Braiseworth for a false presentment, half a mark. **[1191]**[3]	0	6	8
From William of Cotton for the same, half a mark. **[1191]**	0	6	8
From Robert of Thrandeston and William the son of Robert for the same, half a mark. **[1191]**.	0	6	8
From William de Boseuil and Walter of Westhorpe for the same, half a mark. **[1191]**	0	6	8
From William le Potere of Wetheringsett for the same, half a mark. **[1191]**	0	6	8
From Manserus Wygeyn of the same for the same, half a mark. **[1191]**	0	6	8
From Richard of Caldecott and Bartholomew de Brech' for the same, half a mark. **[1191]**	0	6	8

From William Havel of Bacton for the same, half a mark. **[1191]**	0	6	8
From John Cordebof for the same, half a mark. **[1191]**	0	6	8

1 Hugh de Blogate in the text, no doubt correctly. He will have been identical with the Hugh de Blogate of Yaxley who also occurs in the civil pleas, **424**, **1646**.

2 The clerk initially wrote *Polstede*, but for once corrected the name to bring it into line with the main text.

3 This and the eight following entries provide another example of a hundred's jurors being identified by the amercements imposed on them.

Total for the Hundred of Hartismere [38 amercements]	**53**	**11**	**11**
Total for Membrane 56	**80**	**16**	**1**
Sum Total 120 marks, 12 shillings, 5 pence[1]	**80**	**12**	**5**

1 These figures, which are those of the clerk, reveal a shortfall of three shillings and seven pence.

Membrane 56d *AALT 4619–20*

The Borough of Beccles by Twelve

1607.

From Robert Edgard of Beccles and Alan Waghas for false measures, half a mark. **[1218]**	0	6	8
From Robert de Halc for selling cloth contrary to the assize, half a mark. **[1219]**	0	6	8
From Roger of Weston for the same, ten shillings. **[1219]**	0	10	0
From Alexander of Kessingland for the same, half a mark. **[1219]**	0	6	8
From Alan the baker for selling wine contrary to the assize, half a mark. **[1220]**	0	6	8
From Simon Walram, Philip of Ingate and their associates, fine for trespass, sixty shillings, by the surety of Roger[1] the engineer of Weston and Philip the son of William of Beccles. **[1222]**	3	0	0
From John the sheriff for the chattels of Roger Fusel, fugitive, twelve pence. **[1223]**	0	1	0
From Philip the son of William of Beccles, fine for trespass, half a mark.[2] **[1221]**	0	6	8
From John the son of Osbert of the same and Thomas the cook of the same for the same, half a mark. **[1221]**	0	6	8
From Ivo Mulard and Robert de Wathe for the same, half a mark. **[1221]**	0	6	8
From Reynold the merchant and William de la Grene of the same for the same, half a mark. **[1221]**	0	6	8
From Alan the smith, Bartholomew the merchant, William the son of Ernulf of the same for the same, half a mark. **[1221]**	0	6	8

From … [unfinished]

1 Robert in the text.

2 This and the four following entries will represent the penalties imposed upon men of Beccles for their malicious indictment of Adam Talifer and others.

Total for the Borough of Beccles [12 amercements]	**6**	**11**	**0**

The Hundred of Stow by Twelve

1608.

From the same hundred for murder, the liberties excepted, two marks. [**1224**, **1227** and **1241**]	1	6	8
From Buxhall vill because it did not pursue, one mark. [**1226**]	0	13	4
From Thomas the son of Ordiner of the same because he did not come, half a mark. [**1226**]	0	6	8
From John Coppenger and Adam Tytenund of the same because they did not have [Thomas the son of Ordiner] for whom they stood surety, half a mark. [**1226**]	0	6	8
From William Putsoft, fine for trespass, half a mark, by the surety of Stephen le Heyr of Creeting and Alexander de Prato of the same. [**1231**]	0	6	8
From Humphrey Sytte because he withdrew, and from Robert Cokerel, fine for trespass, five marks, by the surety of John of Gedding and Adam Cokerel.[1] [**1232**]	3	6	8
From the tithing of Ralph Oky in Wetherden for the flight of William Fuche,[2] half a mark. [**1235**]	0	6	8
From the tithing of John Heyward for the flight of Thomas Drumbel, half a mark. [**1235**]	0	6	8
From the tithing of Ranulf Yring in Haughley for the flight of John the son of Simon, ten shillings.[3] [**1237**]	0	10	0
From the tithing of Reynold[4] Perdut for the flight of William Scut, ten shillings. [**1237**]	0	10	0
From the tithing of Woolward of Thorney in Thorney for the flight of Peter Ailwin.[5] [**1238**]	0	10	0
From the tithing of Sewal le Noreys in Combs for the flight of Alan the son of Hugh, ten shillings. [**1238**]	0	10	0
From John the sheriff for the same Peter's chattels, three shillings.[6] [**1238**]	0	3	0
From Steeple Creeting vill for trespass, one mark. [**1241**]	0	13	4
From William de Alneto and Geoffrey the son of Clement and their fellows, the twelve jurors, for trespass, forty shillings. [**1241**]	2	0	0

From John the sheriff for the chattels of Thomas Drumbel, fugitive, three shillings. **[1235]**	0	3	0

1 Although the text does not say so, this entry shows a single fine being made by appellor and appellees together.
2 Fyke in the text.
3 This and the following entry are linked by lines to the sum of ten shillings, indicating that a single amercement was imposed on the two tithings.
4 Roger in the text.
5 Again, lines connect this entry and its successor to the sum of ten shillings.
6 This entry has been squeezed in one place in the record too low by the clerk. What is entered as the value of Peter's chattels is the value of his chattels and land together.

Total for the Hundred of Stow [14 amercements]	**10**	**19**	**4**

The Hundred of Mutford by Six

1609.

From Walkelin[1] de Ardern for default, half a mark. **[1244]**	0	6	8
From Ranulf de Maresbarwe for the same, half a mark. **[1244]**	0	6	8
From Hugh of Tynemouth for the same, half a mark. **[1244]**	0	6	8
From the Prior of Broomholm for the same, half a mark. **[1244]**	0	6	8

1 William in the text.

Total for the Half Hundred of Mutford [4 amercements]	**1**	**6**	**8**

The Borough of Bungay by Twelve

1610.

From Bungay vill because it did not pursue, forty shillings. **[1248]**	2	0	0
From Roger of Attleborough for trespass, half a mark. **[1246]**	0	6	8
From Geoffrey le Sour of Bungay and Robert Demur of Elmham because they did not have [Sylvester Hauec, Geoffrey the cooper and William Kenop] for whom they stood surety, half a mark. **[1249]**	0	6	8
From Reynold Godman of Bungay and Geoffrey Godman of the same because they did not have [Benedict Harding] for whom they stood surety, half a mark. **[1250]**	0	6	8
From Adam Cutel of Bungay for selling cloths contrary to the assize, one mark.	0	13	4
From Walter de Florendun for the same, half a mark.[1] **[1251]**	0	6	8

1 Walter appears as Walter Floret of Bungay in the text, while Adam Cutel does not occur in it at all.

Total for the Borough of Bungay [6 amercements]	**4**	**0**	**0**

The Hundred of Claydon by Twelve[1]

[1] In the text Thredling hundred is said to be a third of Claydon hundred. Its pleas are nevertheless entered separately, but here the issues of both hundreds are enrolled together. In what follows, nos. **1264**, **1266**, **1269** and **1270** belong to Thredling.

1611.

From that hundred for murder, liberties excepted, forty shillings. [**1257**]	2	0	0
From Robert the Smith of Sharpstone because he withdrew, four marks, by the surety of Geoffrey of Denton, William of Holbrook, Bartholomew of Tuddenham, Richard de Bosco and Robert of Roding.[1] [**1253**]	2	13	4
From the tithing of Michael Aylward in Helmingham for the flight of John the Fuller, half a mark. [**1256**]	0	6	8
From the tithing of Herbert Pennecake in Barham for the flight of Roger the son of Richard, half a mark. [**1256**]	0	6	8
From Whitton vill because it did not pursue, ten shillings.[2] [**1258**]	0	10	0
From the tithing of William Panel[3] in Thurleston for the flight of John Unsalt, half a mark. [**1258**]	0	6	8
From John the sheriff for John's chattels, four shillings. [**1258**]	0	4	0
From the same sheriff for the chattels of William the tailor, hanged, sixteen shillings and six pence. [**1654**]	0	16	6
From the tithing of William Shori of Thurleston for the flight of Adam Shory, ten shillings.[4] [**1260**]	0	10	0
From the tithing of Justus of Thurleston for the flight of Walter the son of Augustine, ten shillings. [**1260**]	0	0	0
From Thomas the son of Aucher[5] for default, half a mark. [**1262**]	0	6	8
From the tithing of Simon le May in Otley for the flight of Fulk le May, half a mark. [**1263**]	0	6	8
From Geoffrey Carbunel, William the son of Humphrey, William of Claydon and their fellows, the twelve jurors, fine for trespass, forty shillings. [**1258**, **1263**]	2	0	0
From Debenham vill for concealment, forty shillings. [**1264**]	2	0	0
From William Fich of Cotton and his associates, fine for trespass, four marks by the surety of Hubert Gernagan, William of Cotton, Richard the son of Joce of the same, Hugh the son of Richard of the same, Richard the son of Ascelin[6] of the same and Hamo le Neve of Thorney. [**1266**]	2	13	4
From Roger the smith of Debenham, fine for trespass, forty shillings by the surety of Robert of Kenton and Walkelin of the same.[7] [**1269**]	2	0	0

From John Blacheghe for the same, twenty shillings by the surety of Ranulf Wigge and Alexander Moyne. **[1269]**	1	0	0
From William de Rovile of Brandeston because he did not have [Richard the Miller of Brandeston] for whom he stood surety. **[1270]**	0	6	8
From Henry of Barnack and William the son of Henry of the same for the same, half a mark. **[1270]**	0	6	8
From Thomas Doket and Roger de Bovil[8] for the same, half a mark. **[1270]**	0	6	8
From William the miller and Robert de Modidun for the same, half a mark. **[1270]**	0	6	8
From Nicholas Colgrim and William Fide for the same, half a mark. **[1270]**	0	6	8
From Warin the son of the clerk and Geoffrey de Bosco for the same, half a mark. **[1270]**	0	6	8
From Robert the son of the clerk and Thomas Warin for the same, half a mark. **[1270]**	0	6	8
From Gilbert Arnold,[9] Roger Belly and Alan Pullehare for the same, half a mark. **[1270]**	0	6	8

1 An inaccurate entry – in the main text John, not Robert, the smith withdrew his appeal, and in any case it was not he but the men he appealed who made a four-mark fine.
2 In the text this amercement was imposed on Ulveston vill – see the editorial note.
3 In the text he appears as William Daniel, but Panel was probably the correct form of his name. In **1260** the tithing of William Panel in Thurleston is in mercy for the flight of one of its members, but no amercement is entered in this section of the roll, presumably because the tithing had been penalised already.
4 Connecting lines link this tithing to the one in the next entry, showing that together they owed ten shillings.
5 Aunger in the text.
6 Anselm in the text.
7 Another inaccuracy. The fine was not made by Roger the smith but by Roger of Winston who had maliciously indicted him.
8 Roger de Roville in the text.
9 Arum in the text.

Total for the Hundred of Claydon [24 amercements]	**20**	**13**	**10**

Liberty of the prior of Ely: The Hundred of Plomesgate by Eighteen

1612.

From the hundred, the liberties excepted, four marks.[1] **[1275]**	2	13	4
From Rendham vill because it did not pursue, one mark. **[1272]**	0	13	4
From the tithing of Fulk de *Museholt* for the flight of Richard Caperun, half a mark. **[1272]**	0	6	8

From John the sheriff for Richard's chattels, four pence. **[1272]**	0	0	4
From the tithing of William Broc of Rendham for the flight of Roger the son of Hugh, half a mark. **[1274]**	0	6	8
From the tithing of William Knict in Benhall for the flight of John Cucku, half a mark. **[1276]**	0	6	8
From Farnham vill because it did not pursue, half a mark. **[1278]**	0	6	8
From Aldeburgh vill for the same, half a mark. **[1279]**	0	6	8
From the tithing of Nicholas Broc for the flight of William his son, half a mark. **[1282]**	0	6	8
From the tithing of William Bacun in Nortgreneham[2] for the flight of Ranulf Cubbel, half a mark. **[1283]**	0	6	8
From the prior of Ely for an escape, fifty shillings. **[1284]**	2	10	0
From William d'Auberville for the same, fifty shillings.[3] **[1284]**	2	10	0

1 The hundred's murder fine
2 Clearly identical with the *Nordgleman*, that is, Great Glemham, of the text.
3 The justices called for judgment on the prior and William for the escape, for which a hundred shillings was the usual penalty. These two amercements show the two lords paying half each.

Total for the Hundred of Plomesgate [12 amercements]	**10**	**13**	**8**

The Hundred of Carlford

1613.

From the hundred, the liberties excepted, forty shillings.[1] **[1287]**	2	0	0
From the tithing of Roger Nyvi[2] for the flight of Roger Pace, half a mark. **[1286]**	0	6	8
From the prior of Ely for Roger's chattels, four shillings and two pence. **[1286]**	0	4	2
From the tithing of John the son of Reinerus of Witnesham for the flight of Reynold Kelle,[3] half a mark. **[1288]**	0	6	8
From the tithing of Peter Lewin in Kesgrave for the flight of Simon of the same, half a mark. **[1289]**	0	6	8
From the tithing of Luke the son of Humphrey of Otley for the flight of Luke King, half a mark. **[1292]**	0	6	8

1 The hundred's murder fine.
2 *Newou* in the text – 'nephew' in both forms.
3 *Lolle* in the text.

Sum Total 86 marks[1]	**57**	**6**	**8**

1 There are traces of an additional word, now illegible, after the main figure, which may represent a further small sum. As it stands, the clerk's total shows a shortfall of eight shillings and eight pence by comparison with the figures recorded on this membrane.

Total for Membrane 56d	**57**	**15**	**4**

Membrane 57 *AALT 4498–9*

Still Carlford[1]

1 For the whole of this membrane, on both sides, totals are given for each presenting area as well as the usual sum totals for each side of the membrane. They appear to have been inserted by another clerk, writing in a different hand and employing different abbreviations from those used for the individual entries.

1614.

From the prior of Ely for Luke's chattels, five shillings. **[1292]**	0	5	0
From the prior for the chattels of Richard the son of Roger of Kettleburgh, hanged, thirty-six shillings, two pence. **[1293]**	1	16	2
From Ernulf of Kettleburgh, fine for the year and day from Richard's land, thirty-two shillings by the surety of Robert of Roding and Roger of Carlton. **[1293]**	1	12	0
Total 73 shillings and 2 pence	**3**	**13**	**2**
Total for Carlford Hundred [Nine Amercements][1]	**7**	**4**	**0**

1 The clerk gave only the figures for Carlford entered on m. 57, not those already entered on m. 56d, so leaving his total for the hundred incomplete by £3 10s. 10d.

The Hundred of Wilford by Twelve

1615.

From the same hundred for murder, the liberties excepted, sixty shillings. **[1296, 1297]**	3	0	0
From Henry Prat, fine for trespass, half a mark. **[1297]**	0	6	8
From William the son of Hervey[1] for the same, half a mark by the surety of Gervase of Bredfield. **[1296]**	0	6	8
From Pettistree vill because it did not pursue, one mark. **[1298]**	0	13	4
From Loudham vill for the same, ten shillings. **[1300]**	0	10	0
From Ranulf the son of Godwin[2] because he did not prosecute his appeal, and from William Blacsune of Bing and William Kempe, sureties for Richard [*sic*], half a mark. **[1301]**	0	6	8
From Robert the son of Hugh of Pettistree, Roger Copsi of the same and Goscelin the son of Osbert, half a mark.[3] **[1301]**	0	6	8
From the prior of Ely for the chattels of Alexander Wyffin, sixteen shillings, six pence. **[1302]**	0	16	6
From Robert the son of Edward of Boyton and Robert the son of Alan of the same for the same,[4] half a mark. **[1303]**	0	6	8

1 Henry in the text.
2 Godiva in the text.
3 Sureties for Baldwin Buck.

4 Not for the first or only time, the clerk was careless. The two men were amerced because they stood surety for an appellor who failed to prosecute.

Total checked, 6 pounds, 13 shillings and 2 pence [9 amercements]	**6**	**13**	**2**

The Hundred of Colneis by Twelve

1616.

From the same hundred for murder, the liberties excepted, forty shillings. [**1309**]	2	0	0
From Ralph de Hamme of Foxhall and Thomas de Ponte because they did not have [Simon the son of the chaplain] for whom they stood surety. [**1309**]	0	6	8
From Nigel the smith of Trimley for an encroachment, half a mark. [**1311**]	0	6	8
From Gilbert de Blevile of Walton and Bruning of Grimston[1] for default, half a mark. [**1312**]	0	6	8

1 Brun de *Latguine* in the text

Total checked 60 shillings [4 amercements]	**3**	**0**	**0**

The Borough of Orford by Twelve

1617.

From Orford vill, fine for drapers and vintners, four marks. [**1317** and **1318**]	2	13	4
From Eye vill for harbouring Reynold the son of Gilbert outside frankpledge, half a mark. [**1320**]	0	6	8
Total checked 60 shillings [2 amercements]	**3**	**0**	**0**

The Hundred of Loes by Twelve

1618.

From Nicholas of Easton and William le Daneys and their fellows, the twelve jurors, fine for concealment, forty shillings. [**1341**]	2	0	0
From the tithing of Andrew the son of Nicholas of Easton for the flight of Adam the son of Geoffrey, half a mark. [**1326**]	0	6	8
From the prior of Ely for Adam's chattels, six shillings and six pence. [**1326**]	0	6	6

From the prior for the year, day and waste of Adam's land, three shillings and eight pence. **[1326]**	0	3	8
From the tithing of Walter Pillecok[1] in Kenton for the flight of Robert Pepelin, half a mark. **[1327]**	0	6	8
From the prior of Ely for Robert's chattels, four shillings. **[1327]**	0	4	0
From Kenton vill because it did not pursue, ten shillings. **[1327]**	0	10	0
From Andrew the serjeant of Margery la Bigote, fine for trespass, one mark by the surety of William of Holbrook. **[1328]**	0	13	4
From William Brictwald[2] of Ash and Robert Clift of the same because they did not have [William Lanis] for whom they stood surety, half a mark. **[1330]**	0	6	8
From Roger the son of Ayleva[3] of Ash and Robert the son of Roger of Campsey Ash for the same, half a mark. **[1330]**	0	6	8
From Baldwin of Easton for selling cloths contrary to the assize, half a mark. **[1333]**	0	6	8
From the tithing of Robert the carpenter of Framlingham for the flight of Alfred,[4] half a mark. **[1335]**	0	6	8
From the tithing of William the serjeant in Framlingham for the flight of Walter the son of William, half a mark. **[1335]**	0	6	8

1 Pileroc in the text.
2 Bricnoth in the text.
3 Alfred in the text.
4 Another clerical error – the fugitives from this tithing were Hugh and Robert Hachard.

Total checked 6 pounds, 4 shillings, 2 pence [13 amercements]	**6**	**4**	**2**

The Borough of Elmham by Three[1]

1 Six in the text.

1619.

From James King of Elmham and William Blokere of the same because they did not have [Benedict the weaver] for whom they stood surety, half a mark. **[1342]**	0	6	8
From the tithing of Reynold[1] Brun for the flight of Benedict the weaver, half a mark. **[1342]**	0	6	8
From the bishop of Norwich for Benedict's chattels, one mark. **[1342]**	0	13	4
From Elmham vill for murder, one mark. **[1343]**	0	13	4
From that vill because it did not pursue, one mark. **[1342]**	0	13	4
From Henry Buscel of Flixton because he did not prosecute his appeal, half a mark. **[1345]**	0	6	8

From Roger del Hil of Wissett and Andrew the son of Oliver of the same because they did not have [the person[2]] for whom they stood surety, half a mark. **[1345?]**	0	6	8
From Henry the son of William of Elmham,[3] fine for trespass, one mark by the surety of Henry de Bosco and Henry le Sor of Flixton. **[1345]**	0	13	4
From the tithing of Gerard the son of Richard of Elmham for the flight of Robert Bruning and William his brother, half a mark. **[1346]**	0	6	8

1 Roger in the text.

2 A baffling entry. From its position one would expect the man who failed to attend the eyre to have been the Henry Buscel named in the previous entry, but in the text his sureties are said to have been Osbert del Brok and Robert the son of the clerk, both of Elmham, neither of whom occurs elsewhere in the eyre roll. The fact that the man whose appearance they guaranteed is unidentified suggests that the clerk was puzzled too.

3 Henry the son of Roger in the text.

Total checked 4 pounds, 6 shillings and 8 pence [9 amercements]	**4**	**6**	**8**

The Hundred of Wangford by Nine

1620.

From John the sheriff for the chattels of Ivetta of Bures, hanged, twenty shillings. **[1347]**	1	0	0
From Nicholas Newman because he did not have [Avelina the wife of William the Norman] for whom he stood surety, half a mark. **[1348]**	0	6	8
From John the sheriff for the chattels of Robert Woodward, fugitive, two shillings. **[1348]**	0	2	0
From the tithing of Geoffrey Rode in Mettingham for the flight of John the son of Roger,[1] half a mark. **[1349]**	0	6	8
From the tithing of William Garneys in Ilketshall for the flight of Elyas Bissop, half a mark. **[1359]**	0	6	8
From the tithing of William Leverich in the same for the flight of Ralph Tendy, half a mark. **[1359]**	0	6	8

1 John the son of Henry Hakede in the text.

Total checked 48 shillings and 8 pence [6 amercements]	**2**	**8**	**8**

Hundred of Hoxne by Twelve

1621.

From Badingham vill for murder, forty shillings. **[1363]**	2	0	0

From Laxfield vill because it did not pursue, forty shillings. **[1362]**	2	0	0
From Humphrey de *Criketoft* for a false appeal, half a mark by the surety of Benedict de *Bricholt* and Roger le Frances of Earsham.[1] **[1361]**	0	6	8
From Robert Ters, fine for trespass, one mark by the surety of Adam of Mendham and Thomas Sharp. **[1361]**	0	13	4
From Guy the son of Gilbert of Laxton[2] because he did not have [Agnes Litewif] for whom he stood surety, ten shillings. **[1362]**	0	10	0
From Daniel Herre of the same, Walter the carpenter of the same and Geoffrey Hem of the same, half a mark. **[1362]**	0	6	8
From Matthew Ele of Whittingham and William Dole of the same because they did not have [Alexander of Elveden] for whom they stood surety, half a mark. **[1367]**	0	6	8
From Syleham vill for concealment, twenty shillings. **[1369]**	1	0	0
From Richard Stumpecok and Hervey the merchant of Horham because they did not come, half a mark. **[1370]**	0	6	8
From the tithing of William the tailor of Kelsale for the flight of Robert Hagene, half a mark. **[1373]**	0	6	8
From John the sheriff for Robert's chattels, fifteen pence. **[1373]**	0	1	3
From [the tithing of] William Buck in Tannington for the flight of Gerard Ruheved, half a mark. **[1373]**	0	6	8
From the vill of Kelsale for harbouring Richard of Westleton outside frankpledge, twenty shillings. **[1373]**	1	0	0
From the tithing of Simon of Banham in Bedfield for the flight of Adam the son of William, half a mark. **[1375]**	0	6	8
From Hubert of Tannington and his fellows, the twelve jurors, for a false presentment, twenty shillings. **[1367]**	1	0	0

1 An erasure in the main text probably marks the place where the sureties, named here, were to be recorded.

2 Ivo the son of Gilbert of Laxfield in the text. There is no Laxton in Suffolk.

Total checked 10 pounds, 11 shillings and 3 pence [15 amercements]	**10**	**11**	**3**

The Hundred of Samford by Eighteen

1622.

From the hundred for murder, the liberties excepted, five marks. **[1377, 1379, 1382** and **1383]**	3	6	8
From the tithing of Robert de *Saltemede* in Thorington for the flight of Geoffrey de Perer, half a mark. **[1376]**	0	6	8

From Sproughton vill because it did not pursue and for other trespasses, five marks. [**1377** and **1382**]	3	6	8
From Godwin Bullock, fine because he withdrew, one mark by the surety of Roger of Boyland and Michael of Freston. [**1378**]	0	13	4
From William of Badley, fine for a false appeal, half a mark by the surety of Hugh of Badley and Gerard[1] Richaut in Sproughton. [**1381**]	0	6	8
From John the sheriff for the chattels of Michael[2] the son of Godfrey, hanged, seventeen pence. [**1380**]	0	1	5
From Holbrook vill because it did not pursue, two marks. [**1383**]	1	6	8
From Maurice of Dodnash because he did not have [Roger the dauber] for whom he stood surety, half a mark. [**1384**]	0	6	8
From Geoffrey the son of Maurice of Dodnash, fine for trespass, one mark by the surety of Geoffrey de Bosco and Alexander of Stutton. [**1384**]	0	13	4
From Gerard the brother of Richard because he did not have [the person] for whom he stood surety, half a mark.[3] [**1385?**]	0	6	8
From Great Belstead vill because it did not pursue, four marks. [**1388**]	2	13	4
From John the son of John the chaplain, fine for trespass, one mark by the surety of John the son of Richard of Chattisham, Geoffrey the son of John and Thomas Maukel.[4] [**1394**]	0	13	4
From Nicholas the clerk of Hintlesham and Thomas the son of Baldwin of the same because they did not have [Walter the carpenter] for whom they stood surety, half a mark. [**1394**]	0	6	8
From John the sheriff for the chattels of Richard the brother[5] of Walter in Bergholt, forty-three shillings. [**1395**]	2	3	0
From the same for the land[6] and waste of Richard's land, one mark. [**1395**]	0	13	4

1 Geoffrey in the text.
2 Matthew in the text.
3 Another mysterious entry – no Gerard occurs among Samford's pleas.
4 Nauke in the text.
5 Richard son of Walter in the text.
6 *Sic* – a mistake for 'year'.

Total checked, 17 pounds, 4 shillings and 4 pence[1] [15 amercements]	**17**	**4**	**5**

1 The clerk is out by a penny, probably because he misread his colleague's badly formed entry for the chattels of Michael son of Godfrey (**1380**) as sixteen rather than seventeen pence.

Sum Total ——— 3 pence[1]

1 The foot of the membrane has been torn away, and only a few words are legible.

Total for Membrane 57	**57**	**1**	**6**

Membrane 57d *AALT 4621–2*

Still Samford

1623.

From the tithing of Hamo the son of Amice[1] in Freston for the flight of William Sprig,[2] half a mark. [**1396**]	0	6	8
From John the sheriff for the waste of William's land, two shillings. [**1396**]	0	2	0
From the tithing of Selicus Ars[3] for the flight of Simon the fuller, half a mark. [**1398**]	0	6	8
From John the sheriff for Simon's chattels, twenty shillings. [**1398**]	1	0	0
From the tithing of Henry of Wenham in Little Wenham for the flight of Robert Clop, half a mark. [**1399**]	0	6	8
From John the sheriff for Robert's chattels, forty pence. [**1399**]	0	3	4
From the tithing of Sampson of Boyton for the flight of Alan the son of Algar, half a mark. [**1400**]	0	6	8
From the tithing of Geoffrey Sadewe for the flight of Walter the son of Hugh, half a mark. [**1401**]	0	6	8
From William Pipard for default, one mark. [**1403**]	0	13	4
From the abbot of Aumâle for the same, five marks. [**1403**]	3	6	8
From James Lenveyse for concealment,[4] half a mark. [**1389** or **1397**]	0	6	8
From William the son of Robert of Raydon for the same and Walter of Stratford for the same, half a mark. [**1389** or **1397**]	0	6	8
From Alan the son of Roger of Brantham and Stephen Haute of the same for the same, half a mark. [**1389** or **1397**]	0	6	8
From Adam de Vallibus and Thomas of Dodnash for the same, half a mark. [**1389** or **1397**]	0	6	8
From Robert of Raydon and Robert de *Ikelesham* for the same, half a mark. [**1389** or **1397**]	0	6	8
From Osbert of Sproughton for the same, half a mark. [**1389** or **1397**]	0	6	8
From Richard de *Benton* for the same, half a mark. [**1389** or **1397**]	0	6	8
From Roger Iuvencel and John Testepin, half a mark. [**1389** or **1397**]	0	6	8

1 Emma in the text.
2 Spinc in the text.
3 Selicus of Wenham in the text.
4 This and the following seven entries, involving a total of thirteen people, will record the amercements twice imposed on the Samford jury for concealment (**1389**, **1397**).

Total checked 9 pounds, 12 shillings[1] [33 amercements]	**9**	**12**	**0**

[1] This is the total for Samford's amercements on this membrane only, the clerk did not provide one for that hundred's amercements as a whole.

The Hundred of Lothingland by Six

1624.

From the hundred for having a coroner, twenty marks. **[1430]**[1]	13	6	8
From the tithing of Warin Waghe in Somerleyton for the flight of Richard Kue, half a mark. **[1414]**	0	6	8
From John the sheriff for Richard's chattels, eighteen pence. **[1414]**	0	1	6
From Hobland vill because it did not pursue, one mark. **[1414]**	0	13	4
From Richard the son of Richard, fine for trespass, half a mark by the surety of Master Robert de L'Isle, the archdeacon of Colchester. **[1415]**	0	6	8
From Abraham the son of Thomas for the same, half a mark by the surety of the same archdeacon. **[1415]**	0	6	8
From William le Sauvage for trespass and that he may be under surety, twenty pounds by the surety of Alexander Aleyn of Yarmouth, Walter of St Etheldreda[2] of Norwich, John de Beaumes of Ipswich, Adam le Sauvage, Richard his brother, John le Sauvage and William le Leche.[3] **[1416]**	20	0	0
From the tithing of Adam of Corton in Corton for the flight of Gilbert of Kessingland, half a mark. **[1417]**	0	6	8
From John the sheriff for Gilbert's chattels, eighteen shillings. **[1417]**	0	18	0
From John the sheriff for the waste of his land, one mark. **[1417]**	0	13	4
From William Pepudros for selling wine contrary to the assize, half a mark. **[1421]**	0	6	8
From Thomas le Lutre of Little Yarmouth for selling cloth contrary to the assize, half a mark. **[1422]**	0	6	8
From Simon Aysman for the same, ten shillings. **[1422]**	0	10	0
From Robert de *Godinton*[4] for the same, half a mark. **[1422]**	0	6	8
From Thomas of Lowestoft for the same, half a mark. **[1422]**	0	6	8
From John the son of the parson of Somerleyton for trespass, one mark. **[1423]**	0	13	4
From the tithing of William of Thurlton in Little Yarmouth for the flight of Herbert of Raveningham, half a mark. **[1424]**	0	6	8
From John the sheriff for his chattels, thirty shillings. **[1424]**	1	10	0
From the sheriff for the waste of his land, forty shillings. **[1424]**	2	0	0

From the sheriff for the chattels of Walter le Blund of London, hanged, sixteen shillings. **[1425]**	0	16	0

1 See editorial note on **1430.**
2 Literally Aldreth.
3 William de *Leghe* in the text.
4 *Cudinton* in the text.

1625.

From Henry of Blundeston and Geoffrey of Corton[1] for default, half a mark. [**1429**]	0	6	8
From Walter Perebrun and Hugh of Dunston for the same, half a mark. [**1429**]	0	6	8
From Seman Rus and Thomas Ivete for the same, half a mark. [**1429**]	0	6	8
From Osbert the son of Hugh the archer and David Wichaud for the same, half a mark. [**1429**]	0	6	8
From Robert Peny, Adam Thurger and Hervey Godwin for the same, half a mark. [**1429**]	0	6	8
From William Man, Richard the Red and Robert the Red for the same, half a mark. [**1429**]	0	6	8
From John the son of Goscelin of Burgh Castle and John Ledrich for the same, half a mark. [**1429**]	0	6	8
From Robert the brother of the priest of Bradwell and Thomas de *Abelun* for the same, half a mark. [**1429**]	0	6	8
From Robert of Blundeston and Roger of Gunton and their fellows, the six jurors, for concealment, two marks. [**1414**]	1	6	8

1 The text of no. **1429** records only the six vills which failed to attend on the first day. The eighteen men named in this and the following seven entries will have constituted more than half the representatives of those vills – who should each have sent four men and the reeve – who defaulted at the eyre.

Total checked 48 pounds, 2 shillings and 2 pence [29 amercements]	**48**	**2**	**2**

The Hundred of Blything by Twelve

1626.

From the same hundred for murder, the liberties excepted, five marks. [**1433**]	3	6	8
From Bridge vill for harbouring Nicholas de Monay, half a mark. [**1433**]	0	6	8
From John the sheriff for Nicholas's chattels, three shillings. [**1433**]	0	3	0

From Blythburgh vill for harbouring Alan Iambel outside frankpledge, two marks. **[1433]**	1	6	8
From John the sheriff for Alan's chattels, sixteen pence. **[1433]**	0	1	4
From the tithing of Roger Coleman in Stonham for the flight of Robert de Monay, half a mark. **[1433]**	0	6	8
From John the sheriff for Robert's chattels, twenty-three shillings, six pence. **[1433]**	1	3	6
From Matilda the wife of Warin Cek,[1] Richard the son of Bartholomew and Bartholomew of Cove, fine for having an inquest, forty shillings by the surety of Walter Osbern of Northale, William of Childrehus of the same Thorard Herman of the same and Bartholomew the son of Ralph of the same. **[1434]**	2	0	0
From John the sheriff for the chattels of Alice the widow of Alexander Calver, hanged, two shillings. **[1435]**	0	2	0
From Robert Underwode,[2] fine for a false presentment, half a mark by the surety of Richard Champeneys. **[1436]**	0	6	8
From Thomas the son of Walter of Henham because he did not come and Geoffrey Prudekin of the same and Adam Lefkin[3] of the same because they did not have [Thomas the son of Walter of Henham] for whom they stood surety, half a mark. **[1436]**	0	6	8
From Baldwin the reeve of Thorington because he did not prosecute his appeal, half a mark. **[1439]**	0	6	8
From Ralph of Dam and Richard his son, fine for trespass, one mark by the surety of Walter of Dufford and John the son of John [of Cove].[4] **[1439]**	0	13	4
From John the son of Geoffrey, fine for trespass, one mark by the surety of Elyas of Middleton and John Gunnore of [Westleton].[5] **[1441]**	0	13	4
From Middleton vill because it did not pursue, one mark. **[1442]**	0	13	4
From the tithing of Richard Aylnod in Kelsale for the flight of Thomas the son of Richard, half a mark. **[1442]**	0	6	8
From Theberton[6] vill because it did not pursue, half a mark. **[1443?]**	0	6	8
From Walter the son of Richard Pessun because he did not prosecute, together with Richard Pessun and Norman de *Gedeston'*,[7] half a mark. **[1444]**	0	6	8
From Walter de Dede because he did not come, and William Hole of Sizewell and Robert Anketil of the same because they were his sureties and did not have him, half a mark. **[1444]**	0	6	8
From Roger Dade because he did not come, and Roger[8] Bayser of Sizewell and Robert Kempe of the same for the same [as his sureties], [half a mark].[9] **[1444]**	0	6	8

1 Gebe in the text.

2 Sudleboys, also meaning 'under the wood', in the text.

3 Lefwen in the text.

4 Illegible – place-name supplied from the text. From this point the right-hand side of the membrane has often been so rubbed as to be indecipherable.

5 Illegible – place-name supplied from the text.

6 Probably another clerical error – Leiston was most likely meant, as in the text. However, not only is Theberton close to Leiston but the suspected killer whom the men of Leiston failed to pursue came from the former vill.

7 Walter's sureties.

8 Reynold in the text.

9 Because the right-hand edge has been rubbed away, the amount of the amercement is illegible. The sum entered here is hypothetical, but was the usual penalty for an offence of this kind.

1627.

From Richard Dade, fine for trespass, half a mark by the surety of Walter[1] of Knodishall and Philip le Rus of Leiston. **[1444]**	0	6	8
From Elyas Cook of Leiston and his associates, fine for trespass, forty shillings by the surety of Philip Ruffus of Leiston, Robert Kentwin[2] of Aldringham and Richard Gripun of Knodishall. **[1446]**	2	0	0
From the tithing of Geoffrey Crel of Southwold[3] for the flight of William Pestel, half a mark. **[1359]**	0	6	8
From John the sheriff for the chattels of the same William, five shillings [and] six pence. **[1359]**	0	5	6
From Walter the son of Osbert of Knodishall because he did not have [Geoffrey the servant of the abbot of Leiston] for whom he stood surety, half a mark. **[1445]**	0	6	8
From the abbot of Leiston for the flight of Geoffrey his servant, who was of his household, twenty shillings. **[1445]**	1	0	0
From Robert the son of William of Peasenhall, fine because he withdrew, two marks by the surety of Godfrey of [Brundish[4] and] Baldwin Champeneyes of Uggeshall.[5] **[1445]**	1	6	8
From Adam the son of Walter of Knodishall, fine because he withdrew, half a mark by the surety of Adam Fink----.[6] **[1445]**	0	6	8
From Peter the son of Walter of Leiston for being the surety of Adam the son of Walter, twenty shillings.[7] **[1445]**	1	0	0
From Walter de Prato of Theberton for the same ... **[1445]**	0	0	0
From Hamo the son of William of the same and Ranulf the son of William of the same ... **[1445]**	0	0	0
From Robert Otewine[8] of Leiston for the same ... **[1445]**	0	0	0
From Thomas Sudleboys of the same[9] ... **[1445]**	0	0	0
From John Gunnore de *Webeton'*[10] for the same, ten shillings by the surety of ---. **[1445]**	0	10	0
From Alexander Page of the same[11] for the same ... **[1445]**	0	0	0

From John Osgood of the same for the same … **[1445]**	0	0	0
From William[12] the son of Godwin … **[1445]**	0	0	0
From Hervey Sotel of the same … **[1445]**	0	0	0

1 Adam the son of Walter in the text.
2 Lutewine in the text.
3 Sudhal, but clearly a mistake.
4 Place-name supplied from the text.
5 Reading uncertain, in the text Baldwin's toponym is *Bonhill*.
6 The rest of the name is lost. In the text Adam's sureties are recorded as Adam Fikelyn and Thomas Bulsy, both of Leiston.
7 This and the next four entries are connected by lines to the sum of twenty shillings, for which these men (and two others) were jointly liable as Adam's sureties.
8 Botewine in the text.
9 Of Theberton in the text.
10 For an explanation of John Gunnore's appearance here but not in the text see **1445**, note 3. *Webeton* is a mistake for Westleton. This and the next four entries, like the five preceding it, are connected by lines to a sum of money, ten shillings in this case, due from these men together as the sureties of Robert son of William of Peasenhall. Some illegible words may spell this out, or they may name additional sureties for payment of the debt.
11 Westleton in the text.
12 Walter in the text.

Total …[1]	**20**	**18**	**8**

1 There are no legible totals for either Blything hundred or the whole dorse. The figures provided here are editorial ones. The one for Blything covers its amercements up to the end of the membrane.

Total for Membrane 57d	**78**	**12**	**10**

Membrane 58 *AALT 4500–1*

Still Blything

1628.

From Walter the son of Adam of Darsham and William the son of Elfric[1] of the same because they did not have [Gillian the mother of Isabel the daughter of John] for whom they stood surety, half a mark. **[1447]**	0	6	8
From John the son of Richard of the same, Robert the son of Walter of the same and Robert the son of Elfric of the same because they did not have [the person] for whom they stood surety, half a mark.[2] **[1447]**	0	6	8
From William the son of Alexander of Darsham and Robert del Broc of the same, half a mark.[3] **[1447]**	0	6	8
From Robert Temprenoyce, fine because he withdrew, twenty shillings by the surety of William the son of Hubert of Brampton and Alan Jordan of the same. **[1448]**	1	0	0

From Adam the son of Geoffrey Gykel, fine for trespass, twenty shillings by the surety of Geoffrey Gykel and Richard Hayre of the same.[4] **[1448]**	1	0	0
From Walter Burchard for selling wine contrary to the assize, half a mark. **[1449]**	0	6	8
From John de Valonyes of Westleton for default, half a mark. **[1450]**	0	6	8
From Thomas del Gap of Henham and Thomas Holdering because they did not have [Geoffrey of Henham] for whom they stood surety, half a mark. **[1454]**	0	6	8
From Gillian the daughter of Matilda Lauerch and Matilda her mother, fine for a false appeal, half a mark by the surety of John Sprout of Halesworth and Hugh the reeve of the same. **[1455]**	0	6	8
From Hugh the son of Camilla, fine for trespass, two marks by the surety of Hamo Chevre and Robert of Layham. **[1456]**	1	6	8
From Robert[5] Pepper because he withdrew, half a mark by the surety of Richard de *Gosmere*. **[1456]**	0	6	8
From the tithing of Richard de Bruera in Bosmere[6] for the flight of Thomas Stulpard. **[1457]**	0	6	8
From the tithing of John Halyday in Blythburgh for the flight of Arnold Kinchaut, half a mark. **[1459]**	0	6	8
From John the sheriff for Arnold's chattels, sixteen pence. **[1459]**	0	1	4
From Baldwin of Mellis and his fellows, the twelve jurors, for concealment, forty shillings. **[1433]**	2	0	0

1 In the text Walter Kyterel stood surety for Gillian along with Walter son of Adam.
2 These men were not sureties but three out of four neighbours to an accidental death, in mercy for failing to attend the eyre.
3 They were amerced as sureties for the men named in the previous entry.
4 In the text Geoffrey is described as being of Westhall; presumably Richard was likewise.
5 Geoffrey in the text.
6 Reydon in the text – unlike Bosmere it is in Blything hundred.

Total for the Hundred of Blything [53 amercements][1]	**29**	**13**	**4**

1 This sum includes the total for Blything given at the end of m. 57d – the amercements for that hundred on m. 58 amount to £8 14s. 8d. It and subsequent totals are editorial, except for those given at the end of membranes.

The Borough of Exning by Six

1629.

From that vill for murder and because it buried a man without a coroner's view, five marks. **[1460]**	3	6	8

From Geoffrey Bule of Newmarket (half a mark) and Gerard the son of Adam of Exning (forty pence) because they did not have [Martin the son of Eudo] for whom they stood surety, ten shillings. [**1461**]	0	10	0
From Alexander Cheppe and Adam his brother, fine for trespass, ten shillings by the surety of Henry de Cumpenye in Exning and Ralph Cook of the same.[1] [**1461**]	0	10	0
From William de Acre for default, half a mark. [**1463**]	0	6	8
From Geoffrey Canterel for the same, half a mark. [**1463**]	0	6	8
From Nicholas But for the same, half a mark. [**1463**]	0	6	8
From Geoffrey the merchant for selling cloths contrary to the assize, half a mark. [**1464**]	0	6	8

1 The names of the sureties were omitted from the text.

Total for the Borough of Exning [7 amercements]	**5**	**13**	**4**

The Liberty of St Edmund

Double Hundred of Babergh

1630.

From those hundreds for murder, the liberties excepted, six marks. [**1469**, **1471** and **1474**]	4	0	0
From Walter the son of Robert because he did not come, half a mark. [**1465**]	0	6	8
From the tithing of Richard the son of Ralph for the flight of Roger the son of Nicholas,[1] half a mark. [**1468**]	0	6	8
For the chattels of the same Nicholas,[2] from the abbot of St Edmund's, four shillings. [**1468**]	0	4	0
From the tithing of Robert de Forde for the flight of John Ikin,[3] half a mark. [**1468**]	0	6	8
From the abbot of St Edmund's for the waste of John's land, seventeen shillings.[4] [**1468**]	0	17	0
From Polstead vill for a false presentment, twenty shillings. [**1469**]	1	0	0
From Lawshall vill because it did not pursue, twenty shillings. [**1474**]	1	0	0
From Peter de *Langfeld*[5] for default, half a mark. [**1478**]	0	6	8
From Robert of Shelton for the same, half a mark. [**1478**]	0	6	8
From Glemsford vill for many trespasses, twenty shillings. [**1480**]	1	0	0
From the bailiff of the bishop of Ely at Glemsford for the chattels of [John le] Wales,[6] five shillings. [**1480**]	0	5	0

From the tithing of Robert the blanket-maker in Stoke-by-Nayland for the flight of John and William Buffet, half a mark. [**1481**]	0	6	8
From the tithing of Sweyn le Bercher in Stoke-by-Nayland for the flight of Robert Puleyn,[7] half a mark. [**1481**]	0	6	8
From the abbot of St Edmund's for the chattels of John Thoraud, fugitive, and for his land and its waste, forty-six shillings.[8] [**1481**]	2	6	0
From the tithing of Robert Pepper in Little Cornard for the flight of Eustace the miller, half a mark. [**1483**]	0	6	8
From Newton vill for harbouring William Tuttemere, twenty shillings. [**1484**]	1	0	0
From the tithing of Roger Priur of Eleigh for the flight of William Fant, half a mark. [**1485**]	0	6	8
From the abbot for William's chattels, four shillings. [**1485**]	0	4	0
From the tithing of Edric Faderman[9] for the flight of Eudo the son of Henry, half a mark. [**1486**]	0	6	8

1 Nigel in the text.
2 Roger son of Nicholas, *recte* Nigel, is meant. No mention is made of the six shillings due from the year and waste of Roger's lands, but in the next but one entry it has been added to the eleven shillings due from the land of John Chinnere, like Roger a tenant of the abbot.
3 *le Chinnere* in the text.
4 As noted above, the clerk has consolidated the sums due from the lands of Roger the son of Nigel and John le Chinnere.
5 Presumably identical with the Peter Branch listed among the defaulters.
6 Christian name omitted by the clerk and supplied from the text.
7 Frankelyn in the text.
8 The values of John's chattels and land given in the text together amount to 42s. 8d.
9 Fayrman in the text.

1631.

From the tithing of Geoffrey Amfrey for the flight of Thomas Amfrey, half a mark. [**1487**]	0	6	8
From the abbot for Thomas's chattels, six shillings. [**1487**]	0	6	0
From the tithing of Alexander Lewine for the flight of Thomas the son of Roger, half a mark. [**1488**]	0	6	8
From Cavendish vill for harbouring, two marks. [**1489**]	1	6	8
From the tithing of Robert the son of Walter in Glemsford for the flight of William Prat, half a mark. [**1490**]	0	6	8
From the tithing of Roger Goch[1] for the flight of William Goch, half a mark. [**1491**]	0	6	8
From the abbot for William's chattels, ten shillings. [**1491**]	0	10	0

From John de Hodebovile, Adam of Eleigh and their fellows, the twenty-four jurors, one hundred shillings. **[1470]**[2]	5	0	0

1 Roger the brother of William Goche in the text.
2 This case contains the only recorded shortcoming by the Babergh jury.

Total for the Hundred of Babergh [28 amercements]	**23**	**12**	**0**

Hundred of Risbridge by Twelve

1632.

From that hundred for murder, the liberties excepted, four marks. [**1494** and **1496**]	2	13	4
From Reynold the son of Jordan[1] of Withersfield and Thomas of Alby because they did not have [Walter the cook and Hugh the carpenter] for whom they stood surety, half a mark. **[1495]**	0	6	8
From John the Butler for trespass, twenty shillings. **[1498]**	1	0	0
From the tithing of Humphrey of Stutton[2] for the flight of Reynold the shepherd, half a mark. **[1499]**	0	6	8
From the abbot for Reynold's chattels, ten shillings. **[1499]**	0	10	0
From Wratting [Talworth] vill for trespass, one mark. **[1501]**	0	13	4
From the tithing of William Odierne for the flight of Ralph the son of Richard, half a mark. **[1503]**	0	6	8

1 Ralph in the text.
2 Humphrey Strut in the text.

Total for the Hundred of Risbridge [7 amercements]	**5**	**16**	**8**

The Borough of Clare by Twelve

1633.

From that vill for its fine before judgment, two marks. **[1508]**	1	6	8
From William the son of Thomas of Clare for selling cloth contrary to the assize, half a mark. **[1509]**	0	6	8
From Geoffrey Pye and Reynold his associate for the same, half a mark. **[1509]**	0	6	8
From Henry the merchant of Hawkedon for the same, half a mark. **[1509]**	0	6	8
From William Ruffus for wine sold contrary to the assize, one mark. **[1510]**	0	13	4
From Reynold the tailor and William the clerk for the same, half a mark. **[1510]**	0	6	8

From the said abbot for the land of Ralph the son of Roger and its waste, forty shillings. **[1511]**	2	0	0
Total for the Borough of Clare [7 amercements]	**5**	**6**	**8**

The Borough of Sudbury by Twelve

1634.

From that vill for its fine before judgment for drapers and vintners, one hundred shillings. **[1512]**	5	0	0
Total for the Borough of Sudbury [1 amercement]	**5**	**0**	**0**

The Hundred of Thingoe by Twelve

1635.

From that hundred for murder, the liberties excepted, thirty shillings. **[1514, 1515]**	1	10	0
From Hengrave vill for a false presentment, one mark. **[1515]**	0	13	4
From Brockley vill for harbouring John the miller outside frankpledge, one mark. **[1516]**	0	13	4
From the abbot for John's chattels, nineteen shillings and three pence. **[1516]**	0	19	3
From the tithing of Reynold the beadle in Chevington for the flight of Walter Buc, half a mark. **[1517]**	0	6	8
From the tithing of Godfrey [Irich] in Lackford for the flight of Humphrey [the son of Joscelin], half a mark. **[1517]**	0	6	8
From the abbot for Humphrey's chattels, two shillings. **[1517]**	0	2	0
From the tithing of Gilbert Sumer in Lackford for the flight of Aylwin Punge, half a mark. **[1518]**	0	6	8
From Rede vill for a false presentment, half a mark. **[1520]**	0	6	8
Total for the Hundred of Thingoe [9 amercements]	**5**	**4**	**7**
Total for Membrane 58	**59**	7	**11**
Sum Total Eighty-eight marks and nineteen pence[1]	**58**	**14**	**11**

1 The clerk's total represents a shortfall of thirteen shillings from the total reached by adding up the figures presented on this membrane. Given his general standard of carelessness and inaccuracy, perhaps it is surprising that the deficiency was not greater.

Membrane 58d *AALT 4623–4*

The Half Hundred of Cosford by Six

1636.

From that hundred for murder, the liberties excepted, forty shillings. [**1521**]	2	0	0
From Kersey vill for trespass, one mark. [**1521**]	0	13	4
From Gilbert of Manton and Andrew the carpenter of the same because they did not have [Wyot of Kettlebaston] for whom they stood surety, half a mark. [**1523**]	0	6	8
From the tithing of Robert Skep[1] in Kettlebaston for the flight of Wyot of the same, half a mark. [**1523**]	0	6	8
From the tithing of Roger Ailwin for the flight of Peter Han, half a mark. [**1525**]	0	6	8
From the tithing of Thomas of Chilton for the flight of Richard Kebben, half a mark. [**1524**]	0	6	8
From Ralph Kempe for default, half a mark. [**1526**]	0	6	8

1 Chip in the text.

Sum Total for the Hundred of Cosford [7 amercements]	**4**	**6**	**8**

The Hundred of Blackbourn by Twenty-Four

1637.

From the same hundred for murder, the liberties excepted, four marks. [**1527**, **1534** and **1536**]	2	13	4
From Knettishall vill because it did not pursue, half a mark. [**1527**]	0	6	8
From Richard de *Langetot* for the flight of William Welshapen who was of his household, half a mark. [**1528**]	0	6	8
From the tithing of Alexander Barun in Hunston for the flight of Roger the shepherd, half a mark. [**1530**]	0	6	8
From Langham vill for harbouring Anselm Horen, ten shillings. [**1532**]	0	10	0
From Great Ashfield[1] vill because it did not pursue, one mark. [**1534**]	0	13	4
From the abbot for the chattels of Ralph, Peter, Gillian, and Stephen the weaver, thirteen shillings. [**1535**]	0	13	0
From the tithing of Robert le Totere for the flight of Henry the smith, half a mark. [**1537**]	0	6	8
From the abbot for Henry's chattels, twenty-six pence. [**1537**]	0	2	2

From Thomas de Haya, fine for trespass, ten marks by the surety of Adam the Fleming of Exning, Thomas Kenesman of the same, Geoffrey the merchant of Newmarket, John the son of Laurence of Livermere, Richard Malet of Exning and Peter the son of William of the same. [**1539**]	6	13	4
From the vill of Stanton because it did not pursue, one mark. [**1542**]	0	13	4
From Adam the son of Robert of Horringer because he did not have [Robert the son of Robert de Furnaus] for whom he stood surety, half a mark. [**1541**]	0	6	8
From Adam Hovel of Hunston and Andrew the son of Thomas of Ashfield because they did not have [Simon the chaplain of Badwell Ash] for whom they stood surety, half a mark. [**1549**]	0	6	8
From Barnham vill because it did not pursue, ten shillings. [**1551**]	0	10	0
From the abbot for the chattels of an unknown thief, three shillings. [**1552**]	0	3	0
From the tithing of Walter the merchant in Ashfield for the flight of Stephen Thren, half a mark. [**1553**]	0	6	8
From the abbot for [Stephen's] chattels, two shillings. [**1553**]	0	2	0
From Euston vill for trespass, half a mark. [**1556**]	0	6	8
From Henry of Livermere, fine for trespass, forty shillings by the surety of Thomas of Shotford, William le Claver, Warin de *Wadeshill*, William of Langham and Thomas de *Hulme*. [**1539** or **1589**][2]	2	0	0
From Ralph of Cookley for default, half a mark. [**1561**]	0	6	8

1 Little Ashfield in the text.

2 Henry's fine, not referred to in the text, may have been related to his indirect involvement in the affray in which Geoffrey his chaplain was killed (**1539**). Or it could have resulted from his having had his own son indicted for larceny (**1589**). Perhaps he was penalised here for both incidents.

1638.

From Bardwell vill for harbouring Robert Kindel outside frankpledge, twenty shillings. [**1564**]	1	0	0
From Gilbert of Walsham for a false presentment and concealment, one mark.[1] [**1527**]	0	13	4
From Saer of Stanton and Thomas of Stanton for the same, half a mark. [**1527**]	0	6	8
From Warin Outlaw and Robert of Hoo for the same, half a mark. [**1527**]	0	6	8
From William of Wordwell for the same, half a mark. [**1527**]	0	6	8

From John the son of Laurence of Livermere for the same, half a mark. **[1527]**	0	6	8
From John of Lound for the same, half a mark. **[1527]**	0	6	8
From Robert the son of Saer of Stanton for the same, half a mark. **[1527]**	0	6	8
From Robert de Wikes for the same, half a mark. **[1527]**	0	6	8
From William of Norwich for the same, half a mark. **[1527]**	0	6	8
From Robert of Norton for the same, half a mark. **[1527]**	0	6	8
From William le Neve for the same, half a mark. **[1527]**	0	6	8
From Berard of Wattisfield for the same, half a mark. **[1527]**	0	6	8
From Simon of <Ixworth> Knettishall[2] and Ivo of Knettishall for the same, half a mark. **[1527]**	0	6	8
From Guy of Hepworth for the same, half a mark. **[1527]**	0	6	8

1 Gilbert and the sixteen men named in the following thirteen entries will have constituted a large proportion of Blackbourn's twenty-four jurors, amerced in **1527** for presenting Englishry falsely.

2 In the text Ixworth is written above Knettishall. The latter has not been struck through, but from the fact that Ivo is not described as 'of the same' it may be deduced that he alone came from Knettishall, and that Simon came from Ixworth.

Sum Total for the Hundred of Blackbourn [35 amercements]	**23**	**13**	**6**

The Hundred of Thedwestry by Twelve

1639.

From that hundred for murder, the liberties excepted, forty shillings. **[1565, 1566, 1567]**	2	0	0
From Barton vill because it did not pursue, forty shillings. **[1567]**	2	0	0
From [Little] Whelnetham vill for the same, ten shillings. **[1568]**	0	10	0
From the tithing of Richard the son of Hugh in Thurston for the flight of Godfrey the son of Peter, half a mark. **[1571]**	0	6	8
From Adam Bike, Freche the son of Eustace of Thurston, Henry the Smith of the same and Thurkil the son of Leviva of the same because they did not have [Godfrey the son of Peter] for whom they stood surety, half a mark. **[1571]**	0	6	8
From the tithing of Walter Kaym in Fornham St Genevieve for the flight of Robert Kaym, half a mark. **[1573]**	0	6	8
From Robert[1] the son of Hugh for the year, day and waste of the same [Robert's] land, one mark by the surety of Ralph le Estrange. **[1573]**	0	13	4

From the tithing of Nicholas de Spina in Little Bradfield for the flight of Alan Baril, half a mark. **[1577]**	0	6	8

1 Ralph in the text.

Total for the Hundred of Thedwestry [8 amercements]	**6**	**10**	**0**

The Hundred of Lackford by Twelve

1640.

From that hundred for murder, the liberties excepted, forty shillings. **[1586]**	2	0	0
From the tithing of Richard Puttok in Herringswell for the flight of John the carpenter, half a mark. **[1579]**	0	6	8
From Peter Newman and Rogan le Paumer because they did not have [Matilda the mother of Robert the son of Peter of Tuddenham] for whom they stood surety. **[1579]**	0	6	8
From the abbot for the chattels of Parnel, hanged, six shillings. **[1582]**	0	6	0
From Ralph de Berners' portion of Icklingham vill for trespass, one mark. **[1583]**	0	13	4
From the abbot for the chattels of William the son of Peter, hanged, four shillings, eight pence.[1] **[1583]**	0	4	8
From the tithing of Richard[2] Nuvelhume in Icklingham for the flight of Peter the son of Reynold, half a mark. **[1583]**	0	6	8
From the abbot for the chattels of Katherine of Icklingham, three shillings. **[1583]**	0	3	0
From the tithing of Stephen the merchant in Cavenham for the flight of Richard Bakun.[3] **[1588]**	0	0	0
From the tithing of William the smith in Mildenhall for the flight of Robert the son of Gilbert, half a mark. **[1588]**	0	6	8
From the tithing of Peter de Stangno in Icklingham for the flight of Hugh Ernald, half a mark. **[1588]**	0	6	8

1 Fourteen shillings, eight pence in the text, so out by ten shillings – yet another example of clerical inattention.
2 Robert in text.
3 No sum is entered, though half a mark was the usual penalty for this offence.

Total for the Hundred of Lackford [11 amercements]	**5**	**0**	**4**

The Borough of Ipswich[1]

[1] Up to this point the amercements of hundreds and vills have been entered in the order in which they occur in the main text. Ipswich's pleas begin at **1406**. There is nothing among them to explain why its amercements appear almost at the end of the roll.

1641.

From that vill, fine before judgment for drapers and vintners, fifteen marks. [**1406**]	10	0	0
From the tithing of Hervey Ters of Ipswich for the flight of William the fuller, half a mark. [**1408**]	0	6	8
From the tithing of Adam de Campo of Ipswich for the flight of John Bude, half a mark. [**1409**]	0	6	8
From the tithing of Thomas the miller for the flight of John Osmund, half a mark. [**1410**]	0	6	8
From Stoke vill because it did not pursue, forty shillings. [**1410**]	2	0	0
From the bailiffs of Ipswich for trespass, forty shillings [**1408**]	2	0	0
From the same[1] for the chattels of William the fuller, fugitive, twelve pence. [**1408**]	0	1	0
From the same for the chattels of John Bude, fugitive, three shillings. [**1409**]	0	3	0
From the prior of Ely for the chattels of John Osmund, fugitive, twelve pence. [**1410**]	0	1	0

[1] In the text Sylvester the son of Walkelin is to answer for the chattels; he may have been one of the bailiffs.

Total for the Borough of Ipswich [9 amercements]	**15**	**5**	**0**
Total for Membrane 58d	**54**	**15**	**6**
Sum Total eighty-two marks and two pence[1]	**54**	**15**	**6**

[1] For once the clerk and the editors find themselves in perfect agreement.

Membrane 62 *AALT 4508*

Amercements of the Borough of Dunwich for Pleas of the Crown[1]

[1] The amercements of Dunwich are separated from those of the rest of the crown pleas by three membranes containing the issues of the civil pleas. They are written in a distinctive hand which can be recognised in no. **224** among the civil pleas, where it was also responsible for some, at least, of the Dunwich pleas. It also occurs on m. 60, where it wrote some of the issues of the civil pleas.

1665.

From the vill of Dunwich, fine before judgment for vintners and drapers, twenty marks. [**1590**]	13	6	8

From Burghard Gykel because he did not have [Seman Rufus] for whom he stood surety, ten shillings. **[1591]**	0	10	0
From Gilbert de Moref for the same, half a mark. **[1591]**	0	6	8
From Augustine le Angele because he did not come, half a mark by the surety of Gerard the Scot. **[1592]**	0	6	8
From Robert the son of Hubert Gosce and John Frost because they did not have [Augustine le Aungle] for whom they stood surety, half a mark. **[1592]**	0	6	8
From Philip the son of Robert because he did not prosecute his appeal, half a mark by the surety of Michael[1] his brother. **[1593]**	0	6	8
From John the son of Robert and Matthew his brother, sureties for the same [Philip], half a mark. **[1593]**	0	6	8
From Roger le Angele, fine for trespass, ten shillings by the surety of Andrew the son of Augustine. **[1593]**	0	10	0
From Stephen Fress and Richard his brother, fine for trespass, ten shillings by the surety of Gerard of Hazelwood and William Wetecake.[2] **[1593]**	0	10	0
From William Bernard because he did not have [Walter de Gynes and Thomas de Fonte] for whom he stood surety. **[1594]**	0	6	8
From John le Pessuner and Alexander the son of William for the same, half a mark. **[1594]**	0	6	8
(*Blything*) From William Pulleco of Westleton, surety for Matilda the widow of Osbert Scamund, half a mark. **[1595]**	0	6	8
From Peter Robelin[3] and Hubert Ringolf, bailiffs, fine for trespass, two marks by the surety of Thomas the son of Robert and Burchard Gykel. **[1595]**	1	6	8
From the leet of the suburb of the North Gate for the flight of Amisius Scamund, twenty shillings. **[1595]**	1	0	0
From Richard Peculf and Stephen Frese, sureties for Richard the son of Robert, half a mark. **[1597]**	0	6	8
From Thomas the son of Robert, fine for trespass, half a mark by the surety of Thomas of Linstead. **[1597]**	0	6	8
From Alexander the son of Gerard because he did not have [Philip the brother of Thomas] for whom he stood surety, half a mark **[1597]**	0	6	8
(*Blything*) From Robert Snow of Dunwich and William the son of Hugh of Holton because they did not have [Thomas of Creake] for whom they stood surety, half a mark. **[1600]**	0	6	8
From Robert the clerk of Dunwich because he did not have Peter the son of Robert for whom he stood surety, half a mark. **[1600]**	0	6	8
From the North Leet of Dunwich for the flight of Simon the son of Warin and Arnold Illerheyl, two marks. **[1601]**	1	6	8

From Nicholas the son of Matthew, fine because he did not prosecute his appeal, one mark by the surety of John the son of Augustine and Lambert *Olming*. **[1601]**	0	13	4

1 Not named in the text, unlike his two brothers in the next entry.
2 The sureties were omitted from the text, and the clerk may have been slow to discover who they were, since their names were squeezed into a limited space between this and the next entry.
3 Rokelin in the text.

Total for the Borough of Dunwich [21 amercements]	**23**	**10**	**0**
Sum Total for Crown Pleas	**411**	**19**	**2**

GLOSSARY

abjuration: an extension of the right of sanctuary, whereby a fugitive to a church could confess his offences before a coroner and then swear to leave the country.

amercement: a financial penalty, the medieval equivalent of the modern fine; shown as 'in mercy' in the pleas.

appeal: a formal accusation, alleging felony or breach of the King's peace, made in an elaborate set form and often offering battle as the means of proof.

approver: a self-confessed criminal who tries to save his life by securing the conviction of his associates, through either combat or juries' verdicts.

assize: either a form of legal action or a regulation or ordinance.

attach: to require a man or woman to find guarantors of a future appearance in court.

Capitula Itineris: the list of questions, embodied in written articles, to which juries answered when they drew up the presentments they made to the justices at an eyre. See below, ***veredicta***.

clerk: a man who was either in holy orders or possessed of literate skills, commonly both.

Court Christian: ecclesiastical court in which canon law was applied.

default: person or community failing to appear in court when summoned.

deodand: an object or animal responsible for a death of a person, given to God, that is, to charity, as propitiation.

disseise: to deprive someone of freehold land by force and without a judgment.

distrain: to seize lands or goods in order to compel obedience or compliance.

dower: the third of a man's estate to which a wife was customarily entitled on the death of her husband.

Englishry: the process of establishing a dead person's ancestry in order to avoid a murder fine. See below, **murder fine**.

escheat: the reversion of a landowner's property to his or her lord, or to the crown, should he die without heirs or forfeit his estate by legal process.

exaction/exigent: the process whereby suspects were summoned at successive meetings of the county court to surrender to the King's peace, and outlawed if they failed to do so after five summonses. See below, **outlawry**.

felony: a serious crime potentially punishable by death, notably homicide, theft, rape and arson.

franchise: an office or function of government in private hands. See below, **liberty**.

frankpledge: a system of collective responsibility, implemented through tithings in vills or leets in some boroughs. See below, **tithing**.

gaol delivery: a judicial session at which prisoners in a gaol were presented for trial.

household: an alternative to frankpledge for the dependants (or mainpast) of an important person, the latter being held responsible for their good behaviour.

hue (or hue and cry): the alarm obligatorily raised against suspicious or violent behaviour, or when evidence of evildoing was discovered.

hundred: an ancient administrative subdivision of a county, of varying size, each with its own court.

indictment: accusation of felony made collectively by juries in the opening stages of an eyre in order to secure the arrest of suspects. See below, ***privata***.

liberty: the area within which the possessor of franchises was entitled to exercise them. See above, **franchise**.

mark: a monetary unit of account valued at 13s. 4d. (66p).

murder fine: archaic fine imposed on a community which failed to prove that a dead person was English by descent. See above, **Englishry**.

Norman lands: lands forfeited by Normans or other Frenchmen, usually because their lords sided with the French king against King John at the beginning of the thirteenth century.

on the country: submission to a jury's verdict.

outlawry: deprivation of the protection of the law following the process of exigent, accompanied by forfeiture of lands and chattels; an outlaw who was arrested was liable to summary execution. See above, **exaction/exigent**.

presentments: the formal delivery, both orally and in writing (the so-called *vere-dicta*), of the information required by the justices as essential to the conduct of an eyre.

privata: documents given to the sheriff containing the names of men and women indicted by juries at the beginning of an eyre. See above, **indictment**.

seisin: the exercise and enjoyment of the rights inherent in the possession of free-hold land.

serjeanty: a form of tenure whereby the holder of land performed specified services, often but not always non-military, to a lord.

sheriff's aid: a customary due which may once have maintained the sheriff as he performed his duties but by the thirteenth century was paid to the King.

suit: the duty of attendance at a court, usually incumbent upon land.

tenure in chief: land held directly from the crown.

tithing: the building block for the frankpledge system, in Suffolk a group of ten adult males responsible for one another's keeping the peace. Each tithing was referred to by its leading member, or **tithingman**. In Dunwich the same function was performed by the inhabitants of areas known as leets. See above, **frank-pledge**.

tourn: the sheriff's six-monthly visitation of the hundreds under his jurisdiction, to review the maintenance of frankpledge and receive presentments of offences against the peace.

veredicta: answers by juries to questions presented to them in the articles of the eyre. See above, ***Capitula Itineris***.

vill: an area of settlement which was also an administrative unit, the equivalent of a present-day civil parish. The term was used of both rural and urban communities.

villein: an alternative name for a serf, a man or woman unfree in status, and there-fore having limited rights in law and particularly with regard to the lord.

waiver: the equivalent of outlawry for women. See above, **outlawry**.

year and waste: the King's right to hold for a year and a day any free land held by a convicted felon, receiving its revenues and taking every movable asset from it afterwards.

BIBLIOGRAPHY

ABBREVIATIONS

AALT	Anglo-American Legal Tradition. Documents from medieval and early modern England from The National Archives digitised and displayed through the University of Houston, accessible at aalt.law.uh.edu/aalt.html
EcHR	*Economic History Review*
EHR	*English Historical Review*
PSIAH	*Proceedings of the Suffolk Institute of Archaeology and History*
SRS	Suffolk Records Society
VCH	*The Victoria History of the County of Suffolk*, volume II, 1907

MANUSCRIPT SOURCES IN THE NATIONAL ARCHIVES

Chancery:
C 60 (Fine Rolls)
C 66 (Patent Rolls)
CP 25/1 (Feet of Fines)

Exchequer:
E 159 (King's Remembrancer: Memoranda Rolls)
E 372 (Pipe Rolls)

Judicial Records:
JUST 1 (Eyre Rolls)

PRINTED PRIMARY SOURCES

Bracton on the laws and customs of England, edited and translated by S.E. Thorne, 4 vols (Cambridge, MA, 1968–77)

Calendar of Charter Rolls, 1226–1257 (HMSO, 1903)

Calendar of Patent Rolls: Henry III (HMSO, 1906–13)

Calendars of Inquisitions Post Mortem, i–iv (HMSO, 1904–13)

Cartae Antiquae Rolls 1–10, edited by L. Landon, Pipe Roll Society 55 (1935)

Cartulary and Charters of the Priory of Saints Peter and Paul, Ipswich, i, edited by D. Allen, Suffolk Charters 20, SRS (2018)

Charters of Norwich Cathedral Priory i, edited by B. Dodwell, Pipe Roll Society new series 40 (1974 for 1965–66)

Close Rolls of Henry III (HMSO, 1902–38)

Councils & Synods with other documents relating to the English church ii, A.D. 1205–1313, edited by F.M. Powicke and C.R. Cheney, 2 volumes (Oxford, 1964)

Curia Regis Rolls of the Reigns of Richard I, John and Henry III preserved in the Public Record Office, 20 volumes (1922–2006)

1238 Devon Eyre: Crown pleas of the Devon eyre of 1238, edited by H. Summerson, Devon and Cornwall Record Society new series 28 (1985)

English Episcopal Acta 21: Norwich 1215–1243, edited by C. Harper-Bill (Oxford, 2000)

Liber Feodorum, The Book of Fees commonly called Testa de Nevill, 3 volumes (HMSO, 1920–31)

Little Domesday Book: Domesday Book Suffolk, i and ii, edited and translated by Alexander Rumble (Chichester, 1983)

Matthew Paris, *Chronica Majora*, edited by H.R. Luard, 7 volumes (Rolls Series, 1872–83)

Patent Rolls of the reign of Henry III, 1216–1232, 2 volumes (HMSO, 1901–03)

Placita de Quo Warranto, edited by W. Illingworth (Record Commission, 1818)

Rotuli chartarum, 1199–1216, edited by T.D. Hardy (Record Commission, 1837)

Rotuli Hundredorum ii, edited by W. Illingworth (Record Commission, 1818)

Rotuli litterarum clausarum 1224–1227, edited by T.D. Hardy (Record Commission, 1833–34)

Rotuli litterarum patentium, edited by T.D. Hardy (Record Commission, 1835)

Rotuli de oblatis et finibus ... tempore regis Johannis, edited by T.D. Hardy (Record Commission, 1835)

Select cases of procedure without writ under Henry III, edited by H.G. Richardson and G.O. Sayles, Selden Society 60 (1941)

Sibton Abbey cartularies and charters i, edited by P. Brown, Suffolk Charters 7, SRS (1985)

1240 Suffolk Civil Pleas: The civil pleas of the Suffolk eyre of 1240, edited by Eric Gallagher, SRS 52 (2009)

1235 Surrey Eyre: The 1235 Surrey eyre, 3 volumes, edited by C.A.F. Meekings and D. Crook, Surrey Record Society xxxi–ii, xxxvii (1979–2002)

1249 Wiltshire Crown Pleas: Crown pleas of the Wiltshire eyre, 1249, edited by C.A.F. Meekings, Wiltshire Archaeological and Natural History Society, Records Branch xvi (1960)

SECONDARY SOURCES

Allen, M., 'Ecclesiastical mints in thirteenth-century England', in M. Prestwich, R. Britnell and R. Frame (eds), *Thirteenth Century England* viii (Woodbridge, 2001), pp. 113–22

Bailey, Mark, *Medieval Suffolk: an economic and social history, 1200–1500* (Woodbridge, 2007)

Bailey, Mark, 'Villeinage in England: a regional study, *c.* 1250 –*c.* 1349', *EcHR* 62 (2009), pp. 430–57

Blomefield, F., *An essay towards the topographical history of the county of Norfolk*, 2nd Edition, 11 vols (1805–10)

Brand, P.A., *The origins of the English legal profession* (Oxford, 1992)

Brand, P.A., *Observing and recording the medieval bar and bench at work*, Selden Society lecture (1999)

Briggs, K., 'Where in Suffolk was Wicklaw?', *Journal of the English Place-Name Society* 50 (2018), pp. 11–15

Briggs, K., and Kilpatrick, K., *A dictionary of Suffolk place-names*, English Place-Name Society (Nottingham, 2016)

Brodt, B., 'East Anglia', in D.M. Palliser (ed.), *The Cambridge urban history of Britain i, 600–1540* (Cambridge, 2000), pp. 639–56

Cam, H., 'The king's government as administered by the greater abbots of East Anglia', in *Liberties and communities in medieval England* (London, 1963), pp. 183–204

Campbell, J., 'Hundreds and leets: a survey with suggestions', in C. Harper-Bill (ed.), *Medieval East Anglia* (Woodbridge, 2005), pp. 153–67

Carpenter, D.A., *The minority of Henry III* (London, 1990)

Carpenter, D.A., *Henry III: the rise to power and personal rule, 1207–1258* (New Haven, 2020)

Church, S.D., 'Belet, Michael (d. in or before 1247), royal servant', in H.C.G. Matthew and B. Harrison (eds), *Oxford Dictionary of National Biography*, 60 volumes (Oxford, 2004), 4, 887–8

Clanchy, M.T., 'Highway robbery and trial by battle in the Hampshire eyre of 1249', in R.F. Hunnisett and J.B. Post (eds), *Medieval legal records edited in memory of C.A.F. Meekings* (London, 1978), pp. 25–61

Colman, G., and Colman, S., 'A thirteenth-century aisled house: Purton Green Farm, Stansfield, Suffolk', *PSIA* 30:2 (1965), pp. 149–65

Denholm-Young, N., *Richard of Cornwall* (Oxford, 1947)

Dodwell, B., 'Holdings and inheritance in medieval East Anglia', *EcHR* 20 (1967), pp. 53–66

Dyer, C., *Making a living in the middle ages: the people of Britain, 850–1520* (London, 2002)

Fairclough, J., 'The bounds of Stoke and the hamlets of Ipswich', *PSIAH* 40:3 (2003), pp. 262–77

Gabel, L.C., *Benefit of clergy in England in the later middle ages* (New York, 1969)

Given, J.B., *Society and homicide in thirteenth-century England* (Stanford, 1977)

Green, A., 'The stewardship of the eight and a half hundreds', *PSIA* 30:3 (1966), pp. 255–62

Green, T.A., *Verdict according to conscience: perspectives on the English criminal trial jury, 1200–1800* (Chicago, 1985)

Groot, R., 'Petit larceny, jury lenity and parliament', in J.W. Cairns and G. McCleod (eds), *'The dearest birthright of the people of England': the jury in the history of the common law* (Oxford, 2002), pp. 47–61

Hagger, M.S., *The fortunes of a Norman family: the de Verduns in England, Ireland and Wales, 1066–1316* (Dublin, 2001)

Holt, J.C., *The Northerners: a study in the reign of King John* (Oxford, 1961)

Hudson, J., *The Oxford history of the laws of England ii: 871–1216* (Oxford, 2012)

Hunnisett, R.F., *The medieval coroner* (Cambridge, 1961)

Kimball, E.G., *Serjeanty tenure in medieval England* (New Haven, 1936)

Knowles, D., and Hadcock, R.N., *Medieval religious houses: England and Wales* (2nd edn, London, 1971)

Meekings, C.A.F., *Studies in 13th-century justice and administration* (London, 1981)

Miller, E., *The abbey and bishopric of Ely* (Cambridge, 1951)

Moore, T.K., 'The loss of Normandy and the invention of *Terre Normannorum*', *EHR* 125 (2010), pp. 1071–1109

Morgan, M., *The English lands of the abbey of Bec* (Oxford, 1946)

Morris, M., *The Bigod earls of Norfolk in the thirteenth century* (Woodbridge, 2005)
Plucknett, T.F.T., *Edward I and criminal law* (Cambridge, 1960)
Poole, A.L., *Obligations of society in the XII and XIII centuries* (Oxford, 1946)
Power, D., 'The treaty of Paris (1259) and the aristocracy of England and Normandy', in *Thirteenth Century England* xiii, edited by J. Burton, F. Lachaud, P. Schofield and K. Stöber (Woodbridge, 2011), pp. 141–58
Powicke, F.M., *The loss of Normandy, 1189–1204* (2nd edn, Manchester, 1961)
Pugh, R.B., *Imprisonment in medieval England* (Cambridge, 1968)
Sanders, I.J., *English baronies: a study of their origin and descent, 1066–1327* (Oxford, 1960)
Stacey, R.C., *Politics, policy and finance under Henry III, 1216–1245* (Oxford, 1987)
Summerson, H.R.T., 'The maintenance of law and order in England, 1227–1263', unpublished Cambridge PhD dissertation (1976)
Summerson, H., 'The structure of law enforcement in thirteenth century England', *American Journal of Legal History* 23 (1979), pp. 313–27
Summerson, H., 'Maitland and the criminal law in the age of Bracton', in J. Hudson (ed.), *The history of English law: centenary essays on 'Pollock and Maitland'* (Oxford, 1996), pp. 115–43
Summerson, H., 'Burning issues: the law and crime of arson in England 1200–1350', in S. Jenks, J. Rose and C. Whittick (eds), *Laws, lawyers and texts: studies in medieval legal history in honour of Paul Brand* (Leiden and Boston, 2012), pp. 101–27
Summerson, H., '"A photograph of English life"? The trustworthiness of the thirteenth-century crown pleas rolls', in D. Ibbetson, N. Jones and N. Ramsay (eds), *English legal history and its sources: essays in honour of Sir John Baker* (Cambridge, 2019), pp. 100–20
Thomas, H.M., *The secular clergy of England, 1066–1216* (Oxford, 2014)
Vincent, N., *Peter des Roches: an alien in English politics, 1205–1238* (Cambridge, 1996)
Ward, J.C., 'The honour of Clare in Suffolk in the early middle ages', *PSIA* 30:1 (1964), pp. 94–111
Waugh, S.L., *The lordship of England: royal wardships and marriages in English society and politics, 1217–1327* (Princeton, 1988)

WEBSITES

Anglo-American Legal Tradition (AALT): aalt.law.uh.edu/aalt.html
Henry III Fine Rolls Project, research project of King's College London: www.finerollshenry3.org.uk
The 'lands of the Normans' in England (1204–44), research project of the University of Sheffield: www.dhi.ac.uk/normans

UNPUBLISHED MATERIAL

Briggs, Keith, *Suffolk place-names*, draft version, 2020. We are most grateful to Mr Briggs for making available the unpublished fruits of his researches, which have enabled a number of identifications in the text.

ANALYSIS OF CONTENTS

These lists provide a key to the crown pleas, supplementing the index of persons and places by giving access to some of their most significant components. The numbers are those of the pleas within which those components occur but they can give rise to repetition. For instance, the killing or killings recorded in **1433**, and the complicated proceedings to which this case gave rise, have resulted in this single entry being entered among the totals for homicides, felons with no chattels, felons with chattels worth 40d. or less (a rough yardstick for poverty, that sum being the minimum value of property on which the thirtieth of 1237 was levied), felons with free lands, failings by vills, and failings by juries. The coverage of these tables has not been extended to include the amercements but it is hoped that the list of articles to which the jurors answered at the eyre, together with details of the proceedings which resulted, will give additional guidance to the contents of the roll (see Introduction p. lxvii, above).

The prosecution of felonies

(1) Appeals and plaints

Total of actions: 1162, 1168, 1172, 1173, 1177, 1190, 1192, 1193, 1197, 1200, 1202, 1211, 1222, 1231, 1232, 1246, 1248, 1249, 1250, 1253, 1266, 1267, 1272, 1276, 1293, 1294, 1301, 1303, 1321, 1326, 1328, 1329, 1330, 1345, 1361, (1374), 1376, 1378, 1381, 1384, 1385, 1393, 1394, 1395, 1411, 1415, 1431, 1432, 1434, 1439, 1441, 1444, 1445, 1446, 1448, 1454, 1455, 1456, 1461, 1493, 1502, 1540, 1541, 1578, 1579, 1591, 1592, 1593, 1595, 1597, 1600, 1601

Appeals by approver: 1293, 1294, (1374)

Appeals of arson: 1326, 1434

Appeals of felony or breach of the peace: 1200, 1211, 1301, 1592, 1593, 1597

Appeal of ham-soken (house-breaking): 1168

Appeals of homicide: 1162, 1172, 1248, 1272, 1276, 1286, 1302, 1328, 1376, 1395, 1411, 1441, 1468, 1579, 1595

Appeals of rape: 1190, 1197, 1246, 1329, 1431, 1432, 1502, 1578

Appeals of robbery or larceny: 1200, 1211, 1222, 1378, 1381, 1445, 1461, 1591, 1600, 1601

Appeals of wounding: 1177, 1192, 1193, 1202, 1231, 1232, 1249, 1250, 1253, 1303, 1321, 1330, 1345, 1361, 1378, 1384, 1385, 1393, 1394, 1415, 1439, 1444, 1446, 1448, 1454, 1456, 1493, 1540, 1541, 1593

Appeals of wounding and robbery: 1173, 1200, 1211

Plaints: 1266, 1455

(2) Felonies presented or giving rise to indictments

Homicide: 1161, 1163, 1165 (and 1269), 1170, 1181, 1186 (and 1206), 1194 (and 1196), 1198, 1201, 1205, 1208, 1209, 1217, 1226, 1227, 1233, 1247, 1258, 1263, 1264, 1271, 1273, 1277, 1278, 1285, 1298, 1300, 1320, 1324, 1327, 1328, 1342,

1344, 1346 (and 1437), 1348, 1349, 1360, 1362, 1363, 1366 (and 1371), 1377, 1380, 1382, 1383, 1388, 1408, 1409, 1410, 1414, 1417, 1418, 1424, 1433, 1442, 1443, 1452, 1468, 1474, 1483, 1494, 1501, 1511, 1516, 1519, 1525, 1527, 1530, 1531, 1534, 1536, 1539, 1542, 1543, 1546, 1551, 1553, 1560, 1567, 1568, 1571, 1576, 1579, 1586

Larceny: 1181, 1182, 1195 (repeated 1550), 1210, 1212, 1221, 1223, 1235, 1236, 1237, 1238, 1252?, 1255, 1256, 1260, 1268, 1270, (1281), 1284, 1288, 1289, 1290, 1291, 1292, 1295, 1306, 1307, 1308, 1313, 1314, 1315, 1316, 1319, 1335, 1358, 1359, 1372, 1373, (1374), 1375, 1396, 1398, 1399, 1400, 1401, 1427, 1428, 1453, 1457, 1459, 1480, 1481, 1482, 1484, 1485, 1486, 1487, 1488, 1489, 1491, 1492, 1497, 1499, 1503, 1507, 1517, 1518, 1523, 1524, 1528, 1532, 1535, 1544, 1547, 1552, 1557, 1563, 1564, 1569, 1570, 1572, 1573, 1577, 1583, 1587, 1588, 1589

Indictment by a thief: 1281; by an approver: 1374

Proceedings and outcomes

(1) Homicide

Killings by unknown criminals: 1163, 1170, 1201, 1205, 1226, 1247, 1278, 1298, 1300, 1360, 1362, 1363, 1382, 1383, 1388, 1418, 1494, 1519, 1527, 1534, 1536, 1546, 1551, 1567, 1568, 1586

Outlawries: 1248, 1272, 1276, 1286, 1302, 1376, 1395, 1468

Exigents: 1165 (but see 1269), 1172, 1176, 1196, 1198, 1206, 1263, 1264, 1273, 1277, 1320, 1342, 1344, 1346, 1348, 1349, 1366, 1377, 1410, 1414, 1417, 1433, 1442, 1443, 1468, 1501, 1516, 1525, 1530, 1539, 1553, 1579

Abjurations: 1161, 1165, 1172, 1258, 1324, 1327, 1408, 1409, 1424, 1539, 1595

Hanged before or at the eyre: 1209, 1380, 1542

Burnt: 1233

Clerks convicted: 1271, 1328, 1511

Suspect dead: 1543

Killing when insane: 1285

Suicide: 1254, 1280, 1299, 1347, 1435, 1582

Suspects acquitted or licensed to return: 1161, 1186, 1206, 1217, 1227, 1269, 1369, 1371, 1411, 1418, 1433, 1452, 1474, 1483, 1531, 1560, 1571, 1576, 1579

(2) Larceny

Exigents: 1182, 1195, 1210, 1212, 1223, 1235, 1237, 1238, 1256, 1260, 1270, 1283, 1288, 1289, 1291, 1292, 1295, 1314, 1316, 1335, 1336, 1359, 1373, 1375, 1396, 1398, 1399, 1400, 1401, 1457, 1459, 1481, 1484, 1485, 1486, 1487, 1488, 1491, 1503, 1517, 1523, 1524, 1528, 1532, 1564, 1569, 1573, 1577, 1583, 1588

Abjurations: 1404, 1480, 1489, 1497, 1499, 1552

Hangings before or at the eyre: 1181, 1210, 1293, 1308, 1358, 1428, 1482, 1507, 1535, 1583

Acquitted or licensed to return: 1181, 1221, 1236, 1255, 1268, 1281, 1290, 1294, 1306, 1307, 1313, 1315, 1358, 1374, 1427, 1453, 1482, 1492, 1507, 1517, 1518, 1544, 1557, 1569, 1587, 1589

Petty theft: 1216, 1255?, 1315, 1557

(3) Other offences (however accused)

Arson: 1282, 1326, 1434, 1458, 1490, 1522, 1537, 1545
Coining: 1425
Poaching: 1239, 1529, 1544, 1558, 1562
Rape: 1190, 1197, 1246, 1329, 1431, 1432, 1502, 1578

Suspected or convicted felons (including suicides) with no chattels: 1161, 1210, 1212, 1223, 1235, 1237, 1238, 1256, 1260, 1263, 1264, 1270, 1276, 1277, 1280, 1282, 1288, 1289, 1291, 1292, 1295, 1299, 1308, 1314, 1320, 1335, 1336, 1346, 1349, 1358, 1359, 1366, 1373, 1375, 1376, 1396, 1400, 1401, 1414, 1433, 1442, 1443, 1445, 1457, 1458, 1481, 1484, 1486, 1488, 1489, 1490, 1501, 1503, 1518, 1522, 1523, 1524, 1525, 1528, 1530, 1532, 1539, 1564, 1569, 1573, 1577, 1579, 1583, 1588, 1595, 1601
Suspected or convicted felons (including suicides) with chattels worth 40d. or less: 1176, 1209, 1235, 1238, 1272, 1348, 1373, 1380, 1399, 1408, 1409, 1410, 1414, 1433, 1435, 1459, 1517, 1535, 1537, 1553, 1583
Suspected or convicted felons with free lands: 1172, 1181, 1195, 1196, 1198, 1223, 1238, 1274, 1293, 1326, 1395, 1396, 1417, 1424, 1433, 1468, 1481, 1573
Members of the clergy involved in wrongdoing: 1168, 1186, 1200, 1237, 1239, 1248, 1249, 1252, 1271, 1273, 1321, 1328, 1366, 1393, 1408, 1411, 1415, 1448, 1451, 1454, 1511, 1522, 1539, 1541
Liberties exercised, claimed or usurped: 1259, 1263, 1267, 1284, 1334, 1339, 1353, 1402, 1404, 1411, 1413, 1426, 1430, 1460, 1466, 1502, 1511, 1529, 1571

Failings by vills

Allowed suspect's escape: 1404, 1408, 1570?
Buried corpse without coroner's view: 1241, 1460, 1501, 1556
Defaulted from eyre: 1370, 1429
Failed to make arrest: 1521
Failed to present to county court: 1185, 1264, 1279, 1320, 1369, 1414, 1474
Failed to raise hue and/or pursue: 1161, 1162, 1170, 1226, 1227, 1258, 1272, 1278, 1298, 1300, 1324, 1327, 1342, 1377, 1382, 1383, 1388, 1410, 1414, 1442, 1443, 1527, 1534, 1542, 1543, 1551, 1567, 1568
Harboured men outside frankpledge: 1165, 1198, 1273, 1320, 1373, 1433, 1480, 1484, 1489, 1516, 1532, 1564
Made false statement at eyre: 1362
Made malicious indictment: 1221
Presented Englishry falsely: 1469, 1515, 1520

Failings by juries

Concealed attachment: 1367
Concealed death: 1241
Concealed infringement of assize: 1464
Concealed killings: 1263, 1320
Concealed Norman lands: 1341
Concealed presentation to church: 1389
Misrepresented abjuror's chattels: 1258

Misrepresented suspects: 1453
Presented Englishry falsely: 1162, 1191, 1226, 1527
Presented wrong first finder: 1414

Accidental and natural deaths presented at the eyre

Burnt: 1230
Drowning: 1164, 1166, 1167, 1169, 1174, 1175, 1191, 1199, 1203, 1204, 1225, 1242, 1243, 1257, 1275, 1279, 1296, 1297, 1309, 1322, 1323, 1343, 1364, 1365, 1368, 1379, 1407, 1447, 1469, 1470, 1471, 1496, 1513, 1515, 1554, 1556, 1566, 1580, 1585, 1594, 1598
Crushed: by a beam: 1325, 1500, 1520; by an oak tree: 1467; by a stack of corn: 1548
Died in prison: 1162, 1416
Falling sickness: 1171, 1189, 1241, 1460, 1598
Falls: over a beam, 1265; from a ladder, 1495; when pursued, 1553; from a building, 1596
Horses and carts: 1185, 1187, 1387, 1438, 1440, 1472, 1473, 1533
Injured by a lance: 1549
Mills: 1207, 1310, 1386, 1436, 1565, 1581, 1584
Palsy: 1531
Stillbirth: 1369
Suddenly fell dead: 1224, 1521
Unspecified – found dead: 1207, 1229, 1287, 1367, 1514, 1538

Deodands

Beam: 1265, 1325, 1500
Beam of a press: 1520
Boat: 1174, 1585
Cart: 1387
Cart and horse: 1365, 1438, 1440, 1580
Cart, two horses and a load of herrings: 1368
Ladder: 1495
Horse: 1185, 1364, 1470, 1472, 1473, 1533, 1554
Iron mill-spindle: 1565
Mill wheel: 1310, 1386, 1436, 1581
Oak tree: 1467
Sail-yard of windmill: 1584
Stack of corn: 1548

Presentment of Englishry

Not presented or presented falsely: 1164, 1191, 1224, 1226, 1227, 1241, 1257, 1275, 1287, 1296, 1297, 1309, 1343, 1362, 1363, 1377, 1379, 1382, 1383, 1414, 1433, 1460, 1469, 1471, 1474, 1494, 1496, 1514, 1515, 1520, 1521, 1527, 1534, 1536, 1565, 1566, 1567, 1586
Presented: 1161, 1162, 1163, 1166, 1167, 1169, 1189, 1203, 1205, 1208, 1225, 1242, 1243, 1247, 1322, 1349, 1360, 1513

INDEX OF PEOPLE AND PLACES

The names of people and places are presented in alphabetical order with numbers referring to the pleas (and their accompanying notes) in which they occur; each entry is accompanied by a brief identifier. Roman numbers are those of pages in the introduction. Personal names are entered under under toponyms where these exist, otherwise under surnames, occupational names, or the names of parents. People recorded as being 'in' a place (this applies especially to the heads of tithings) have been treated as having been 'of' it. Where a man or woman is recorded as having both a toponymic name and a surname, he or she is presented under the toponym, with a cross-reference to it from the surname; thus the primary entry for Robert Ordrich of Barnham is under Barnham, with a cross-reference to that place from Ordrich. As an aid to making identifications or connections, cross-references signalled by the phrase *See also* are also provided from the particular places, occupations or families under which men and women are primarily indexed, to differently formulated entries recording people of the same origin or employment.

Every place-name which has been identified is entered in its modern form, followed by the hundred – signalled by the letter 'h' – in which it occurs, and then by the form or forms found in the original text (a few minor variants have been omitted). But where modern and medieval forms are identical (Brome for example) there is no repetition. Unidentified place-names which are not of foreign origin have been italicised. Some important places, for instance Ipswich, have produced a number of entries of different kinds; in such cases the personal names are presented first, in alphabetical order under forenames, followed by the rest, again in alphabetical order.

It was noted in the introduction that the clerk responsible for the text of the crown pleas was often inaccurate and inconsistent in his presentation of names, sometimes remarkably so. This has created severe problems for the indexer. The differences in spelling or presentation which have sometimes resulted from this clerical incompetence, especially those between entries among the pleas and in the amercements section, are not often such as to render identifications impossible, and where they have been made the forms have been cross-referenced, as a link between a main entry and a minor, abbreviated, one. But occasionally the differences are so great that it has been thought advisable to provide a full entry for each form, though again with a cross-reference linking them. Some errors and omissions have probably escaped detection. When comparing dictionaries to watches, Samuel Johnson said that 'the worst is better than none, and the best cannot be expected to go quite true.' He could easily have been talking of indexes.

THE SUFFOLK RECORDS SOCIETY

For over sixty years, the Suffolk Records Society has added to the knowledge of Suffolk's history by issuing an annual volume of previously unpublished manuscripts, each throwing light on some new aspect of the history of the county.

Covering 700 years and embracing letters, diaries, maps, accounts and other archives, many of them previously little known or neglected, these books have together made a major contribution to historical studies.

At the heart of this achievement lie the Society's members, all of whom share a passion for Suffolk and its history and whose support, subscriptions and donations make possible the opening up of the landscape of historical research in the area.

In exchange for this tangible support, members receive a new volume each year at a considerable saving on the retail price at which the books are then offered for sale.

Members are also welcomed to the launch of the new volume, held each year in a different and appropriate setting within the county and giving them a chance to meet and listen to some of the leading historians in their fields talking about their latest work.

For anyone with a love of history, a desire to build a library on Suffolk themes at modest cost and a wish to see historical research continue to thrive and bring new sources to the public eye in decades to come, a subscription to the Suffolk Records Society is the ideal way to make a contribution and join the company of those who give Suffolk history a future.

THE CHARTERS SERIES

To supplement the annual volumes and serve the need of medieval historians, the Charters Series was launched in 1979 with the challenge of publishing the transcribed texts of all the surviving monastic charters for the county. Since then, twenty-one volumes have been published as an occasional series, the latest in 2020.

The Charter Series is financed by a separate annual subscription leading to receipt of each volume on publication.

CURRENT PROJECTS

Volumes approved by the Council of the Society for future publication include *Monks Eleigh Manorial Documents*, edited by Vivienne Aldous, *The Records of Medieval Newmarket*, edited by James Davis and Joanne Sear, and *The Incorporated Hundreds of Suffolk*, edited by John Shaw; and in the Charters Series, *Bury St Edmunds Town Charters*, edited by Vivien Brown, *Documents of the Franciscans in Bury St Edmunds*, edited by Francis Young, and *Rumburgh Priory Charters*, edited by Nicholas Karn. The order in which these and other volumes appear in print will depend on the dates of completion of editorial work.

MEMBERSHIP

Membership enquiries should be addressed to Mrs Tanya Christian, 8 Orchid Way, Needham Market, IP6 8JQ; e-mail: suffolkrecordssociety@gmail.com

The Suffolk Records Society is a registered charity, No. 1084279.

OBITUARIES

Joy Rowe 1926–2020

Joy Rowe, who died on 7 September, a few weeks short of her 94th birthday, was a founding member of the Society. She remained as a council member until 2008 and was then invited to become a vice-president. She was an honoured guest at the 60th anniversary celebrations of the Society in 2017.

The Rowe family moved into Ixworth Abbey in the early 1960s where Joy became an expert in securing grants and other funding from various bodies to continue the restoration of this important house and the associated ruins of the Augustinian priory. Her whole life reflected her interest in and love of history, whether teaching at Hengrave Hall, working as an archivist at West Suffolk Record Office under Martin Statham or researching and writing many books and articles. She was an active member of many societies including the Suffolk Institute of Archaeology and History and for many years was on the grants committee of the Suffolk Historic Churches Trust. She was elected a Fellow of the Society of Antiquaries of London in 2002.

Joy Rowe's research covered the early modern history of Catholicism in East Anglia, drawing attention to the families of recusants and their networks of chapels and travelling priests. Her work on recusancy led to many contributions to books and journals including the Norfolk and Suffolk historical atlases as well as eight entries in the *Oxford Dictionary of National Biography*. In 2016 she was the General Editor of the Society's volume 59 *Rookwood Family Papers, 1606–1761*, edited by Francis Young.

CB

William Serjeant 1921–2020

We record with sadness the death, on 19 January at the age of 98, of William R. (Bill) Serjeant, formerly joint archivist of the Ipswich and East Suffolk Record Office, 1970–74, and first county archivist of Suffolk, 1974–82.

Bill Serjeant was honorary secretary of the Suffolk Records Society for seventeen years from 1970 to 1987. He had previously held a similar position with the Thoroton Society in Nottinghamshire, a county of which he had been county archivist from 1962 and, prior to that, librarian-archivist and assistant director in the Manx Museum and the National Trust.

At SRS, working alongside some of the great names of Suffolk history – Norman Scarfe, Geoffrey Martin, Leslie Dow, David Dymond – he made an invaluable contribution to its development. Meanwhile, he sat on the council of the Suffolk Institute of Archaeology and History and the Suffolk Local History Council, for which he edited *The Suffolk Review* for twelve years.

After retirement, he continued to work for archives and local history in Suffolk, remaining as a council member of SRS until 2009 and acting, for many years, as honorary archivist to the Tollemache and de Saumarez families. In collaboration with his wife, Ruth, and M.E. Grimwade he took on the task of overseeing the publication of a four-volume index of the entire series of probate records of the archdeaconries of Suffolk and Sudbury, from 1354 and 1444 respectively up to 1700, issued in four volumes by the British Record Society between 1979 and 1984.

VG